Principles of Management
in Export

Principles of Export Guidebooks

Series Editor: Michael Z. Brooke

Principles of Management in Export

James Conlan

First published 1994

Blackwell Publishers
108 Cowley Road
Oxford OX4 1JF
UK

238 Main Street
Cambridge, Massachusetts 02142
USA

British Library Cataloguing in Publication Data
A CIP catalogue record for this book is available from the British Library.

Library of Congress Cataloging-in-Publication Data
A CIP catalog record for this book is available from the Library of Congress.

ISBN 0-631-19194-1

Typeset in 11½pt on 13½pt Garamond Light by Aitch Em Wordservice, Aylesbury, Buckinghamshire, Great Britain.

Printed in Great Britain by Hartnolls Limited, Bodmin, Cornwall.

This book is printed on acid-free paper.

Contents

List of Figures and Tables

Foreword

The final book in the export series commissioned by The Institute of Export is a far-reaching review of the management of a company's trade. It is written by James Conlan of Buckingham College Business School, which has a fine reputation for expertise on international business.

I can commend Mr Conlan's writing as a sound and common-sense introduction to export management.

The Earl of Limerick, President,
The Institute of Export

Series Editor's Introduction

In launching the seventh book in this series of guidebooks to the profession of exporting, the series editor – along with others associated with the project – is pleased to welcome James Conlan as its author.

Like the books on marketing, *Principles of Management in Export* is a general overview of its subject. The author's contribution to the development of you, the reader, rests on his long experience as a manager and teacher and I present this book with great pride to the exporting public.

All the books in this series are preoccupied with bringing products to foreign markets (what else is export about?) and this book – which reviews the whole subject of export management – is concerned with maintaining and servicing the markets by effective management.

May I welcome you, the reader, and hope to meet you again when you read the other books in the series which cover all aspects of export which you need to know – law (for the non-lawyer), transport and distribution, international marketing, market research and trade and payments, in addition to the first book in the series which is a review of the whole subject.

The main focus of James' book (as with the other books in the series) is on the market itself – how to manage within it. Adapting is half the battle.

Michael Z. Brooke

About The Institute of Export Examinations

The Institute is grateful for the initiative of Michael Z. Brooke, the series editor, and Blackwell Publishers in publishing this unique series of books specially written for the Professional Examinations.

The authors for the series have been carefully selected and have specialized knowledge of their subjects, all being established lecturers or examiners for the Professional Examinations.

The books have been written in a style that is of benefit not only to students of The Institute but also to commercial organizations seeking further information about specific aspects of international trade.

Professionalism in export is vital for every company if they are to compete successfully in world markets and this new series of books provides a sound basis of knowledge for all those seeking a professional qualification in export through The Institute of Export's Professional Examinations.

The book covers the following parts of The Institute's syllabus.

Principles of Management in Export

Objectives of the Syllabus

To put into an organizational, commercial and management context the knowledge and skills covered in the other papers. This is achieved by examining:

1 The political, legal and organizational environment of an export business and the analysis of profitable export trading.
2 The basic principles of measuring profitability and the documents recording it.
3 The more important concepts guiding commercial decision making, management control techniques and the setting of budgeted targets.
4 Some basic tools of longer term planning including the application of information technology.

The nature of a profitable business

1 The application of the resources of finance, of technology, and of people's knowledge and skills to the supply of goods and services to identified markets at a profit.
2 The different legal entities; sole traders, partnerships, private and public companies.
3 The company as a 'legal person' and its relationships with its shareholders, its directors, its employees, its customers and suppliers, and with the providers of debt capital.
4 The basic legal requirements arising from incorporation.
5 The variations in the legal status, and in financial reporting in different countries including those of the European Union.
6 The definition of commercial success, and management's role in converting the inputs: capital, technology, knowledge and skills, into profitable growth.
7 The information flows within a business that enable it to run and to be controlled.

Financial aspects of management

Assets and liabilities

1 Profitable growth defined as the growth of the net assets of the company.
2 The balance sheet as a statement of the assets and liabilities of the company at a point in time, divided into longer term and 'current'. The conventional forms of the balance sheet as laid down by the Companies Act 1985, as modified by any subsequent legislation.
3 The effect of individual transactions on the individual elements of the balance sheet, distinguishing those which change the net asset value from those which do not.
4 Working capital and its significance for the operations of the business.

Profit and losses

1 The relationship over time between the balance sheet and the profit and loss account. The importance of the accounting period.
2 The conventional forms of the profit and loss account as laid down by the Companies Act 1985 or as required by management.
3 The distinction between the trading account, the profit and loss account and the appropriation account.
4 The distinction between financially significant and other acts of the company.
5 The effect of profitable trading on the closing balance sheet for the period, particularly on reserves.
6 The distinction between capital and revenue expenditures.
7 The flow of information from transactions, through day books and the ledger system, to the trial balance, and then to the two main final statements.

The principles underlying the profit calculation

1 The accrual and the matching concepts.

2 The going concern concept.
3 The money measurement and realisation concepts.
4 Stock valuation methods and their significance to the calculation of profit.
5 The setting of standards in the UK, the role of the ASB, SSAPs and FRSs, and variations in other countries including the USA and those of the European Union.

Costing for decision making

1 Costs or expenses? Cost allocation, cost centres and cost units. Direct costs and overheads. The need to apportion overheads.
2 Costing for pricing and for control. The techniques of apportionment, cost absorption and the underlying assumptions.
3 Costing for decision making and longer term planning. Fixed and variable costs, the break-even chart.
4 Contribution to fixed costs or to overheads. Unit and total contribution. Contribution from a mix of products. Using contribution for targeting profit.

Working capital and cash flows

1 The effect of changing levels of activity on working capital. Overtrading and the management control of working capital, stocks, debtors and creditors.
2 Sources and application of funds statement (excluding the details of FRS 1).
3 The preparation of the cash flow forecast.
4 Cash control options for the exporter, their advantages and their costs.

Some objectives and techniques of management

Profit maximisation

1 Price/demand relationships and their effect on the break-even chart.
2 Maximising turnover or maximising profit.

3 Margins v. turnover; optimising the mix.
4 Profit sharing between exporter and distributor. The concept of transfer prices.

Decision making under uncertainty

1 Basic concepts, rules for mutually exclusive and independent events, probability trees.
2 Expected monetary value, criteria of choice in decision making. Risk strategies.

Performance assessment and the use of ratios

1 Indicators of profitability.
2 Indicators of liquidity.
3 Indicators of efficiency.
4 Indicators of security.
5 Ratios for investors.
6 The uses and deficiencies of 'ratios analysis'.

Longer term investment assessment

1 The characteristics of investment in overseas markets. The costs, time and risks involved.
2 Simple measures of investment assessment; average return, pay-back period.
3 The time-value of money and borrowing costs as the basis of discounting techniques.

Some management tools

1 Information technology in the export office; the application of word processing, spreadsheets, data processing, electronic mail, telex, fax.
2 Information systems; data flows, MIS, company data bases, system design.
3 External links; the technology, ISDN and other public facilities, public data bases, links with banks, Customs, forwarders.

4 Electronic Data Interchange (EDI), the role of VANS, benefits and requirements for exploitation.
5 Budgeting; the function of budgets in a commercial organization, the management of the budgeting process, the elements and their inter-relationship, budgeting as an on-going tool of management.

R.T. Ebers FIEx,
Director of Education & Training,
The Institute of Export

Introduction

What This Book is Designed to Achieve

This book's contents are based on two simple but important ideas. The first is:

Exporting is the ordinary form of business

One of the clichés of current business writing is that trade is now global and that markets are international. In practice, export trade is too often seen, particularly by politicians, as somehow special, requiring special skills and special support. Exporting is often seen as some specific cure for national economic ills including unemployment, an adverse balance of (visible) trade and a dearth of 'strategic industries'. In short, these attitudes betray a yearning for 'macho', national economic planning, attitudes which seem to look back to the 18th Century mercantilist economic theory that imports impoverish a nation but exports enrich it. Governments may then attempt to implement this obsolete theory by policies of 'balanced' or 'managed' trade.

The opposite view, which is the view expressed in this book, was spelt out some time ago by the head of the Hong Kong Trade Development Council: 'I'm not interested in balancing trade in any bilateral sense. Our aim is just to increase the total volume of trade.' So prosperous economies are founded on prosperous trading which, in turn, is founded on the efficiency of individual business organizations supplying markets where ever they may be found. To misquote Gertrude Stein: 'A customer is a customer is a customer.'

Therefore, this book concentrates on the basic principles of entrepreneurial management, ignoring the simplicities and easy options of only trading in one's home market.

The second basic idea underlying the writing of this book is:

The function of a business is to make money

Were one to ask amongst one's friends 'What is the function of a business?' the responses would almost certainly be varied: to provide employment, to offer a fulfilling career, to benefit the national economy, to give opportunities for personal development, and so on. To state bluntly that the function is money making would certainly be regarded by some as too narrow, too materialistic and effectively 'politically incorrect'.

But it should be noted that all of these alternative and indisputably laudable aims cannot be achieved if the business in question does not generate a financial surplus on its trading activities. If it does not do that it will not provide adequate returns to its employees, to its suppliers (and their employees in turn), and to investors who will include pension funds. We should not forget the Inland Revenue whose thankless task it is to collect the money by taxing the profits earned to pay for all those public 'goods', from unemployment benefits, to subsidies for opera.

Not only do we, as ordinary citizens, consciously or unconsciously, expect our enterprises to produce this flow of financial benefits, but we should also remember that any such enterprise can only become established by the provision of finance in the first place. That there must be some investment in physical assets may be regarded as obvious; less obvious is the investment in technical research and development and also in marketing research and in training. What is often forgotten is the investment in that abstraction – 'working capital'.

Businesses also rely on public and private investment in the 'infra-structure' which will include everything from airlines to waste disposal, and investment in the training of the working population as a whole, at school or after. Which ever way we look at the enterprise, it is finance that is put in and it is finance that comes out and it is the basic minimal requirement of management to ensure that what comes out is greater than what is put in.

It is the aim of this book to offer some assistance in the achievement of that aim in a global context.

Part 1

The Business and Management Background

In these first four chapters we take a look at what a business is meant to achieve. By a business, we mean an export business because that is the only form of business to be interested in. Justifying that claim will set the scene for the rest of the book.

We will then justify the existence of such an export business by showing that the whole reason for being in business at all is to become more prosperous, individually, nationally and globally.

We will also look at the environment, mainly the legal environment, in which the activities of an exporting business must operate.

The job of the four chapters in this first section of the book is to lay the foundations for the more technical topics which will be developed in Part 2.

1

What an Export Business is All About

What Does a Business, Any Business, Actually Do?

This book is entitled 'The principles of management in export' so you, as the reader, are entitled to some explanation as to:

1 what 'management' is;
2 any definable – or even describable – principles that may be offered to those attempting the management task; and
3 what is so special, if anything, about an 'export business' ?

What is Management?

Well, we all know what a manager is. It is someone who sits in an office with a telephone and a computer on the desk and with a filing cabinet in the corner, who tells his or her sub-ordinates to do this or not to do that, and in the intervals covers sheets of paper with reports, financial analyses and proposals, before rushing off to the next presentation. So is that a manager?

No! A manager is an effective entrepreneur, someone who has the creative flair of the entrepreneur combined with the technical knowledge and ability to turn the entrepreneurial ideas into reality.

So what's an entrepreneur then? Nolan Bushnell, one of the legendary figures of the Silicon Valley in the 1970s, defined an entrepreneur, not as a specialist of any professional or technical kind, but as someone who can apply the talents of such specialists to a business idea. An entrepreneur is just that, someone who senses an opportunity, locates the technologists he or she needs, recruits the best finance talent, adds in the best marketing talent, gets the team together and says 'This is what our company is going to do!'. A business plan is roughed out and then a plan for raising the finance, and that's the start of it all. So what did the entrepreneur do? He or she did not provide the technology, nor the finance, nor the marketing expertise. All the entrepreneur did was to make it happen – and that was the most important bit of all.

A nice story, but one which needs just two other things to complete it. Is there really a market for left-handed widgets and, if so, where is it? Secondly, what skills do the technologist, the marketing guy and the finance guy really need to possess so that it can all be put together?

So, in order to round out the picture of the effective, entrepreneurial manager, just two more quotes. Peter Drucker said a long time ago that 'The job of a manager is not to solve problems. His job is to exploit opportunities.' Someone else said an equally long time ago: 'The task of a manager is getting people to do things.'

So that is the ultimate aim of this book. To state it more accurately, the aim is to offer some ideas that will enable you to use your talents more effectively to exploit opportunities for reward.

Are There Any Such Things as Management Principles?

If the manager is to make it all happen he or she must know:

1 what it is that he or she wants to make happen;
2 why that thing is worth achieving;

3 what is required to make it achievable; and
4 where to obtain the necessary resources.

In this book we will give some help in acquiring this knowledge, either directly or by indicating where help may be found.

What Is So Special About an Export Business?

The general underlying theme of this book is that there is actually nothing special about an exporting business; rather, it is the non-exporting business that needs to justify its narrow view of the exploitable opportunities open to it. Given the descriptions of entrepreneurship and the management task that we quoted above, any identification of a business opportunity is one to be seized and exploited, whether it is pizzas in Papua New Guinea or Marxist memorabilia for Muscovites.

Nevertheless, it must be admitted that it is a commonly held view that exporting is perhaps, a little peculiar and the statistics can confirm this. In 1992 only 50 companies were responsible for 44 per cent of UK exports. Government sponsored promotions were therefore targeted at smaller companies but often with limited success. Perhaps many small companies feel that their business is unsuited to exporting. But perhaps not. Let us take as an example an actual word processing agency, a business which is the archetypal neighbourhood supplier. But one such agency, based in Belfast, built up a business, aimed first at the whole UK and then North America, accepting work by fax and delivering the finished product using British Telecom's KiloStream service.

But a more ambitious entrepreneurial aim does demand more knowledge, more skill, more patience and more managerial ability than simply sticking to a single familiar market. So what we will be doing in this book is to provide a basic foundation of some important aspects of the management task in the context of global trading.

How This Book is Organized

This book is not intended, single handed, to turn you into a successful and wealthy international trader. What it does aim to do will be to concentrate on some fundamentals of international business that it is very important to get right most of the time. The things we will be looking at include:

1 the legal context in which businesses must operate;
2 measuring and recording progress;
3 defining and measuring profitability;
4 managing costs and managing cash;
5 coping with uncertainty;
6 performance and return on investment;
7 the application of information technology; and
8 planning it all.

The design of this book reflects that it is part of a series. Therefore this particular volume concentrates on the **principles** of profitable export trading. The companion volumes in the series cover marketing and market research, the law governing overseas trade, distribution, and international trade and payments. The details of these other books in the series are given at the beginning of this volume, and the series should be seen as a whole, covering the totality of the principles and practice of international trade.

From time to time reference will be made to these other volumes, which tackle the more technical aspects of export trading in some depth. We will also refer you to other sources where appropriate.

It is also important at this stage to note what this book does not cover. Since it is but a slim volume the book concentrates on some core principles of profitable management and this implies an emphasis on financial management. Get that right and you, as a manager, will be able to concentrate on the detailed attainment of planned targets; get it wrong and you may soon not have a business at all.

So we will not cover:

1 Those detailed, technical matters covered by the other books in this series.
2 Pure management theory, or any classification of management styles or organizational structures.
3 Theories of 'organizational behaviour', of the way people behave in organizations, although we will make limited reference to such factors where they may have a direct impact on the export operation.
4 Financial accounting techniques. This volume will not tell you how to do your book-keeping, but it will make clear why that task needs to be done and, more importantly, how to use the figures that the accounting process throws up.
5 The specific products, services, markets, distribution chains and the company set-up that you, as an individual, are daily involved with. But it is our intention that, having read this book, you will find it easier to apply management principles to your own personal work.

A Bird's-eye View of
What an Export Business Does

To exploit the opportunities that an export business has identified, management must put in some resources in the expectation of getting more resources out. What comes out will then be distributed to many people and organizations including, of course, the shareholders.

The inputs may be summarized as:

1 Some set of specific products or services, delivery of which is what your business is all about.
2 Identified markets, whether defined geographically, technically or commercially, which can be expected to demand the products or services on offer.
3 Knowledge and skills that will make possible that transfer of products to those markets. Exporting requires a greater variety of 'know-how' and skills. Therefore much of what is required will be obtained from outside the firm – from researchers,

distributors and agents, specialist bodies such as freight forwarders, banks, insurers, and from SITPRO, THE and so on.
4 Finance, inevitably, will be required and it will take two forms;
longer term **investment funds** and short term **working
capital**.

The skills and the inputs which they generate are often insepar-
able. In the 1980s a textile trader built up a worldwide business
based on personal contacts, built up by energetic globetrotting,
but he also knew how to operate the business from London
using, not without technical hassles, just 'phone and fax. In a
not dissimilar way, a successful export business was born when
the founder, 'on a whim', took samples of top-quality chamois
leather to Sweden and found a market. Having identified the
potential demand in that country he later exploited the opportunity by cold-calling importers in the United States and found
another new market there.

As management uses its skills to garner together these inputs,
so the business will produce the outputs that, taken together,
define a profitable business. We may briefly summarize these
outputs as:

1 Delivery of the products and services to the markets that
demand them, when and in what form demanded. The essence
of a trading business is delivery.
2 Collection of the revenues earned by delivery. This is something that cannot be taken for granted when exporting.
3 Gross margins, the difference between the revenues and the
cost of the goods or services sold. These margins are needed
to pay the costs of operating the business as an organization,
in brief, to pay the overheads.
4 Interest paid to all sorts of providers of finance. In addition
to the interest payable on loans, many export procedures carry
an implicit interest charge, for example, discounting bills
of exchange or deferred payment letters of credit.
5 Wages and salaries. It is useful when considering such organizational costs to think in terms of added value; do we
as employees of the organization produce as individuals
enough added value between what the product cost and

what it earned in revenue?

6 Share dividends which the owners of the business hope to get after all the other contributors have taken their cut.

The task of management is to ensure, consignment by consignment, year by year, that the inputs match the outputs. It follows that there must be a common system of measurement to record that match, or mis-match. That system is money and the management of the system is financial management. It is an imperfect system. It leaves a lot out of account; it involves past, historic costs and revenues whereas the entrepreneurial manager is targeting future revenues and profits. It also appears complicated and this is because business operations themselves are complicated. But the money measurement system, for better of for worse, is at the centre of profitable management. Furthermore it makes possible two things:

1 Quantified management control. Qualitative judgements can easily degenerate into guesswork. Quantitative measures – costs, margins, budgets, risks, percentage returns, may be miscalculated, they may be mis-applied, but properly used they are objective and verifiable.
2 Giving due consideration to the time factor. Our inputs and our outputs do not take place simultaneously. From that initial trade mission to receiving the sterling for the repeat order, there will always be a long span of time. We can measure the implications of that span, principally by a discounting technique based on interest rates.

So What Is the Point Of It All?

We work hard at our global enterprise, partly because it is fascinating, and partly in order to have a bigger, better, more valuable business next year than we had last year. So, what do we mean by the value of the business? Looking at it from the point of view of the shareholders, the value is the discounted value of all realized future earnings – both dividends and capital gains.

So management is primarily interested in the future but has only past, historic records on which to base its decisions. It is rather like driving a car using only the rear view mirror! Nevertheless, it can be done successfully, as tens of thousands of profitable export businesses demonstrate. But it also means that we should never lose sight of the complex and difficult task we have undertaken, nor fail to make use of the techniques available to us to avoid disaster and ensure success.

Now that we know what it is that we are trying to do, we can, in the following chapters of this book, set about deciding how to do it.

Questions for Discussion

1 Describe in your own words the difference between:
   (a) An administrator.
   (b) A manager.
   (c) An entrepreneur.
2 In the context of the European Union in the 1990s, state your views on whether the sales of products or services of United Kingdom origin to other Union countries should or should not be regarded as 'exports'.
3 An export manager, in reviewing the work of his department, said: 'When I watch my staff at work on all the variety of jobs that exporting involves, I am thinking all the time: What Added Value is being generated?' Why should he say that?

2

Companies and Businesses

What This Chapter, and the Next Two, Are All About

The background to the management control of an export business. If you are managing or helping to manage a business you will need to know three kinds of things:

1 What is the nature of the organization that you are involved in, and what is the consequential nature of the relations it has with all the various outsiders, people as well as organizations, that you as a manager and your company have to deal with.

2 What is the foundation of the control system that you must use. As we saw in the last chapter any quantified control system will mainly use money as its measuring stick. Other, non-monetary, data such as stock turn round, promotional activities or delays in processing export documents will have a significance that needs to be thought about in monetary terms. Therefore we need to understand thoroughly the nature – and deficiencies – of this monetary control system.

3 When we have a grasp of these two we will then be able, as exporters, to deal with foreign organizations that have different legal characteristics and operate with different systems of financial control. If we do not understand our

own systems it will be very difficult to recognize, let alone see the significance of the foreign ones.

Therefore in this chapter we will look at the ways in which a UK company can be formally established and look at the operating implications of its legal status. Using these as models, we will examine some foreign variations.

After reading this and the following two chapters you will be able to:

1   understand the nature of the responsibilities of the manager to his or her colleagues, to distributors and customers, and to suppliers;
2   see why the financial recording system known as 'the accounts' is organized in the peculiar way that it is; and
3   know what you might expect to find when you have dealings with foreign companies and foreign managers.

A 'Business' or a 'Company'?

Let us make this distinction clear before we go any further.

A 'business' is a collection of people, skills, knowledge and expectations that together create the trading situation. This trading situation results in 'customers' obtaining goods or services at a price that enables the 'supplier' (that's you) to pay for the running of the business.

The 'company' is the formal (or sometimes informal) organization established to operate that trading activity. The way companies are formally set up will vary even in the same industry or trading context.

For instance, one might establish a company first and then set about building up a business using the company as the vehicle for doing so. Alternatively, as many exporters have done, one might develop a business first as a one-man-band with no formal arrangements and only later, when the business relationships are well established, set up the company in the formal, legal sense.

Why do we have to bother with these legal formalities?

It is quite possible, one Monday morning, to go out collecting orders and arranging deliveries with no more than a letter head and a visiting card. Such a person would be a sole trader and we will look at that and at other methods of doing business in a moment. But this simple style of trading is unsatisfactory for several reasons. For example:

1 Customers, suppliers and banks would like to know who they are dealing with, the 'entrepreneur' or his company if he has one.
2 When loans are arranged, when suppliers demand payment, when customers send in cheques, who is responsible for paying or receiving the money?
3 If the entrepreneur joins forces with a partner, what would be the mutual relationship if there was a dispute?

So sole traders, necessarily, have a restricted mode of operation. It was this fact that hindered economic development in medieval times when English law recognized only a restricted range of 'corporations'. Change came with the development of chartered companies at the beginning of the seventeenth century, but company formation was still a cumbersome business, involving grants of Royal Charters or special Acts of Parliament until the middle nineteenth century. Then, and with subsequent Companies Acts, the joint stock company with limited liability for its members became the usual, but not the only, form. Let us now look at the five ways we might formally establish an exporting company.

Types of UK Businesses

The sole trader

There are no legal formalities to observe when running a business as a sole trader. The disadvantage is that the law regards the trader and his business as one; the trader has sole responsibility for the business and for its liabilities; the assets of the trader and the business are likewise treated as those of the trader himself which can mean personal bankruptcy if the business fails. On the other hand, a sole trader can employ other people, and the expenses of the business are deductible when calculating the trader's personal liability for income tax.

A partnership

As with a sole trader, no legal formalities are required to establish a partnership although a formal partnership agreement is highly desirable in case the partners fall out. Not only are the partners personally responsible for the business, they are **jointly and severally** responsible for all the debts and other liabilities, so creditors can claim off any one of the partners individually. Another odd feature of partnerships is that a partnership may in law be deemed to exist whenever two or more persons carry on a business in common. Thus it is possible to incur the unlimited liabilities of a partnership without intending to do so.

Because of the serious disadvantages of being a sole trader or a partner, any serious export business is almost certain to be **incorporated** under the rules of the Companies Acts. So from now on we will assume that any export business under discussion is such an incorporated, limited liability company. Sole traders and partnerships are not companies in the legal sense.

A private company

A private company is recognizable as it has Limited or Ltd in its name. As far as company management is concerned, the main distinguishing feature of a private company is that it cannot 'invite the public to subscribe for its shares or debentures (loans)'. Raising capital for expansion is therefore restricted. Private sales of shares to potential business partners is also difficult because the new shareholders may find it difficult to sell their shares at some future date. They are thus locked in to the company. In any case, private company rules usually restrict the right of shareholders to sell their shares.

Private companies can range from individuals who prefer to be 'incorporated' even though in the business sense they are actually sole traders, to very large companies operating internationally.

A public company

A public company is distinguished by having 'public limited company' or 'plc' in its name. The important feature of a public company is that it can offer its new share issues to the public at large, and individual shareholders can sell their shares to anyone else without restriction.

A 'listed' public company

A public company can only obtain a real benefit from its ability to raise share capital if it is 'listed' on a stock exchange; in the case of UK companies, usually the London stock exchange. A public company may also be listed on a foreign exchange, to improve its access to additional share capital. Nearly all public companies in the UK are 'listed'.

The Significant Characteristics of Incorporated Companies

By incorporated companies we mean businesses legally incor-porated under Companies Acts or their foreign equivalents, almost always in their home country. Different countries impose different rules for incorporated companies. There is a major distinction in the legal and accounting requirements for com-panies between Anglo-Saxon countries and the others. We shall use the term Anglo-Saxon to denote the UK, Ireland, the USA, Canada, India, Australia and New Zealand. These countries share a legal tradition based on English Common Law and have a pragmatic approach to financial reporting. Other countries have legal traditions based on codified Roman Law or on some other system and often exhibit a legalistic approach to financial reporting.

For the moment we will only discuss UK private, public and listed companies. The characteristics that are significant to the management of these companies are:

1   A company is a **distinct, legal person**, quite different from its shareholders, its managers or its employees. The assets are the property of the company, its debts are the liabilities of the company, not of any or even all of the shareholders. You will see in chapter 5, where we examine the way the financial accounts of a company are organized, that financial transactions between the 'company' and everyone else – shareholders, directors and managers – are transactions between legally separate 'persons' and must be recorded as such. This is important; if you forget this you will find the later chapters confusing.

2   A company has shareholders who contributed the original share capital that financed the business. The company may subsequently issue, that is, sell, more shares to raise more capital. If those shares are issued at more than face value (which is usually the case) the difference between the nominal value of the share and the money paid per share is recorded as **share premium**. The shareholders are legally known as the 'members of the company'.

3   The shareholders own the company but they do not run it. Instead they vote to appoint **directors** who run the company through its managers and other employees. However, one single individual may be simultaneously a shareholder, a director, and an employee. Managers are employees. Almost always with UK and US companies the voting by the shareholders at the Annual General Meeting (AGM) or Extraordinary General Meeting (EGM) is on the basis of one vote per share. This is not the rule in many other countries.

4   The shareholders' liability for the debts of the company is limited to the nominal value of their shares. If the company fails, the shareholders lose their investment but no more. Hence: limited liability.

5   Under the Companies Acts every company is required to

keep proper financial accounts. These accounts are the accounts of the company and are **not** the accounts of the members, directors or anyone else. We shall see in chapter 5 that the organization of the accounting records reflects this fact. Among many other requirements, the UK Companies Acts require that the accounts give a **true and fair view** of the state of the company and of its transactions. This is a peculiarly 'Anglo-Saxon' concept.

6   If a company makes a 'profit' it may distribute this to the shareholders' as dividends or it may 'retain' that profit in the business. We will see how that works in chapter 6. A company cannot normally pay back its share capital to its shareholders.

7   A company continues to exist irrespective of changes or the death of its members, until it is formally 'wound up'. Therefore the accounts of the company assume that the company will continue as a going concern. Hence the accounts of the company must take into consideration all future known or estimated revenues and expenses.

8   One company may be a shareholder of another company. If one company holds more than half of another company's share capital or enough to control it, then the latter is a subsidiary of the former company, the parent company. Any group of parent and subsidiary companies must also pre-pare consolidated accounts, that is, a set of accounts for the group as a whole. Outside the 'Anglo-Saxon' countries and the Netherlands, consolidation of group accounts is either rare or only a recent requirement.

Chapters 5 to 14 are designed to show, amongst other things, the way managers can use financial figures to monitor the progress of their businesses and we shall assume the pragmatic, Anglo-Saxon approach to financial reporting. But as **export** managers we must be aware that the companies we are dealing with may prepare their financial figures differently. For instance, these differences may be particularly significant in assessing the financial strength of prospective agents or distributors, or in assessing the credit worthiness of potential customers.

Manufacturing versus service companies

It will be useful at this stage to mention one other distinction we need to note between two categories of companies; manufacturing companies and service companies. This significance of this distinction is quite independent of nationality, legal status or size.

Manufacturing companies will almost certainly have a higher proportion of fixed assets in their total assets, and it is likely to follow that such companies will therefore have a higher proportion of fixed costs among their total costs.

In contrast, service companies will have fewer fixed assets and lower fixed costs as a proportion of the totals. It is to be expected that distributors or agents will behave as service companies except when that service role is played by an indigenous manufacturing company.

As we will show in subsequent chapters, this difference in asset and cost make-up affects the way the companies think about prices, volumes, discounts, innovation and risk. Why this is so is partly what this book is about.

National Variations in Financial Reporting

Before we look at national variations in the way companies are established and financed, and in the way in which financial data is (or is not) reported, there are three general aspects of the global situation to bear in mind.

1   The fundamental necessities of running a profitable business are both ancient and universal. It is the modes of presentation, even when taking the form of apparently comprehensible numbers, that can be and often are misleading. The trick is to see through the national 'colouring' to the trading realities behind.

2   The basic accounting process, invented by the Italian city states in the fourteenth century, using double entry bookkeeping to generate financial data founded on the twin

concepts of assets and liabilities, may be regarded as universal practice. You should, in theory, be able to understand financial figures from any country. However there remain problems of availability, of subtle differences in terminology, in reliability, and in the significance of specific measures in different national commercial contexts.

3 The English language is widely used worldwide for management and financial practice but closer examination will show that it is often, in fact, American English and American business concepts that are being used. Oscar Wilde described Britain and the United States as two countries separated by a common language, and that is particularly true for financial management. A short glossary of some British/American confusions can be found in appendix A.

National legal systems

As we have already mentioned, these may be divided into two types. Some countries have a legal system based on a limited amount of statute law which is supplemented by case law or judicial precedent developed by the courts in individual judgements. These are the Anglo-Saxon countries mentioned earlier. Other countries, particularly those of the European Community, have, to a greater or lesser extent, a system of codified law based on and developed from Roman Law. The difference is in practice between a pragmatic and adversarial approach as compared with prescriptive and morality-based systems. This is reflected in the approaches to legal requirements for company financial reporting.

Types of companies

The basic business unit in all countries will be incorporated companies with limited liability issuing shares. The major exception to this rule is the existence in some countries of public corporations, or of 'parastatal' organizations – usually exercising some degree of monopoly power.

All western countries except Sweden distinguish between private and public companies. However, the proportions vary from country to country with relatively fewer public companies in European continental countries, reflecting the less developed stock markets. For instance in 1993 only 425 German companies were listed compared with, at the same date, 1,950 companies in the UK's smaller economy. However at the time of writing, these difference were beginning to diminish partly due to the wish of more countries to have active stock markets, and partly due to an increasing number of multinationals wishing to be listed on US or UK stock exchanges.

Variations in financing

Anglo-Saxon companies tend to have a higher proportion of their longer term financing from share capital in contrast to others where bank or loan capital is more the norm. For example, in the early 1990s 70 to 75 per cent of the capital of German '*Mittelstand*' firms came from loans as opposed to shares.

The sources of share capital also varied. In the UK, 'institutions' were providing 70 per cent of stock market investment in shares, whilst in Japan and Germany a significant proportion of shares were held by associated companies or by banks. Another feature of Swiss, Spanish, and German company financing is the issuing of either non-voting shares or of bearer shares. The effect of these differences is to diminish the influence of the private shareholder on larger corporations as compared with the United States.

Taxation

The variations in taxation include variations in both direct tax on corporate profits and indirectly through social security payments. In 1992 corporate tax rates varied between nearly 60 per cent in Germany down to less than 40 per cent in the US and 33 per cent in the UK. French rates were similar to those of the UK but, in addition, companies there funded much of the social security system by additional payments. Another national variation was the limitation of corporate tax to retained profits in Germany and Italy but on all profits in the UK.

Accounting philosophies

The way the law in different countries requires companies to prepare and publish their accounts reflects different political philosophies. On the one hand we have the Anglo-Saxon countries where we find a pragmatic, commercially driven approach to accounting systems. In the United States and Canada the federal SEC plays a guiding role that in the others has been the responsibility of professional bodies. Ideas of economic theory have had a larger influence in the Netherlands, which falls between these two extremes.

In contrast to the Anglo-Saxons, we have countries where statute law and taxation have a large influence on the way companies present their accounts. This is typically so for Germany and Japan. The French *Plan Comptable Gènèral* has in the past regulated in fine detail the whole accounting process, with similar codified practices in Belgium, Spain and Italy. Sweden is another intermediate case with the aim of national economic policy making having an influence on the regulation of businesses.

The Implications of National Variations

Which accounts are we talking about?

Different national regulations can determine either the way the accounts are kept or the way the final accounting statements are published, or both. As pointed out above, commercial realities mean that, whatever the national system, managers in those countries all have the same tasks of controlling costs, of budgeting and so on. But if the UK export manager is using data derived from foreign *published* accounts to assess distributors or competitors, he or she needs to take national differences into account.

For whom are the accounts prepared?

Anglo-Saxon thinking is in favour of the full and unambiguous disclosure of information with only minor differences in legal requirements between public and private companies, and between small companies and the rest. In countries where statute and taxation are the major influences, the role of the accountant and the auditor is to ensure compliance with the law. So the UK financial analyst, looking at a set of foreign published accounts might ask 'These accounts are "correct" but are they useful and informative?'

What decides the style of presentation?

On the one side we have had the extreme case of the 'Plan Comptable Gènèral' where uniformity of presentation is regarded as of major importance. On the other we have the Anglo-Saxon view that accounting information is provided primarily for the owners of the business and, because business is an intuitive art not susceptible to theory, flexibility is essential. This view is enshrined in the concept of 'a true and fair view' of the situation of the company, and the requirement that UK auditors must certify that the accounts show this. However the harmonization Directives of the European Community have made changes to that general picture.

What might the accounts fail to show?

European continental practice exhibits a higher level of conservatism in calculating profits. The valuation of stocks, provisions for bad debts and other contingencies, calculation of depreciation and so on will tend to produce lower profit figures and the phenomenon of hidden reserves. The presence of these characteristics is at least partly due to the lower importance of share prices in showing company performance (because of less developed stock markets) and partly due to the indirect effect of taxation regulations. The net result is that, for instance, many German companies are financially stronger than one might suppose.

What changes are taking place in this international scene?

At the time of writing (1993), there were two factors at work. In the first place the increasing desire of multinational companies to be listed on Anglo-Saxon stock exchanges with their more 'open' listing requirements, and the desire in the major European countries for their stock exchanges to attract international investors, has meant a shift of emphasis away from law and tax to the interests of the ordinary share holder.

The second factor was the initiatives within the European Community to increase commercial competition, and achieve greater harmonization in financial reporting. These initiatives found expression in the series of company law Directives. The more important of these were the Fourth Directive, covering the contents and form of annual accounts, and the Seventh, on group accounts and consolidation.

The effect of these Directives extends beyond the twelve countries of the 1992 Community to all other European counties as well. For the UK export manager an important change has been the general acceptance of the 'true and fair view' in the Fourth Directive. This is a total change for published accounts in France, Germany, Italy, Sweden and Switzerland.

What We Have Learned from this Chapter

To put it briefly, there were two major ideas to be grasped from this chapter:

1 What is meant by a 'company', and what are the implications of that concept for the relationships between the company, the company's business, and the company records (mainly financial) that management uses to control that business.
2 The general ideas which we have just introduced, and the application of those ideas which we will examine in the next few chapters, are subject to some national variations across the world.

Questions for Discussion

1 In discussions of the fundamentals of business, the term 'Stake-holders' is often used. Can you find out what it means and what is its relevance to the longer term strategy of a business?
2 Jack Spratt buys and sells bulk spirits worldwide through his private company, Mackerel Ltd, of which he is the sole employee. Taking the day off to go to Ascot, he draws £10,000 from the bank with a cheque drawn on the company's account. Describe four different ways in which that cash transaction might be described when the company's end-of-year accounts are prepared.
3 Great aunt Matilda, who provided 20 per cent of the share capital of Mackerel Ltd, was horrified at this extravagance and said to Jack: 'You are robbing the shareholders! If you don't pay back that £10,000 I will sue you.' Can she?

3

How We Measure
Our Progress

In this chapter we will look at the task of turning an export 'idea' into a business. The background to that task has been briefly described in the previous two chapters. Now we will make a closer examination of the task to see what is involved. Then we will be able to find ways of successfully tackling many of the facets of the exporting task.

'It Seems Like a Very Good Idea!'

Arthur Brown is a systems analyst and designer who has been working in France for three years on computer system development for a French manufacturing company. This has recently involved the installation of a new piece of British software with an advanced technical application. What Arthur Brown has noticed is that, for certain types of installation, a relatively small but sophisticated add-on module would materially enhance the performance of the original software package.

Arthur Brown has now returned to the UK and, with the encouragement of the producers of the original software, has designed the add-on module to the stage where a prototype could be programmed and tested. Because the new module would help the sales of the original software, the company has promised support in finding customers. They themselves are not interested in getting directly involved as the new add-on software would be too small a scale business to be attractive, nor would it fit in with the British company's longer term strategy. Arthur himself has saved up enough money (he thinks!) to get the business going on his own.

So Arthur Brown now has a potential business. More specifically, he has:

1 A product that works, or at any rate will work as soon as the coding is complete and tested. Based on his experience in France he knows that the product offers a genuine advantage to an identifiable group of potential users.
2 A market. The users of the original software are known and the benefit of the additional module is demonstrable, as Arthur Brown's experience with his former French employer has shown.
3 Access to that market. The British producers of the original software have promised a mailing list (for a fee, of course!) of the French users. Arthur Brown himself is familiar with that industrial sector in France and has sufficient command of French to oversee the production of sales literature and technical manuals, and to conduct presentations and demonstrations to potential 'clients'.
4 The technical ability to organize the programming and testing, to train any employees that the business may need to employ, and to seek further markets or applications in the longer term.
5 The finance to make it happen.

Turning a Business Idea into a Business

So, Arthur Brown has a product, a market, the technical ability to put the two successfully together and some cash. All that is needed is the management expertise to complete the task. But now comes the stage which many entrepreneurial spirits find frustrating. That longer term target, of realizing the fruits of one's enterprise and efforts, seems to recede further and further into the future whilst the entrepreneur himself must devote his attentions to dealing with people and organizations other than the customers where the 'business' really resides,

Arthur Brown finds he has the opportunity to outline his ideas to his bank manager in the informal and slightly alcoholic atmosphere of a Christmas party. Arthur expands on the software details that he knows and loves so well but is disappointed to find that the conversation seems to go off in quite another direction. 'I suppose you're incorporated by now – if not, I can give you the name of a first class solicitor. Who's your accountant? Get him to send me your business plan as soon as its ready. Oh!, and let me know what you want to do about remittance transfers. Being a computer expert you won't have any problems with this Intrastats pantomime of course! One big advantage you'll have, being a service company, is that you can keep your gearing pretty low. You've got all the addresses you need? – Inland Revenue, Customs & Excise, the employment people and the rest ...'.

Incorporated? Business plan? Solicitor? Accountant? Remittances? Intrastats? Gearing? **Inland** Revenue? (I thought we were exporting for heaven's sake!) National Insurance contributions? What has all this got to do with supplying products to meet market demand?

In order to convince Arthur Brown that this world is not designed to prevent entrepreneurs from exporting anything at all, we will take each of these 'peripheral distractions' one by one, to see how they affect the management of an export business, and their significance to its success.

What is a successful business?

Arthur Brown, like every other enthusiastic entrepreneur, is hoping for 'success' in the not too distant future, but how do we measure 'success'? What is success any way? The only objective measure of success is the value of a business to a disinterested outsider, which means 'What would he pay for the business if it were offered and if he could afford it?' At the moment the value of Arthur Brown's business is exactly zero.

Later on he will have software to sell, a reputation in the market place, customers paying him money, cash in the bank (less some debts to pay), and a few other things as well. So **one** measure of a business is the value of its **assets** less the value of its **liabilities**. This is not the only measure of success but it has the virtue of being an objective one. It is also the basis of the accounting process, and it is the measure that outsiders (like the Inland Revenue for example) will expect the business to use. The basic justification for this was explained in chapter 1.

Because our financial measuring stick is founded on the twin ideas of assets and liabilities, all measured in money terms, it follows that the statement of a company's assets and liabilities is the starting point for monitoring its financial progress. That statement is called the **Balance Sheet**, and we will explain the significance of that document in chapter 5. In that chapter we shall make use of a very important, fundamental idea: profit is an increase in net assets.

If you keep that in mind you will find the rest of this book easier to understand. You will also have a sharper idea of what the management of a business organization is all about.

Do we need a 'Company' as well as the business?

Arthur Brown's bank manager seemed to assume that 'incorporation' was an obvious first step but was this reasonable? Arthur Brown will be seeking co-operation from the software producer, he will be offering his services to French companies, he will continue to talk to his bank manager, he will commission someone to programme, code and test his own software, and he may wish to employ people to help him run the business. The question is: Will all these potential collaborators take him seriously?

As we said in chapter 2, a serious export business of this type or larger is almost certain to be incorporated as a limited liability company. Because Arthur Brown is a British citizen now based back in Britain, the company will be incorporated under the UK Companies Acts by registering with Companies House.

This requires some formalities such as making an Annual Return each year, but provided someone takes responsibility for it, the small amount of paper work should never be a deterrent to incorporation.

In what way is the company seen to be making profitable progress?

If Arthur Brown is steering his company towards success, he needs some method of knowing that he is indeed moving in the right direction. That method is the company's accounting system combined with a number of other techniques. The 1985 UK Companies Act (the relevant Act at the time of writing) is a substantial document but a copy should be on the shelf of any chief executive. The single most significant requirement for us at this point is contained in Section 221 of the 1985 Act; that every company is required to keep accounting records sufficient to show and explain the company's transactions, so that, at any time, it should be possible to determine the company's financial position and to ascertain that the company's balance sheet and profit & loss account have been prepared in accordance with the Act.

In effect this requirement only asks that a company should be run at the minimum level of competence. The people who need to know that proper accounts are being kept include:

1   The managers of the company. They need to supervize the day to day operations of the company and to plan its future operations effectively. If they don't have the figures, they can't.
2   The shareholders, who have a statutory right under the Act to be informed as to what the directors of the company have done with their investment. If Arthur is going to be the major shareholder he will need to be sure that he is getting a better return on his investment than he would have done if he had kept the money in the building society.
3   All the providers of finance to the company, the bank, invoice factors or forfaiters, and other providers of export or general

finance or short term credit will need evidence that the company can pay the interest and repay the loans.

4   The Inland Revenue who will be assessing the company for Corporation Tax.

5   Customs & Excise who will be interested in the company's records for collecting and paying VAT.

6   Trade contacts of any kind who will be as interested in his company's financial stability as he is in that of his own customers.

7   The employees of the company who have a very personal interest in the efficient management and healthy prospects of the business.

8   Companies House, where the Registrar of Companies will be expecting to receive the company's Annual Return and the copies of audited accounts as laid down by the Companies Act.

In chapter 6 we will see how that profit figure, which is the measurement of the company's progress, is arrived at. We will also look at the generally accepted conventions used in the calculation – essential for the correct interpretation of the figures – and also at the possible ambiguities that must be resolved.

How may management monitor the day-to-day operations?

Almost every day, Arthur Brown will be making decisions that will have an impact on his longer term success, but he will not be doing his accounts every day. How will he know if he can afford to offer a discount for a larger order? What will it cost him if he has to wait an extra fortnight for a payment? Is it worth while buying some fancier software for processing his orders? Every week the question is: 'Which is the profitable decision?'

Knowing in retrospect that the company made a profit or a loss last month or last year is only of indirect assistance to a manager who has to decide now whether a particular order or a new price list will contribute to the company's profit or diminish it. In chapter 7 we will look at the way individual transactions individually affect the company's profit. Then in chapter 8, by examining the concepts of 'cost' and 'contribution', we will see how the financial figures can be used in day to day decision making.

Getting the prices, costs and volumes right

Arthur Brown's venture depends to a large extent on co-operation with the British producer of the original software. That company has suggested that its home, UK market should not be neglected even though, as Arthur Brown already knows, UK prices are more competitive and margins are slimmer. 'But' they say 'you need the extra volume to spread your overheads and lower your break-even volume'. He has to consider strategic issues. For example, is the type of business that he originally planned the right sort of business for his proposed company? Perhaps a very expensive foray into the very competitive North American market is desirable; or perhaps it is suicidal. How can Arthur Brown decide these sorts of questions?

In chapter 12 we will look at the way prices, costs, sales revenues, and profits interact and at the way we can use the concept of 'contribution' not just to achieve profits, but to maximize our profits.

Why he must keep a (very close) eye on the cash

Arthur Brown's bank manager was taking a close interest in the project not simply out of Yuletide goodwill but because there was one very important element in planning the business that Arthur Brown did not mention – that was **time**. Arthur knows how to get the business going but, however smart he is, it will take time. In the interval programmers, translators and printers will need to be paid. Arthur can share a trade exhibition stand with the software company but they will want his share of the cost to be paid up front. The office needs to be established and who is going to hold the fort when Arthur is in France? And

Arthur himself needs to eat during this period, not to mention his family. The bank manager knows two other things that every start-up entrepreneur also needs to know:

1   The money starts to come in a long time after it starts being paid out – so what happens in the meantime?
2   No bank or other institution will provide all the capital needed, but almost certainly Arthur Brown will be borrowing some money to supplement his own investment.

How much he will need to borrow can only be decided if Arthur knows the difference between liquidity and profitability, and if he also knows how to prepare and use (that's the difficult bit) a cash flow forecast. If he borrows too little the business may fail, not because it was not profitable but merely because it was broke (and the bank will lose the money it loaned). If he borrows too much, the interest charges will impose an unnecessary cost burden on his business.

Forecasting and then controlling the cash situation, or to express it more usefully, controlling the working capital of the company, is something that we will examine in chapters 10 and 11.

How can Arthur Brown keep a continuous grip on things?

There are two things that may tempt Arthur to throw all the plans and forecasts and cost sheets into the waste paper basket. They are:

1   Whatever Arthur plans, howsoever carefully, things will never, but never, work out the way originally planned.
2   Arthur's skills are those of a software designer, so he has no desire, ability or opportunity to be a financial analyst – and his business would probably collapse if he tried. But he does need some practical pointers that will continually guide him, and continually reassure him that he is doing it right or warn him when he is not.

We will explain how both these difficulties can be coped with in chapters 13 and 14.

Can he cope with that 'time' thing – in the long term?

We explained just a moment ago that Arthur Brown can be sure that cash will only start to flow in a long time after it started to flow out. Nevertheless he must not have to wait too long before receipts catch up with payments. How long is 'too long'? That particular problem faces anyone engaging in the export business. Exporters are, by the nature of their trade, engaged in the long term business of opening up and developing many and distant markets. Chasing after 'the quick buck' is not for them.

Therefore in the management of an export business we need a technique that will reconcile the conflicting costs of time and interest charges. This can be done by applying the ideas of **investment appraisal** to the marketing strategy, and this will be discussed in chapter 14.

Can Arthur use Information Technology in his business?

He is a software designer so, of course he can! Or can he? Information technology in export management is more about management than about technology. An understanding of the technology will help us to understand what can be done and what cannot, and it will also stir up the imagination to produce better and more effective ways of running the business. But it is not information technology we should be mainly interested in but rather its **application**. This will be examined in chapter 15.

Will it all fit together in practice?

Familiarity with the components of an export business is the professional and valuable skill of the technical experts. As may be seen from what we have talked about already in this chapter, the management of an exporting company needs to be familiar with those technical skills, but in addition needs to have the vision to see how they may all be fitted together. The place where they may be seen to fit together is in that document often referred to as 'the budget'. A little caution is necessary when discussing the budget. In commercial organizations the budget may sometimes be regarded as a weapon of mass destruction in the battle of corporate politics; in bureaucratic organizations it may be a Maginot Line behind which administrators defend their individual territories or attempt to annex those of others.

In chapter 14 we will instead attempt to direct attention towards the use of the budgeting **process** as a tool of business development and the management of change.

Why is it always so complicated?

The short answer to that question is that any business, even a very small one, consists of a complex web of linked activities. If those activities are to be monitored, steered and evaluated there must be some 'system' in place.

A true story: This writer when first in business as a young man, had to organize a rush print job for a prestigious American customer. It was delivered to the customer, at his London hotel, on time. Regrettably the Production Director was not impressed. 'Where's the delivery note?' 'The delivery note? Well, er ...!' With no delivery note how could Accounts invoice the customer or, later, ensure that the customer paid? With no delivery note how would the factory know that the job had been dispatched? If the factory does not know what has been dispatched how can they cost the work they have done or keep track of their use of machine time and of materials? And, what does the Chief Accountant tell the VAT inspectors at the next visit?

This sounds like a plea, a very familiar plea, for better communications. However, if a company holds a committee meeting about every order or every project we may be sure that very little productive work will get done at all. Although we do need communication, a business needs a communication system that is effective and efficient. This means that only that which needs to be communicated is actually communicated, that each member of the staff can rely on getting the information he or she needs, but no more. The information system must be effective but minimal.

We will look at this requirement in a little more detail in the next chapter. However, knowing that a company needs an information system does not tell you what information should be processed by the system. That major requirement is the underlying topic of all the subsequent chapters of this book. A company does not run an accounting system to provide occupational therapy for its book-keepers – it does it because it wants (or should want!) to see the output figures and knows how to use them. Therefore the information system needs to be carefully designed with content and application clearly in mind.

What a Financial Management System Does Not Measure

One very useful skill for managers is knowing what they do not know. If you know that, you also know who you need to ask and what it is you must ask for. If nobody has the answer, then at least you know that it is necessary to devise a decision strategy which takes that state of ignorance into account. So what is it that financial management does not tell us as managers?

1 It does not say what will happen in the future, but making things happen **in the future** is what management is all about. However it will provide data that will help management to make estimates about the future – typically in planning and budgeting.
2 It will not provide quantified information about the preferences and idiosyncrasies of agents, distributors and end users. But all such people have their own businesses to run and if we can understand our business thoroughly we stand a better chance of forecasting how they will respond to us. Furthermore, a good cost analysis system will tell us how

much it is costing the company to gather such useful (or perhaps not so useful?) information by other means.

3   It will not tell management how to motivate the export salesmen or the export office staff. But with an effective information and control system in operation more can be delegated to more junior employees because they know what is required of them and management knows what they are achieving. That should give the export manager time to attend to the effectiveness of his or her department without being distracted by continual 'fire-fighting'. Remember – management is getting people to do things.

Questions for Discussion

1   So you have this wonderful export business idea, but the thought of preparing a 'business plan' seems so tedious when you would much prefer to be drumming up business in exotic overseas markets. What advantages would a business plan have that would make the tedium worthwhile?

2   When small companies grow up they often change from being 'Limited' to being a 'Plc'. Give two advantages and two disadvantages of making the change.

3   You have, by means of patience and plain hard work, built up an export business that turned in a profit of £87,000 last year. A friend said: 'Eighty seven thousand earned in one year! You must have money coming out of your ears!' Suggest three possible reasons why you still can't afford that Rolls in spite of being so profitable.

4

Organizing the
Information Flows

We have seen what, in general terms, a commercial export business actually does and how its 'success' may be defined. We can now start to look at how these broad principles may be put into practice. Chapters 1 to 3 of this book gave the context of the export manager's task; chapters 5 and onwards deal with the techniques of planning, control and evaluation of performance. However the detailed implementation of an export strategy will involve individual people exercising particular skills.

Introduction

In this chapter we will examine the way in which the many and varied individual activities of an export operation impinge on the overall success of the business and what this implies for the recording and control systems that management must operate. We will do this by listing some of the typical operations required to exploit an export market, and by showing how the impact such operations may have on the overall success of the business may be recorded.

What you will learn from this chapter, supported by what you have already learned from the three previous ones, is the relevance of the individual techniques (which we will look at later in this book) to the overall target of business success.

Management Information and Control

You were reminded in chapter 1 that the task of the manager is getting people to do things. Achieving that involves:

1 providing the environment in which those individuals can effectively and efficiently exercise those skills;
2 providing the information system so that it can be seen (immediately or many months later or both) that those skills have been exercised; and
3 providing the recording and evaluation system that will demonstrate that the activities of all persons involved contributed to the success of the business, whether looked at consignment by consignment or looked at year by year.

In practical terms that means management must have a system of recording and evaluation that will:

1 Keep a record of the investment in the export markets. A lot of money must be spent on research, on product development, perhaps on manufacture, on selling, on supply and distribution, and on meeting the cost of providing finance for all of that. Remember what we said in the last chapter about **time**?
2 Keep a record of the costs and the revenues of the consignments or of the service commissions that are the exporter's business, so that for each of them management will know the extent to which they are individually contributing to the success of the business.
3 Keep records of overall company performance that will enable both the management and the shareholders to see that the total operation was worthwhile. The availability of such records will, incidentally, keep our bank manager happy, as well as other providers of export finance, Customs & Excise, the Inland Revenue and the Registrar of Companies.

What will be assumed here and in the rest of this book is that the detailed operations of the export task are being competently performed in the technical sense. These operations are all well described in the companion volumes of this series on exporting. Just to remind you, those volumes are:

Principles of Marketing
Principles of International Trade and Payments
Principles of Law Relating to Overseas Trade
Principles of International Physical Distribution
Principles of International Marketing
Principles of International Marketing Research

All the operations described in the companion volumes are the essence of the exporter's trade. However in any particular market or with any particular product any one of these operations may be either important or less important, may be either to the detriment or to the benefit of the business. They all involve costs which the exporter hopes will be recouped in the final analysis, and it is therefore the responsibility of the export manager to ensure that this happens. However different markets, different industries, different countries all have their own peculiar characteristics and what may be essential in one may be merely an expensive luxury in another.

To quote a few examples, one company for which the author worked had little need for sophisticated market research or even for sophisticated marketing simply because that particular industry worked in a uniform way from Tokyo to Valparaiso and many of the senior managers were personally acquainted with each other. In another case, a friend of the author financed a holiday in south-east Asia by cold calling, while he was there, selling stationery items by sample on open account - and he got paid! On another occasion this author was involved in machinery exports where the names and addresses of all potential customers worldwide were obtainable from desk research, but where sales were handicapped by the prices being **too low**, customers often preferring the expensive option of a 'Rolls-Royce' product from a Swiss competitor.

Note that in the illustrative analysis that follows we will refer to the 'product' and to the 'distributor'. The product, of course, could be anything from a 20-tonne machine to a box of plastic toys or (in the case of a service company) something as 'invisible' as a consultancy contract. In a similar way, the distribution of the product or service could involve anything from a one-off contract with a foreign buying house in the UK, to the establishment of a wholly-owned subsidiary in the overseas market. Therefore, when following the narrative below you should treat the implied export exercise as a stereotype of just one possibility out of many.

We must now consider how the three types of records – the investment in overheads, the direct costs of individual consignments and profitable performance – relate to some typical activities.

Export Activities and Management Records

We could list the various activities required to exploit a particular export market like this:

1 Initial desk market research.
2 Field market research.
3 Development of the product and promotional material.
4 Appointing distributors or agents.
5 Field sales activity.
6 Agreeing a sales contract and payment arrangements.
7 Credit checks and getting credit cover.
8 Arranging any necessary working capital financing.
9 Order notification leading to order confirmation.
10 Purchase or manufacture of the goods.
11 Finished goods assigned to the order.
12 Export packing.
13 Documentation, insurance, shipping arrangements.
14 Order dispatched.
15 Title to the goods passes.
16 Installation, training, spares orders.
17 Invoices and other bills to pay are received.

18 Payment received from the customer or bank.
19 Follow-up: service, repairs, accessories.
20 Repeat orders.
21 Longer-term growth in trade to that market.
22 Financial growth of the distributor or whosoever.

Each of these activities may be well or badly performed. The technical requirements in each case, the options open to the exporter, the necessities for any market, distributor or consignment, are all matters that are well covered in the companion volumes in this series. We shall concentrate on the information flows that will enable management, week by week or year by year, to see that all the activities are making an effective contribution to the long-term success of the business. In doing so we will outline some of the organizational decisions that have to be made to ensure that the company has an efficient and effective management information system.

Investment in the Market and in the Distributor

Items 1 to 6 in our list represent the company's investment in one particular market and probably in one particular local representative. All these activities involve the expenditure of money now (plus, we hope, some help from the DTI). Management must therefore:

1 Ensure that all such expenditures are recorded so that, perhaps two years later if necessary, the company knows that it spent so much on achieving – or failing to achieve – a target market opening. We need an accounting system to do this.
2 Check that such expenditure is within sensible limits. What those sensible limits are would have been established earlier when the initial budgets were drawn up following initial market projections. Therefore we need profit and cash forecasts so that management can compare 'actual' with 'budget' figures.

3 Decide what proportion of these expenditures represent the acquisition of an objectively valued, long term asset in that market (establishing a subsidiary or building a warehouse for instance) or for the product (technical improvements that will be valuable in other, un-exploited markets). We must therefore make the distinction between current and capital expenditure. If it is current expenditure a decision must be made whether or not it is to be recognized as a cost to that distributor's agreement, to that market as a whole, or to be spread equitably over all the company's export markets. We will have the problem of cost apportionment.

4 Reflect on the time factor, using the ideas of investment appraisal, to establish that those initial market development costs, paid so long ago, really represented a sensible investment in the light of the sales revenues actually achieved several years later.

Keeping An Eye on the Profitability

Items 7 to 14 in our list can all be regarded as related to one particular consignment (or perhaps to one service project). So, in order to ensure that the order was profitable we add up the costs, subtract them from the revenue, and that's the profit! Well, not quite.

1 Some of those charges will be easy to identify and to allocate to one particular order. These are our 'direct costs'. However one of those 'direct costs' will be the value of goods assigned to the order when taken from a larger stock in the warehouse. Therefore we need records of manufacturing costs and records of the valuation of the 'finished goods' stock in order to arrive at the cost of goods sold.

2 But what about the cost of the export office and of activities like the time spent preparing those dreaded second, correct, letter of credit details? What about the insurance cover if the company has an open policy for all its consignments? Such expenditures will have to be apportioned to the various activities we are considering. But any one of these

expenditures may have been paid against a single invoice – and properly recorded of course! If we are to 'cost' the consignment we need both an accounting system and also a costing system that will analyse the costs in the many different ways management needs.

Keeping An Eye on the Cash

Items 15 to 18 relate to the cash coming in. This cash is the means of recouping the initial investment in the market, of paying the costs of the consignment just delivered, of paying the company overheads, and of providing the profit which was the original point of it all. Therefore management must have a system that:

1   Tells them just how much cash is expected and when. This, obviously, is particularly true if the company has, for instance, hedged its foreign exchange risk by selling forward.
2   Will provide action reports on a regular basis on the progress of these expected cash inflows. This is all part of the technique of the control of working capital, and the successful juggling of working capital underlies decisions about hedging exchange exposure, credit insurance, factoring, and export finance in general.

The Basis of Longer-term Planning

We have already indicated that many of the figures that pass across the export manager's desk are there to be compared with the budgeted or with the forecast figures previously prepared. Longer-term planning is a continuous process, repeatedly using the 'historic' figures already generated by past business activities to build plans for future business activities, which will then be formalized in quantified budget plans. To do that management must have:

1   The overall performance records of the business, which are

summarized in the profit & loss statement, in the balance sheet, and in the cash flow statement.

2   The ability to interpret and to see the significance of the individual items in those documents.

3   The knowledge to see how any one of those figures may be beneficially or adversely affected by possible non-financial decisions about new markets, new products, changes in volumes, changes in price, changes in exchange rates and so on.

4   Sufficient overall 'feel' for the whole business operation to see how those summary figures, taken in conjunction with the company's plans, will look to the providers of the finance that powered the enterprise, that is the shareholders and the banks.

The Business as a Machine

A machine is a collection of mechanical parts, all designed to work together to produce a desired output, whether it is an aluminium extrusion, a colour magazine or a safe road journey. All the parts must mesh together, efficiently converting the inputs into the required output. A business is just such a machine. In chapter 1 we gave a bird's-eye view of the inputs and outputs. Simplifying it even further, we can say that the inputs are knowledge, skills and finance, and the output is profit.

The staff involved will be both using information and generating it. For instance, the credit status and agreed payment terms for a customer, or the weights and cubes for a bill of lading must all have been prepared prior to when an order is confirmed or a bill.

In the same way, decisions about packaging, about transport, about insurance cover all imply the acceptance of costs either in money or in time. The costs must then be fed back into the information system, so that sales performance may be monitored, orders evaluated for profit, slow payers chased, prices revised, discounts agreed, forward financing arranged, future promotions budgeted for.

All the time operating staff and management will be feeding

in and extracting information from the system. If the company implements EDI those information flows will also involve suppliers, customers, banks, and Customs & Excise.

The management task, as we stated at the beginning of this chapter, is to ensure that all those involved simultaneously have available and are producing the necessary information flows. The management can then get on with its other job, that of evaluating the recorded performance and using those records to plan future improved performance. This is what Part 2 of this book covers.

Questions for Discussion

1   Look at the list shown in this chapter under the heading 'Export activities and management records'. For each of these 22 activities state what organizations or which persons may be responsible for ensuring that they happened or helped to ensure they happened.

2   Bernie Cornfeld, when he was running his very profitable international investments organization in the late 1960s, said: 'The less my salesmen know about investments the better. It only takes their minds off selling.' Would knowing too much about the intricacies of exporting be a similar distraction to a company's export salesmen?

3   List the people and organizations involved in the sequence of events for a company exporting high value, low weight goods by air freight, from the initial receipt of a request for a quotation from a new customer to the arrival of the shipment at the overseas airport ready for customs clearance.

Part 2

The Basic Tools for Profitable Management

The previous chapters set the target for an export manager as the achievement of a 'profitable business'. To achieve any target it is necessary to be sure precisely what that target is, and to be sure that you will know when you have hit that target.

In this section we will see how the target of profitability is to be quantified and why it is quantified in that particular way. Knowing that will enable us to grasp three things about the export business we are involved in.

First we will see how the balance sheet of a company will tell us whether we have arrived at where we wanted to get.

Secondly we will see how the profit and loss account will tell us how we got there (or perhaps why we failed to get there). Either way it will give management guidance for the future.

Thirdly we will see how to strike a sensible balance between, on the one hand, that vital but abstract concept of profit and, on the other hand, that useful and very tangible thing, cash in the bank.

5

Management, the Business and the Finance

Introduction

In that famous, fictional trial scene, the King of Hearts was asked by a witness where to begin. 'Begin at the beginning, and go on till you come to the end: then stop' he was told. Not being in a looking-glass world and because we are interested in the management of an export business, we will turn that excellent advice around and start right at the end and work backwards from there.

The management of a business will only spend good money on an information system when it has defined and established the need for the end results. The end results are conventionally called the 'final accounting statements' consisting of: the balance sheet; the trading and profit and loss account; and the cash flow (or 'funds flow') statement.

These three statements show the assets of the company **now**, how the company arrived at that situation, and, more specifically, how the company arrived at its present cash situation. Taken together, they indicate where the company might go next.

We will look at the second of these, 'the P & L' as it is usually known, in chapters 6 and 7, and we will look at recording cash flows in chapters 9 and 10.

This chapter will explain:

1 The way in which an understanding of the balance sheet will enable you to understand the way the conventional financial information system works.
2 What is to be included in the balance sheet and the way in which the items are arranged.
3 The very close connection between this 'final statement' and the day to day transactions of the business.
4 The relationship between the balance sheet figures and the liquidity of the company and the profitability of the company.
5 The necessary conventions that need to be observed in drawing up a balance sheet to achieve consistency and to make it comprehensible both to management and to outsiders.

What is a Balance Sheet?

Quite simply, a balance sheet is a list of assets and liabilities. But whose assets and whose liabilities?

The assets and liabilities are those of the company, not of the shareholders, the managers, or anyone else at all. Remember what we explained in chapter 2 when we listed the more significant characteristics of an incorporated company? A company is a distinct legal person which can own things, can get into debt, can buy things, or can be sued in the courts.

Therefore a balance sheet is a list of **what the company owns and what it owes**.

Why a 'balance' sheet? Because the balance sheet explains where the money came from and what it was used for. These two totals must add up to the same – they must balance.

Because the situation of any company that is not 'dormant' is continuously changing, this statement of assets and liabilities must refer to a **specific point in time**. You should always note the date that appears at the top of every balance sheet.

Because the balance sheet tells us what the company owns and what it owes, it cannot also include business assets which it does not own. The company does not own its employees, not since the abolition of slavery! Nor does it own their knowledge and skills. Hence the old joke about advertising agencies (or similar purely service companies) that 'all the company's assets walk out of the door at 5.30 every evening'. In the same way a company does not own its presence and its reputation in any of its export markets since competitors can take these without obligation. However a company can own patents and trade-marks and therefore, indirectly, can own named brands.

One last point and a most important one: The everyday business transactions of a company all, individually, potentially affect the balance sheet of a company. In theory, every time goods are shipped, materials received, invoices sent out or received, people employed, electricity used, every time that anything is done that has a financial implication, then the company's balance sheet could be re-drawn. In practice, of course, it is up-dated at set intervals; once a month? once a quarter? once a year certainly. Thus there is an observable and direct connection, that can be traced right through the financial re-cording system, between what the employees and directors of the company do and what appears on that 'final statement', the balance sheet. We will now see how it works in practice.

We will use the example of a small, incorporated private company. The operations of a sole trader or of a partnership are legally simpler but, because the law makes no distinction in such cases between the financial affairs of the business and of those managing it, the financial information system in such cases is more confusing.

The Story of a New Exporter

Anthony Aldine is going to be an exporter, an exporter of small books, initially to North America. Anthony has a friend who has written a small training manual for a particular minority sport most of whose practitioners belong to identifiable clubs up and down the length of the United Kingdom. The friend has got the book printed, holds stocks of the book and supplies them to customers by mail order. Anthony suggested that his friend could also sell the books abroad where the sport is often organized in the same way, and his friend responded in the traditional way – 'well, perhaps, or alternatively, perhaps not?'.

So Anthony immediately realizes he has an opportunity to exploit. He can become the entrepreneurial manager of an export business provided he can come to an agreement with his friend over handling the export sales. He guesses that the North American market is ideal because that market is accessible – research will discover the relevant clubs, mail order is feasible, and there is no language problem.

After initial research at the DTI's Export Market Information Centre in London he draws up his business plan. He will initially buy a small stock from his friend, prepare his sales literature, take a trip to the United States in the guise of a lecture tour around the clubs, and then send mail-shots to all the clubs he can identify in the States and in Canada. Sales terms will be 'cash with order' and he will arrange with his local bank to accept the dollar cheques coming in.

Anthony Aldine's business plan indicates that it will cost £10,000 to get going, a sum of money which he has available in his Building Society account. His bank manager is happy to open a new business account for the new company because it looks as though the bank can make promises of support without actually risking any of its own money.

The only thing left is for Anthony to formally incorporate his business as a private limited liability company. Because Anthony has read the first part of this book he knows that this is the sensible way to do things, especially as his wife will act as unpaid company secretary.

We will now observe Anthony Aldine's progress by drawing up a succession of balance sheets.

Note that for the rest of this chapter and in the next we will introduce a number of new technical terms and some accounting conventions. These will be explained as we go along but you can also refer to the appendices at the end of this book for a glossary of technical terms.

The balance sheets that we will present to show Arthur Aldine's progress will be laid out using the 'horizontal format' rather than the vertical format. The latter, vertical layout is the usual one but mainly because it fits an A4 sheet of paper more conveniently. On the other hand, the old fashioned, horizontal format makes the logic of the balance sheet much clearer.

Aldinc Activities Ltd: Act 1, Scene 1

Arthur has taken the first steps to set up his company which will operate his export business. These steps were:

1 Register the company with Companies House.
2 Appoint himself and his wife as directors.
3 Appoint his wife as company secretary.
4 Open a bank account in the name of the company.
5 Pay in the £10,000 as share capital which, of course, was paid from his own personal resources into the company's bank account.

We can now start to draw up a balance sheet, arranged with the **liabilities** (where the money came from) listed on the left hand side and the **assets** (what the money was used for) on the right. If we lived on the other side of the Straits of Dover it would be the other way round – like driving on the roads there!

LIABILITIES	ASSETS

We will divide both the 'liabilities' and the 'assets' into the longer-term items and the shorter term items.

Longer-term 'liabilities' will include share capital, longer term loans and profits ploughed back into the business. We will call them the 'sources of finance' of the company.

Short term 'liabilities' will include money owed for unpaid debts, overdrafts at the bank, and short-term loans and other similar finance obligations such as bank advances on a particular export consignment or bills of exchange to be paid. We will call these 'current liabilities'.

Some of the company's assets are naturally to be considered long term. These would include buildings, machinery and equipment, and investments in subsidiary companies such as overseas subsidiaries. These we will call 'fixed assets'.

Short term assets include raw materials, goods ready for sale, money owed by customers or bills of exchange maturing soon, payments in advance that the company may have made, and above all, cash in the bank or in short term investments. These are all 'current assets'.

So it is very useful to think of the balance sheet split two ways; long term above and short term ('current') below, and with liabilities on the left set against the assets of the company on the right, like this:

LIABILITIES	ASSETS
Sources of finance	Fixed assets
Current liabilities	Current assets

So the new company can now start trading with effect from the 1st of May. Because it does now exist it must have a balance sheet, so if we now record the first transactions of the new company we get:

SOURCES OF FINANCE		FIXED ASSETS	
Share capital	£10,000		
CURRENT LIABILITIES		**CURRENT ASSETS**	
		Cash at Bank	£10,000
Total liabilities	£10,000	Total assets	£10,000

Arthur's company has not bought any long term assets nor has the company incurred any short term liabilities, so these are both zero.

Now for some explanations!

Why 'liabilities'? If the left-hand side of the balance sheet is to show where the money came from this implies that the company has a liability to acknowledge and (in the case of loans or other debts) to repay that money.

The fact that Arthur Aldine could reasonably argue 'It's my money any way!' does not alter things. Remember that the company is a distinct legal person, distinct from anyone or any thing else. Therefore Arthur, wearing his director's hat, has a 'fiduciary duty' to the company and thus to its shareholders (that is, to Arthur wearing his shareholder's hat) to exercise his director's powers in the interests of the company. The balance sheet records that liability.

'Sources of finance'. If the Liabilities side of the balance sheet shows where the money came from it thereby shows what the **company owes**. We will use the term 'sources of finance' or 'sources of longer term finance' to refer to the longer term and permanent funds that are the basis of the company's finances.

'Assets' are things the company owns and, at this early stage, all the company owns is its bank account balance. But why 'current assets'? It is important always to be able to distinguish between short term and long term assets and liabilities. How 'short' is short term? Current assets and current liabilities are those assets and liabilities that may be expected to change their nature in the course of normal trading within one year.

Arthur intends to use that money in the bank. For a start he intends to convert some of it into books for sale, thus changing cash into stock for sale.

Aldine Activities Ltd: Act 1, Scene 2

Arthur gets down to business. He wants to plan his initial sales trip (disguised as a lecture tour) to the United States and he wants to take a small quantity of books with him to display and, he hopes, to sell. Since it is a new company, he cannot expect to get credit from his supplier, that is, his author friend. So he pays cash, £1,000 in fact. So our new balance sheet looks like this:

SOURCES OF FINANCE		FIXED ASSETS	
Share capital	£10,000		
CURRENT LIABILITIES		**CURRENT ASSETS**	
		Stocks	£1,000
		Cash at Bank	£9,000
Total liabilities	£10,000	Total assets	£10,000

Arthur has converted £1,000's worth of one asset (cash) into a similar amount of another asset (a stock of books ready for sale). Let us look at this new balance sheet in more detail.

We have valued the stock of books at what was paid for them; the stock is **valued at cost**. It may be argued, and Arthur probably would, that this stock is worth more to his company than that. But we are following two, related accounting principles:

1 The prudence concept: where alternative valuations or procedures are possible we should select the most conservative.
2 The standard for the valuation of stocks: stocks and work in progress should be valued at the lower of cost or net realisable value. (Accounting standard SSAP 9.)

These principles are important. Stock can only be **proved** to be of value when they are sold, so in the mean time only the cost figure is recorded. Furthermore, if Arthur were to decide at any time that the stock he had bought was only saleable for less than he paid for it, he should **write down** the value to what he could realistically expect to get, net of the expenses of getting rid of it.

However the major reason for being careful in the valuation of stock relates back to our definition of 'profit' in chapter 3 as 'an increase in net assets'. If we overvalue stock we automatically generate a fictitious, 'paper' profit. The fraudulent overvaluation of stock is one of the favourite methods of dishonest directors claiming fictitious profits.

The 'total assets' figure has remained unchanged from the last balance sheet, and so it should. In running a business, management is continually changing one asset into another: buying machinery for cash, paying off debts, changing raw materials into finished goods. None of these earns a profit because there is no change in net assets. That means that a profit is only earned by trading profitably, not by shuffling assets.

Note that in spite of the activities of our Managing Director the balance sheet still balances – it always does as a matter of arithmetic. Even companies descending down into the black hole of liquidation still have a balanced balance sheet till they finally disappear from sight.

Aldine Activities Ltd: Act 2, Scene 1

Arthur gets into business. In the course of transatlantic telephone calls arranging his lecture tour of the sports clubs he finds that there is already a demand for the manual as the result of press reviews of it in a British magazine that was seen in the States. Arthur has made some sales ('Cash with order, plus post and packing, please!') for half his stock of books. These he then posts off to the American customers. Unfortunately he knows that his next bank statement will show a charge for the dollar/sterling conversion. So instead of banking, after conversion, the expected £700, Arthur only expects to see £670.

Noting these facts, we now get (leaving out the £ signs):

SOURCES OF FINANCE		FIXED ASSETS	
Share capital	10,000		
Reserves	170		
CURRENT LIABILITIES		**CURRENT ASSETS**	
		Stocks	500
		Cash at Bank	9,670
Total liabilities	10,170	Total assets	10,170

The two balance sheet totals have now changed; that is because Arthur has been **trading**. More precisely, he took out of his stock books valued at £500 and received in return a net £670, which indicates a profit of £170. But, strictly speaking, it was not necessary to calculate that profit. The profit figure was immediately visible on the right hand, or assets side of the balance sheet. What was happening on the other, left-hand side, will need some explanation.

With regard to the current assets, stocks have gone down simply because only £500's worth of books remain on the shelf. There's no argument about that. Nor is there about the bank balance; the bank will confirm that. So the assets of the company have gone up and that means, by definition, a profit has been earned. A reduction in one asset (stock) of £500 (the books shipped) has been offset by an increase in another asset (cash) of £670.

It now seems that our balance sheet no longer balances. That is because we have not taken into consideration the undoubted profit of £170. It is this profit that has given a bank balance of £9,670. If Arthur had sold those books 'at cost', there would have been no profit and the bank balance would have been £9,500. So profit is one of the places that the money comes from, and therefore should be recorded on the left hand side of the balance sheet.

There are several different descriptions of that balancing profit figure, such as 'retained profits' or 'balance on the profit & loss account' or 'reserves'. This last often puzzles people. The only sense in which it is a 'reserve' is that it shows the amount by which losses can whittle away past profits before the shareholders find that they have partially or wholly lost their original investment. However we will use the term 'reserves' because it is so commonly used and it is short.

You might justifiably argue at this point that the profit figure is only a balancing figure and therefore has no objective value. But against that argument it can be seen that the recorded assets of the company have indeed gone up by that amount, and that constitutes a profit on our original definition. In practice we will calculate the profit figure quite independently in the trading and profit and loss account, and we will find that this alternative method produces exactly the increase in net assets that the balance sheet shows. We will see how that is done in the next chapter.

Aldine Activities Ltd: Act 2, Scene 2

Arthur Aldine gets down to the hard graft of selling (which also means spending a lot of money). The transactions he has carried out were:

1 He has completed his lecture tour and has managed to sell all of his original stock of books. This produced only £660 net sterling.
2 He took delivery of £5,000's worth of additional stock but only promised to pay for it 'soon'.
3 He has however paid the bills arising from his American trip. They came to only £1,600 thanks to local American hospitality.
4 He has also had to get printed a quantity of sales leaflets and that cost £550.
5 He paid a telephone bill of £300.
6 He has asked his author friend to send another £5,000's worth of books as soon as they are printed.

However things seem to have got a bit fraught, cashwise both as far as the company and his home life are concerned.

7 At his wife's insistence he has drawn £1,500 from the company account as salary to pay the grocery bills.
8 He has only paid his friend £3,000 of the £5,000 owed, promising to pay the balance as soon as the next batch is ready.
9 He has however sold £1,000's worth of the second delivery of books and received the money and converted it into sterling. The bank was getting a bit more co-operative on those charges and credited his account with £1,350 this time.

Things do seem to be getting complicated, and Arthur Aldine could be forgiven for wondering whether he is winning or losing. To decide that we really ought to do the job properly by preparing a cash account and a profit and loss account for this first period of hectic trading. Instead we will take a short cut and see how each transaction directly affected the balance sheet and thereby indicated an overall profit or loss.

Book-keeping Without Keeping Any Books

Taking each transaction in turn, we will note its effect on any relevant balance sheet item. You might find it useful to sketch each of the nine balance sheets yourself as we go, in order to see how the (simple) arithmetic works.

1 Book stocks were cleared so the stock value reduces to zero. But cash has gone up by more than that; by £660 to £10,330. The difference goes into 'reserves', increasing them by £160 to £330.

SOURCES OF FINANCE		FIXED ASSETS	
Share capital	10,000		
Reserves	330		
CURRENT LIABILITIES		**CURRENT ASSETS**	
		Stocks	0
		Cash at Bank	10,330
Total liabilities	10,330	Total assets	10,330

2 More books have been delivered so the stock value now must be £5,000. But Arthur has not paid for them so the cash figure is unchanged. Arthur nevertheless has a liability to pay and this should be recorded. Because it is a short term liability (his friend certainly thinks it is!) we will include it under 'current liabilities' as 'trade creditors', showing the amount due of £5,000.

SOURCES OF FINANCE		FIXED ASSETS	
Share capital	10,000		
Reserves	330		
CURRENT LIABILITIES		**CURRENT ASSETS**	
Trade creditors	5,000	Stocks	5,000
		Cash at Bank	10,330
Total liabilities	15,330	Total assets	15,330

You will notice that total assets and total liabilities have increased by £5,000. The increase in physical assets is quite obvious. We described the liabilities side of the balance sheet as indicating **where the money came from** but no money has changed hands. The explanation is that Arthur Aldine is financing a slightly enlarged business **by not paying his supplier**. He is using his friend's working capital! When we look at the control of working capital in chapter 9 we will see that the timing of payments is significant. Depending on how management organizes the cash flows the exporter may be using the working capital of his own company, that of his suppliers or his customers, or effectively borrowing it from the bank or trade factor in the guise of export finance.

3 Paying those bills reduced the cash by £1,600 to £8,730. Unfortunately there is no corresponding asset which we can put into the balance sheet; the expenditure is an irrecoverable outlay which Arthur hopes will bear fruit in some as yet undetermined way at some unknown date in the future. So, quite simply total assets have gone down by £1,600. Just as an increase in assets is a 'profit', so a decrease is a 'loss' which reduces the reserves by that amount to minus £1,270. We will use the convention of putting negative money figures in brackets, so we write £(1,270). Note that we subtract that negative figure to get the total of £13,730 on the left hand side.

SOURCES OF FINANCE		FIXED ASSETS	
Share capital	10,000		
Reserves	(1,270)		
CURRENT LIABILITIES		**CURRENT ASSETS**	
Trade creditors	5,000	Stocks	5,000
		Cash at Bank	8,730
Total liabilities	13,730	Total assets	13,730

Before we go any further we need to see make some sense of these 'negative reserves' that have appeared in Arthur's balance sheet. Remember the 'reserves' normally show the amount of profit that the company has ploughed back into the business, rather than distributed to the shareholders as dividends on their shares. The reserves figure shows the **cumulative** retained profits since the business started. But if a company has made more losses than profits – a pretty usual initial situation in exporting – then a negative reserves figure indicates a cumulative loss.

In Arthur's case, he can see that, whereas he originally invested £10,000 in the company and then a further £330, the assets have subsequently declined (because of all those expenses) down to a recorded total of £13,730, £5,000 of which is owed to his friend, his supplier. That leaves Arthur's investment (Arthur is wearing his shareholder's hat at this point) reduced to £8,730 recorded assets.

4 A similar situation to the previous one as far as cash is concerned; a £550 reduction to £8,180. This time, however, we do have an asset to show for this outlay; Arthur has the leaflets. But since Arthur intends using these leaflets over the next few months, that asset will disappear into mailings to customers. If Arthur was preparing monthly balance sheets then the residue of the stock of leaflets might be shown temporarily but this could hardly be regarded as 'material'. So this asset will be 'written off against profits' at once and thus we get a further reduction in reserves of £550 to £(1,820).

This 'writing off' applies the **materiality principle** which says that small 'capital' items may be written off as soon as purchased. For the same reason small items may be aggregated together rather than separately distinguished and separately recorded in the accounts.

SOURCES OF FINANCE		FIXED ASSETS	
Share capital	10,000		
Reserves	(1,820)		
CURRENT LIABILITIES		**CURRENT ASSETS**	
Trade creditors	5,000	Stocks	5,000
		Cash at Bank	8,180
Total liabilities	13,180	Total assets	13,180

5 The telephone bill is a pure expense just like the travel expenses. So cash and reserves both go down by £300 to £7,880 and to £(2120) respectively.

SOURCES OF FINANCE		FIXED ASSETS	
Share capital	10,000		
Reserves	(2,120)		
CURRENT LIABILITIES		**CURRENT ASSETS**	
Trade creditors	5,000	Stocks	5,000
		Cash at Bank	7,880
Total liabilities	12,880	Total assets	12,880

6 Placing an order does not change any asset or liability values. No money is paid and no liability is incurred. Until the goods are actually delivered and title passes, Arthur as the customer has no liability to pay. Therefore there is no change in the balance sheet.

However the terms of any particular contract of sale may change this situation and it is for this reason that export sales contracts and the use of Incoterms need to be carefully considered. A sale should not be recorded as such until the exporter is confident of receiving his money.

7 Arthur, in his capacity as director of the company and authorized signatory, writes a cheque drawn on the company's account, payable to himself as an employee of the company and crediting his personal bank account. As it is a salary payment the company will also have to settle with the authorities for the Income Tax and National Insurance contributions, but we will leave that complication firmly on one side.

Again we have a pure expense reducing the net assets of the company by the amount paid. Thus both cash and reserves go down by £1,500 to £6,380 and £(3,620) respectively.

SOURCES OF FINANCE		FIXED ASSETS	
Share capital	10,000		
Reserves	(3,620)		
CURRENT LIABILITIES		**CURRENT ASSETS**	
Trade creditors	5,000	Stocks	5,000
		Cash at Bank	6,380
Total liabilities	11,380	Total assets	11,380

8 Paying part of the amount owing on the last delivery of books obviously reduces cash by £3,000, down to £3,380. But it also reduces the debt by the same amount. Therefore 'trade creditors' goes down from £5,000 to £2,000.

SOURCES OF FINANCE		FIXED ASSETS	
Share capital	10,000		
Reserves	(3,620)		
CURRENT LIABILITIES		**CURRENT ASSETS**	
Trade creditors	2,000	Stocks	5,000
		Cash at Bank	3,380
Total liabilities	8,380	Total assets	8,380

9 Finally we do have some sales producing a profit. Stocks go down by £1,000 and this decrease is technically known as the **cost of goods sold**. The stock value is now £4,000. Cash goes up by the amount received, £1,350 (to £4,730), and the difference between the cost of goods sold and the cash received is once again the profit. Therefore reserves go up by £350 to £(3,270). The final balance sheet, looking rather battered as compared with the earlier ones, is this:

SOURCES OF FINANCE		FIXED ASSETS	
Share capital	10,000		
Reserves	(3,270)		
CURRENT LIABILITIES		**CURRENT ASSETS**	
Trade creditors	2,000	Stocks	4,000
		Cash at Bank	4,730
Total liabilities	8,730	Total assets	8,730

Where has Arthur Aldine got to, so far?

Arthur is, no doubt, keeping proper accounting records as required by the Companies Acts but we can see what progress he has made simply by looking at his latest balance sheet. We will go through it, item by item.

Share capital

The owners of the company are the shareholders who have invested £10,000. Share capital is not normally repaid so if an individual shareholder wants his money back he can achieve that only by selling his shares to someone else at an agreed price. As far as the company is concerned the only change is the name on the Register of Members; the figure on the balance sheet does not change in such an event.

Reserves

This figure is the cumulative profits earned, net of losses suffered, since the formation of the company. This company shows a cumulative net loss of £3,270; not unusual in the early days of an export venture. It is easy to see how that came about. The company had total sales receipts, net of currency conversion costs, of £2,680, for £2,000's worth of books supplied, which gave a gross profit of £680. But the company also had over-heads totalling £3,950. Subtracting that from the gross profit figure confirms the loss of £3,270.

Current liabilities

These are debts that should be repaid in the next twelve months. The amount owing on the latest delivery of books, £2,000, we will call 'trade creditors' as the debt has been incurred by the purchases of goods for resale, that is, tradable goods. Other short term debts like an unpaid telephone bill would simply be 'other creditors'.

Stocks

Arthur Aldine purchased a total of £6,000's worth of books, in the sense that he took delivery and added the books to his existing stock. It is true that he has not yet paid for them all and this is acknowledged by the 'creditors' figure of £2,000.

Cash at the bank

This means what it says. Retail operations usually need to record, in addition, 'cash in the till'.

Some General Points to Consider

Always remember that a balance sheet shows the assets and the liabilities at a specific point in time so there should have been a date at the top of this one. Never mind! Arthur has only been trading a few weeks so there is plenty of time to time to do it all properly at the end of his first quarter's operations.

What the balance sheet, on its own, does not tell us is how the company arrived at the situation portrayed. Because we already have the details we have been able to confirm that it all makes sense. In practice we will need a properly drawn up 'trading and profit and loss account' to show what happened in the period prior to the balance sheet date. This we will look at in the next chapter.

The aim of any business is to make a profit or, at least, avoid making a loss. When that happens the 'reserves' figure changes. You may have noticed that in these examples the reserves only changed when the company made a trading profit or had to pay expenses. When it purchased stocks or paid off debts the change in one asset or liability was exactly matched by a corresponding change in another leaving the total reserves unchanged.

We must therefore think of the four categories of financially significant transactions: revenues, which increase the net asset value and profit; expenses, which decrease the net asset value and profit; purchases of assets; and, discharge of liabilities, which always involve an equal and opposite change in some other asset or liability, often in the cash figure, so no profit or loss is involved.

The numbers that appear in a balance sheet are essentially

cumulative ones. The share capital, the reserves, and 'fixed assets' such as machinery represent the net cumulative values of monies invested, profits earned and machinery bought less disposals. In the same way stocks, cash, debts owed to and by the company are carried forward until added to or subtracted from by a new transaction.

Consequently the closing balance sheet figures at the year end on the 31st of December are the opening figures for the start of the new year on the 1st of January.

Aldine Activities Ltd:
First Three Months of Trading

Business was now picking up. Dispatches to the United States of books that had cost £3,000, brought in £4,000 net cash. An enquiry from a reputable Swedish publisher, prepared to take English language training manuals, resulted in sales of £5,000's worth for £6,500 but payable by a 90-day bill of exchange. This meant an urgent £10,000 order from the printer who not only needed to be paid in cash on delivery but also needed payment of the still outstanding debt of £2,000.

Arthur made a quick visit to the bank to organize a three year, £2,000 loan on the (informal) strength of the Swedish order, in preference to getting the bank to discount the bill. But that loan still left a cash shortfall in prospect, as he explained to rich uncle Algernon Aldine. Uncle Algernon had hitherto invested exclusively in wine, women and song but with advancing years this was no longer practical so Aldine Activities looked like an alternative. So it was agreed that the company would sell him 2,500 £1 (nominal) shares, giving him a 20 per cent stake in the business. Because uncle Algernon was indeed rich, Arthur set the price at £1.20 per £1 share making the total investment £3,000.

Although Arthur had only been in business for less than three months he decided, looking ahead, that he could use a computer to do his accounts and later to help with export documentation. He therefore decided to buy one now, with only limited software, in order to gain experience ready for the time when it would really be needed. In view of the cash situation he chose hire purchase for the computer, printer and software, repayable over three years at £105 per month starting in July.

How should he record both the purchase and payments and the future liabilities arising from the hire purchase deal? The relevant accounting standard (SSAP 21) defines this type of purchase as a 'finance lease' but the complicated requirements of the standard apply effectively only to the published accounts of public companies (Plcs). So Arthur could choose to treat the total of the 36 monthly payments (£3,780) as the cost of the installation, a debt to be paid off over three years. The payments split into three:

1 A single first payment of £105 already paid in July.
2 Eleven more payments due in the next twelve months, which is a 'current liability' amounting to £1,155.
3 The balance of 24 payments which constitute a longer term liability of £2,520.

The payment and the unpaid liabilities add up to the cost of the asset. Consequently there is no change in net assets, so there is neither a profit or a loss on the deal. This is always the case with purchases of assets which the company intends to keep, that is, 'fixed assets'. Arthur still had to pay £300 for miscellaneous expenses and he took a modest £500 for himself to tide him over until the end of July. Those plus the first HP payment reduces the cash balance to £825.

Arthur could now complete his balance sheet for the end of his first three months. In doing so it was obvious that these last transactions must have earned a profit of £1,700 because the negative reserves had improved from the last figure of (3,270) to (1,570). The balance sheet now looked like this:

Aldine Activities Ltd
Balance Sheet, as at the close of business, 31st July

SOURCES OF FINANCE			FIXED ASSETS	
Share capital	12,500		Computer installation	3,780
Share premium	500			
Reserves	(1,570)			
Total equity		11,430		
Long term loan	2,000			
HP balance				
payable	2,520			
		4,520		
Total funds employed		15,950	Total fixed assets	3,780

CURRENT LIABILITIES		CURRENT ASSETS	
Trade creditors	0	Stocks	6,000
HP payments due	1,155	Bills receivable	6,500
		Cash at Bank	825
Total liabilities	17,105	Total assets	17,105

We know that the company must have made a cumulative loss of £1,570 because that is the difference between the total investments in the company of £18,675 (we include the longer term three year bank loan and the HP debts), and the total assets of £17,105. What we now need is a method of independently calculating profits or losses. The method must indicate how, in detail, any such profit or loss happened. This is the subject of the next chapter but there are still two topics to cover.

Working Capital

We will examine the significance of 'working capital' in chapter 9 but we can already see the size of working capital just by looking at the balance sheet. The definition of working capital is: current assets less current liabilities, or net current assets (which is the same thing).

It is the bottom half of our balance sheet taken as a whole. Going back to our original sketch of a balance sheet, we can amend it slightly like this:

LIABILITIES	ASSETS
Sources of finance	Fixed assets
Working Capital	
Current liabilities	Current assets

Working capital represents the resources the management uses for the day-to-day control of the business. The longer term liabilities and assets are changed infrequently; for example, raising longer term finance or buying fixed assets. You can see from the 31st of July balance sheet that the working capital of Aldine Activities amounted to £13,325 less £1,155, equalling a net figure of £12,170.

The Alternative Layout of a Balance Sheet

At the beginning of this chapter we said that the 'side-by-side' presentation of a balance sheet showed more clearly how the liabilities of a company (where the money came from) were balanced by the assets (what the money was used for). But we also said that a 'vertical' presentation was much more common, and there are three reasons:

1 It fits the conventional A4 page more easily.
2 It brings together the current assets and current liabilities, so that the net figure, the working capital is shown as a sub-total.

3 The vertical format can be arranged in two ways:
  (a) either to set the fixed assets and working capital against the sources of long term funding; or
  (b) or, to set net assets (fixed assets plus working capital less long term debt capital) against the shareholders' investment.

The first format (a) is essentially the management's way of looking at the company, and the second the shareholders' or investors' view of the company. It is quite easy to re-cast the 31st July balance sheet to the vertical format and we will use the first of the alternatives (format (a)) here:

Aldine Activities Ltd
Balance Sheet, as at the close of business, 31st July

FIXED ASSETS
    Computer installation   3,780

CURRENT ASSETS
    Stocks of books   6,000
    Bills receivable   6,500
    Cash at bank   825

                            13,325

Less **CURRENT LIABILITIES**
    HP payments due   1,155

WORKING CAPITAL   12,170

TOTAL ASSETS EMPLOYED   15,950

WHICH ARE FINANCED BY:
    Share capital   12,500
    Share premium   500

                            13,000

    Reserves   (1,570)

Total shareholders' funds   11,430

Long term bank loan	2,000	
HP balance payable	2,520	
Total debt capital		4,520
TOTAL FUNDS EMPLOYED		15,950

Sometimes it worries people that the 'grand totals' are not the same in the different layouts. That is merely the result of arranging the four major divisions of the balance sheet in different ways. Provided assets and liabilities are not confused the result will always make sense.

Questions for Discussion

1 Prepare a simple, common sense answer to someone who has said: 'Accountants put the profits on the "liabilities" side of the balance sheet, and when the company is paid the company's cash is "debited". This is upside-down record keeping. It makes no sense at all.'

2 Without referring back to the text of this chapter (or looking at the glossary at the end of the book) write down definitions of:
  (a) Fixed assets.
  (b) Current assets.
  (c) Reserves.
  (d) Creditors.
  (e) Working capital.
  (f) Share premium.

3 Why does a balance sheet always balance?

6

The Trading and Profit and Loss Account

What this Chapter Will Enable You to Discover

In the last chapter we followed the early progress of the establishment of a small export business. We could see that the proprietor and manager made a small loss on the first six month's activities and we could put a figure on that loss. Now we will develop the standard procedure for an independent calculation of the profit figure. This calculation will achieve two things:

1   it will confirm that the change in net asset value was indeed the correct profit figure,
2   it will start the process of explaining how and why the company made that profit and loss.

But first we need to clarify some basic ideas about the calculation of profit figures so that we can be sure to get sensible answers. We will also adopt the conventional label for what is formally known as the trading and profit and loss account; we will henceforth call it simply 'the P & L'.

The 'Accounting Period'

In the last chapter we pointed out that a balance sheet must refer to a specific point in time, simply because a company's assets and liabilities are constantly changing. In contrast the P & L refers to a **period of time** and summarizes the financially significant transactions that took place during that period. An accounting period is any that is convenient to the management; it can be a week, a four-week period, a calendar month, a 'quarter' of three months, or a year. The requirements of the Companies Acts and of the Inland Revenue impose a maximum of one year, but quarterly VAT returns effectively impose a maximum of three months.

The Link with the Balance Sheet

Because the P & L tells us what happened during the accounting period it also explains the difference between the balance sheets at the beginning and at the end of the period. Therefore a company with a quarterly accounting period would produce its 'final statements' like this:

Year 1	31st December	Balance sheet
Year 2	First quarter	P & L for 1st January to 31st March
	31st March	Balance sheet
	Second quarter	P & L for 1st April to 30th June
	30th June	Balance sheet
	Third quarter	P & L for 1st July to 30th September

... and so on. At the end of each period the company will prepare a P & L for the period just completed together with a balance sheet for the situation of the company 'at the close of business' on the last day of the period. If the company were to prepare weekly accounts the 3-month P & L would be a summary of the thirteen weekly ones and the end of period balance sheet would be the thirteenth one of the series.

The 'Accruals Concept' – This is Important!

The point of a P & L account, quite apart from statutory and tax considerations, is to tell management how well it is doing. Therefore the profit figure for, say, July to September must assess the effect of the management decisions in those three months. Unfortunately the financial consequences of such decisions do not always appear neatly in the paperwork for those same months. A sub-contractor may not submit his invoice for work done until the 10th of October. A annual insurance with NCM may run from August 1st to July 31st. Electricity is normally billed after the end of the supplier's period which in any case need not synchronize with the customer's accounting period.

Therefore if the profit figure is to be a measure of management performance it must relate to the effect of management decisions on the same period. We therefore apply the 'accruals concept' in calculating profits. This states that revenues and costs are to be recognized as they are earned or incurred, **not** as money is received or paid, and dealt with in the P & L of the period.

This idea is closely associated with the 'matching concept' by which the expenses incurred in any period are matched with the revenues achieved in the same period in order to arrive at the profit for the period.

Of course it is perfectly possible for a business to restrict its management records to 'cash accounting'. This implies recording only those transactions where cash changes hands, ie. receipts and payments. This, in turn, means that the 'cash at bank' figure is the only measure of success or failure, all other assets and liabilities being ignored. This was the traditional method for local government bodies which, being primarily spending organizations operating on annual budgets, regarded it as adequate. However the investment of longer term 'liabilities' (loan and share capital) in longer term fixed assets gets ignored with any such system of so called 'cash accounting' and is particularly inadequate for the management of an exporting business.

Which Figures Do We Include?

We pointed out in the last chapter that only some transactions change the net asset value as shown on the balance sheet. For many transactions a change in one asset is balanced by an equal change in another. When a company borrows money its cash goes up by exactly the same amount as its liabilities – what it owes. When a customer pays (either directly or via the bank) for goods previously shipped, the 'debtors' total (an asset) goes **down** by the same amount as the cash goes up.

But other transactions always imply a change in the balance sheet total of net assets. The most frequent of these are making sales. When the company invoices a customer for goods shipped that were valued at cost, net assets go up by the amount of the gross profit. In contrast, incurring expenses for which there is no balancing asset, such as paying wages or an insurance premium, reduces net assets by the amount of the cost. It is these revenue and expense items that we include in the P & L calculation because it is the change in net asset value that management is monitoring. The detailed organization of this aspect of financial record keeping, normally called book-keeping, we will look at briefly, later.

Which 'Profit' Figure Should Management be Interested In?

Up to now we have merely considered the final profit figure as a measure of the change in overall net assets after everything is taken into account. But management should also be interested in the potential profit earned before paying, for instance, profit on long term loans, or before paying for the company's overheads. So we the get a hierarchy of profit figures the usefulness of which depends on the point of view of the person calculating them.

The gross profit

The essence of any business is to supply goods or services to customers at a price that is greater than the cost to the company in purchasing or manufacturing them. That is the basic profit on trading and is calculated as sales revenue, less cost of goods sold.

The gross profit earned has to pay for all the other expenses of the business; overheads of all kinds, interest payments, Corporation Tax, dividends for the shareholders and leave a bit on the side so that the business grows. If there is no gross profit you are simply not in business at all. Note that the term 'cost of goods sold' is usually shortened in colloquial speech to 'cost of sales', which is not to be confused with the cost of selling!

The operating profit (sometimes called the trading profit)

If we deduct the costs of running the company; the research and marketing costs, administration, rent, power, depreciation of assets, salaries etc., we get the profit earned by the business as an organisation. The size of this operating profit depends entirely on the skills of the management as no outsiders, so far, have taken anything away. We may alternatively call this 'the net profit before interest and tax'.

Net profit after interest but before tax

Three categories of outsiders have an interest in their share of the operating profit and the first of these are the providers of longer term loan capital, that is, the banks. If we deduct the interest payable to them we get the net profit before tax.

Profit attributable to the ordinary shareholder (or net profit after tax)

This is the profit out of which dividends are paid. Because of the statutory restrictions on paying back share capital, dividends are the route by which profits (if there are any) are channelled back to the shareholders who provided the original investment in the company. In theory the shareholders should be indifferent to how much of this profit is distributed as a dividend and how much is retained in the business. Because the business belongs to them they have the profit either in cash (the dividend) or as a continuing investment in the business (the retained profits).

Retained profit

This is what is left after all the deductions from the profit have been taken into account; direct costs, overheads, interest paid, Corporation Tax and also dividends paid to the shareholders. It is this profit that gives the increase in net assets that we used originally to define the term. This figure may alternatively be called 'transfer to reserves' or something very similar.

What About Accounting for Value Added Tax?

Something that often surprises the newcomer to financial management is that VAT appears to be excluded from financial reports and statements in spite of the fact that VAT amounts appear on purchase invoices. They may also appear on export sales invoices, the company must also prepare VAT returns to the Customs & Excise, and usually send a cheque as well. The explanation is that the monies involved do not belong to the company which merely acts as a tax collector on behalf of the Excise.

In the simplest case, that of home sales in the UK, the

company collects VAT along with the sales revenues from customers, it pays a smaller amount of VAT when it buys goods or services, and it pays the VAT difference to the Excise once every three months. For exporters the situation becomes more complicated depending on whether the exports are to the European Community countries or to elsewhere. In theory, and usually in practice, the management of profitable trading is not affected by these VAT transactions; it is almost as if the company is running two businesses, its profitable export business and, along side that, a non-profit making tax collecting business.

However the VAT complication does involve the ordinary operations of the exporter in three ways:

1   The company's administration must keep the VAT records and make the quarterly return to the Excise. So there is a hidden overhead cost arising from being an un-paid tax collector.
2   The money collected from customers belongs to the Customs and Excise (that is, to the Government) but for a short while is sitting in the company's bank account. Consequently the VAT receipts and payments may cause ups and downs in the company's cash balances, ie. in its liquidity.
3   All the above assumes that the VAT paid on purchases is less than the VAT collected. If this is not the case the company will not be a collector but will be a payer of tax. That net payment will then be a cost to the business like any other tax.

Calculating the Profit
(or Loss, as it May Be)

Armed, as we now are, with these concepts and principles we can now calculate the profit or loss arising from the first three months of trading by Aldine Activities Ltd.

We will start with the sales revenue. We **always** start with the sales revenue which, after all, is the foundation of any business. We will use the figures of net cash receipts that Arthur Aldine has extracted from his bank statements.

We will then calculate the gross profit by subtracting the 'cost of goods sold' (which means the recorded stock value of the goods shipped out to customers) from the sales revenue.

We will then subtract the **expenses** of the business from the gross profit to arrive at the net profit before interest, tax and dividends. We will stop there because no interest, tax or dividends have yet been paid.

We will not include those transactions that did not change the net asset value. We include only 'revenues' and 'expenses' which do change the net asset value.

Therefore we get:

Aldine Activities Ltd
Trading and Profit and Loss Account: May to July

Sales revenue		13,180
less cost of goods sold		
Purchases of books	16,000	
less closing stock	6,000	
Cost of books sold		10,000
Gross profit		3,180
less distribution & administration expenses		
Sales promotion (US trip)	1,600	
Other promotion (leaflets)	550	
Telephone expenses	300	
Salary	2,000	
Miscellaneous expenses	300	
Total expenses		4,750
Net loss before interest and tax		(1,570)

However this profit statement is not quite complete. The sales revenue figures should not be collated by inspecting bank statements. After all, a company needs an independent basis to check those bank statements. In order to compile proper records the required cost and revenue figures should be taken from original documents such as the telephone bill or Arthur's collection of receipts to support his claim off the company for what he spent in the United States.

So, in practice, the sales revenue total is arrived at by adding up the amounts due on all the invoices related to each order. These would be, of course, pro-forma invoices since the company had specified cash with order. The total amount in each case would be before deduction of bank charges for currency conversion and would also include the postage cost for each packet sent. When Arthur checked into it, he saw that total bank charges came to £150 and total postage (including the bulk shipment to Sweden) amounted to £340.

Therefore we must correct the revenue and cost figures to include these additional figures, but this change will not affect the calculated profit. The bank charges have already been allowed for (but not explicitly stated) and the postage was charged at cost, so there was no profit or loss on that expense item.

Making these three adjustments we get the full picture:

Aldine Activities Ltd
Trading and Profit and Loss Account: May to July

Sales revenue		13,670
less cost of goods sold		
Purchases of books	16,000	
less closing stock	6,000	
Cost of books sold		10,000
Gross profit		3,670
less distribution & administration expenses		
Distribution expenses (postage)	340	
Sales promotion (US trip)	1,600	
Other promotion (leaflets)	550	
Telephone expenses	300	
Salary	2,000	
Bank charges	150	
Miscellaneous expenses	300	

Total expenses	5,240
Net loss before interest and tax	(1,570)

When the company makes up its accounts for the whole year, at the end of next April, there will be many more items appearing on both the balance sheet and on the P & L. Amongst those additional items there will be:

1   A depreciation charge on the computer installation which will be more than nine month's old by then. As a fixed asset the cost must be gradually written off over its expected life by means of a series of depreciation charges.
2   An interest charge for the £2,000 bank loan. Interest payments are a pure expense; paying them reduces net assets. In contrast, repaying the loan will be a pure cash transaction and net assets will not change since 'liabilities' and 'cash at bank' will both go down by the same amount.
3   A Corporation Tax charge, since we assume that the company will soon start making enough profits to more than wipe out that initial loss suffered in the first three months.

There may also be a dividend to be paid to the shareholders (to Arthur himself and to Uncle Algernon) but that would depend on approval at the Annual General Meeting by the (same two) shareholders.

What Does the P & L (and the Balance Sheet) Tell Us?

The function of these two 'final statements' is to present a summary presentation of what happened to the company during the last, three-month, accounting period and of where it is now. We will analyse some of the more relevant items starting with the P & L.

Sales revenue

The most crucial figure for any business. Is it what was expected? Is it enough? What might happen if it were a bit higher or a bit lower? What was budgeted anyway? As this P & L covers only the first three months of trading we cannot draw any firm conclusions without considering the gross profit calculation.

Cost of sales, and gross profit

There is a gross margin of 27 per cent or, looking at it another way, a mark up of 37 per cent on cost. Gross margins reflect the combination of two factors; the cost of acquiring goods and what price any market will bear. Both factors may be difficult for management to influence and it may find itself squeezed between costs which are too high and market forces dictating too low a price.

However in this case the core problem is the other major cause of an inadequate gross profit – inadequate sales volume. If Arthur Aldine could have sold 50 per cent more books with the same percentage gross margin, the figures would have been:

Sales revenue (50% up)	20,505
Gross profit (27% margin)	5,536
Less expenses (perhaps?)	5,240
Net profit (not a loss!)	296

Distribution and administration expenses

These expenses are the 'overhead' which the company has to pay for, irrespective of whether it is doing a little business or a lot. But they are also expenses over which management has, in theory at any rate, more control. So one of the never-ending tasks of management is to keep these overheads in line both with the needs of the business and with the gross profit which provides the means to pay for them.

If Arthur Aldine did manage to sell 50 per cent more it is easy to see that the total overhead expense would not have conveniently remained the same. The distribution and bank costs would also have increased but hopefully higher volumes would have won better terms for both items, so the increase would not have been in direct proportion. In contrast, some expenses will not vary as the volume of business increases – they will be fixed costs or semi-variable costs and we will examine the implications of that in chapter 12.

Net profit

The fact that a net loss has been recorded does not mean that the company is facing disaster. It does mean however that the company has shrunk a little – net assets are down, as we noted at the end of the last chapter, from £18,675 to £17,105. But in the long run generating losses will produce a shortage of cash and that will then indeed be a disaster. Therefore the longer term prospects of the business will depend on two things:

1 Its presence in the market place. A successful exporter should be able to attract any necessary additional investment provided the investors can reasonably expect profits in the not-so-long run. What constitutes the not-so-long run is something we will examine in chapter 14.

2 Its current liquidity. There is nothing like a fat bank balance to tide a company over a sticky patch. On the other hand, excessive liquidity is likely to represent an inefficient use of resources which could be otherwise put to better use in expanding the business. The management of working capital will be examined in chapter 11.

So we will now transfer our attention to the balance sheet and to working capital in particular.

Fixed assets

This company had made a modest investment in a computer system. Now fixed assets are the assets that make a company what it is; they should be the business generating expression of the longer term investment in the business – provided, that is, they do indeed assist in building the business. Otherwise they represent assets locked up and not performing.

Working capital

This was £12,170 net at the end of July, of which over half (£6,500) was devoted to financing sales, although this was helped a bit by the short-term finance on the computer HP agreement. Only a small proportion, £825 out of £12,170, was still held as cash available to pay immediate bills, but the stock of books represents about two month's sales at current rates. Therefore the 'bills receivable' are likely to be turned into cash before it is necessary to order more stock for sale.

Current liabilities

These stand at £1,155 and must be repaid over the next 12 months. So therefore they will take a substantial proportion of the incoming cash which Arthur would prefer to spend on stocks for sale and on sales promotion. This illustrates the continual need for management to strike a nice balance on the monthly sources and demands for cash. It also shows the difficulty of expanding a business rapidly because of the need to pay for further stocks whilst waiting for the money from previous sales to get into the bank account.

Sources of longer term finance

It is always nicer to have plenty of money invested in a business so that it is not constrained by temporary cash shortages –

provided of course any interest or repayment requirements can be met. Aldine Activities' longer term invested funds consist of 72 per cent share capital, 12 per cent long term loan capital (neither of which should be a problem), but also 16 per cent medium term liabilities on the HP agreement. If Arthur can build up sales in his second year the HP repayments should not be a problem – but they might be! Hence the need for realistic cash flow forecasting in order to spot trouble well in advance.

What We Have Not Covered in this Chapter

The transactions of Aldine Activities Ltd in its first three months of trading were few and simple. In the next chapter we will look at some of the complications of any business that make it difficult for managers to recognize the more important features of their struggle for growth; complications that make it difficult 'to see the wood for the trees'.

These complications include:

1 The legacy of the effects of previous decisions carried over from the last balance sheet into the current accounting period.
2 The lack of synchronization between selling and sales and the receipts from the sales; between running up bills and paying for them.
3 The technical task of recording the effects of this lack of synchronization.
4 The difference between 'discretionary' spending and those automatically accumulating liabilities like bank charges and telephone bills that may be left out of an inadequate cash flow forecast.

Questions for Discussion

1 During one month a company did the following things:
    (a) Supplied goods invoiced at £135,000.

(b) Incurred general operating expenses that totalled £62,000.

(c) Took delivery of goods for resale that were invoiced at £50,000.

(d) Took out a five year bank loan of £20,000 that more than paid off an overdraft that had stood at £12,350.

(e) With the help of the loan money paid off two month's arrears of interest on the overdraft that amounted to £400.

(f) Stocks at the end of the month, of goods for resale were valued at £6,500 (as compared with £2,000 at the beginning of the month).

In addition the company has fixed assets, which originally cost £72,000, and which are expected to have an eight year operating life.

Calculate the gross profit and the net profit for the month before tax but after depreciation calculated on a straight line basis.

2 Which of the following transactions will have an effect on the calculated profit for the relevant period:

(a) Paying the forwarder's outstanding invoices.

(b) Paying the salaries of the office staff.

(c) Paying an advance of £2,000 to cover personal expenses to a salesmen due to go abroad.

(d) Not paying the business rates for the offices because the company knows the local authority will not notice for at least four months.

(e) Taking delivery of four boxes of photocopying paper.

(f) Receiving back one of its own invoices marked by the Post Office: 'Gone away. No forwarding address.'

3 A company is paying, by quarterly payments every February, May and so on, for the hire purchase of a company car.

How would such payments be accounted for when calculating the profit for the three months commencing April 1st?

7

How We Calculate the Profit

Where Have We Got To So Far?

In this chapter we will look at the practical task of calculating the profitability or otherwise of the management decisions that we take in the day to day task of running an export operation. So, before we get too involved in that task, a summary of what we have established so far would be useful.

1   Any business exploits market opportunities, and we engage in exporting because the potential market is many times larger than one, single home market.
2   'Exploiting a market' means supplying that market with goods or services at a price which is greater than the total costs of acquiring and delivering those goods or services.
3   Successful trading means profitable trading. A profitable business is a business that is growing. The growth is objectively measurable in financial terms. It is the growth of net assets, the net recorded value of what the company owns, that we call profit.
4   Profit is not the accumulation of cash at the bank although it may be associated with it. In fact, the more profitable a company is, the more likely it is that it will be financed with someone else's money.
5   A serious export business is normally incorporated as a private (or sometimes as a public) limited liability company. This

determines its legal status and the way in which it keeps its financial records.

6 Financial records are only one part of the elements of a successful export business. However every export business starts with an initial financial investment, its growth may be measured by its net financial assets, and the final payoff is the financial rewards obtained by employees, suppliers, bankers and shareholders (not forgetting the taxman as well).

7 We summarize the net assets of a company in its successive balance sheets. The balance sheet tells us where the company has got to by the balance sheet date.

8 Every financially significant action of management potentially produces a change in a company's balance sheet. That fact underlies the accounting process. If you can remember that you can understand accounting records.

9 We summarize the growth of net assets in the Trading and Profit and Loss account for any specified period. The P & L tells us how it was that the net assets grew from the date of the previous balance sheet to that of the latest one.

10 Financially significant management decisions do either one or other of two things. They change one asset (or liability) into another asset (or liability), in which case there is no change in total net asset value. Alternatively they do change the net asset value by profitable trading (net asset value goes up) or by incurring expenses (net asset value goes down).

11 Profits can only be earned by profitable trading, not by merely reshuffling the company's assets and liabilities. That latter method has been attempted over the centuries by failing managers and it has never worked.

What we will do in this chapter is to see how the profit calculation process works in practice, using the example of an established exporter. But first we must explain how the paper work is carried out.

How Do the Financial Figures Reach Your Desk?

In chapter 5 we showed the link between individual transactions and the 'final statement' which we know as the balance sheet. In chapter 6 we showed the same linkage with the 'P & L'. But a business cannot operate its management control system in that simple way. In any business there is a continuous sequence of financially significant transactions taking place so there must be a system to direct that flow of data to where it is needed and in the required form. Management will certainly need those summary statements; the balance sheet, the P & L, and the cash flow statement. It will also need other reports on market or product performance, on consignment or project profits achieved, or on any other key numbers needed to assess performance and act as a basis for decisions.

The system that does this is the accounting system; a system which provides a data base for the management control of the financial situation of the company and for its future plans. To the non-accountant the accounting system often seems to be both complicated and illogical. It is complicated only because even the smallest business is complicated. It will not seem to be illogical provided you can keep in mind two things:

1 Business success means profitability which means growth in assets. That means promoting sales (which increase net assets) and controlling expenses (which diminish them), and at the same time providing the fixed assets and working capital that make sales possible.
2 You must also keep in mind the way the accounting process works in directing the flow of data from its origin in business transactions through to the final statements or other reports. This we will now explain.

The way the system works is like this. It starts when the staff of the company and outsiders do things, things such as paying a bill, arranging a shipment, taking delivery of goods from a supplier. Each operation will generate a record of some sort, a completed cheque stub, an invoice, a goods received note or whatever is appropriate. Those initial documents are collectively known to accountants as 'vouchers' and contain the information that will then flow through the system. It then goes like this:

> Business transactions
> Documentation, the 'vouchers'
> Data entered daily into 'Day Books'
> Data extracted weekly or monthly and 'posted' in ledger accounts

The ledger accounts thus hold an accumulating record of the financial transactions to date under different headings; 'wages', 'exhibition expenses', 'sales of spares' and so on. There will be a ledger account for every category of revenue (different types of sales), of expenses (including non-cash items like depreciation), of assets (especially 'cash at bank'!), and of liabilities (for example loans and unpaid bills).

The information in these individual ledger accounts must be brought together at the end of the accounting period so as to ascertain the financial situation of the company as a whole. The first step is to extract the balance (the difference between total debits and total credits) of each ledger account and list all these balances in the 'trial balance'. Because the data has been 'posted' to the individual ledger accounts using the double entry system ('for every debit there is a credit'), the net debits and credits must equal each other. If they do not, there has been an arithmetical or clerical error which needs to be put right.

There will then be some 'end of period adjustments' to be made. The money owed by customers may need adjusting to allow for possible bad debts; there may be expenses relating to the period which have not yet been invoiced and therefore not yet recorded; fixed assets need to be depreciated to recognize the passing of time.

When the adjustments are complete the balances of the revenue accounts and of the expense accounts are brought together to form the trading and profit and loss account. That gives the profit for the period.

Finally, the balances on the asset and on the liability ledger accounts, together with the 'P & L' balance, are brought together to form the end-of-period balance sheet.

Completing our original sketch, we now have:

Business transactions
Documentation, the 'vouchers'
Data entered daily into 'Day Books'
Data 'posted' in ledger accounts
Ledger totals checked in the Trial Balance
End of period adjustments
Revenue and expense balances to the P & L
Asset and liability balances to the Balance Sheet

The technical skill of the accounting book-keeper lies in the accurate and logical postings of the original data to the individual ledger accounts and in making accurately and logically any necessary adjustments. It is not necessary to concern ourselves with that process because we know the principles underlying it and we are therefore able to interpret the figures that the system places on our desk.

We can see that more detailed breakdowns of revenues, of expenses etc. can be extracted from the ledger system provided there are separate ledger accounts for all the distinguishable parts of the business that management might be interested in. Such breakdowns are routinely required by cost accountants in manufacturing companies, but other breakdowns are equally routinely required by management to monitor, to control, and to plan any segment of the business.

It is now time to apply all these ideas to the activities of an exporter who thinks he has had a profitable year and is somewhat puzzled, not to say irritated, that the bank has told him that his current account is overdrawn. We will prepare his balance sheet to see where he is now, but before that we must calculate his profit for the year just completed to show how he got there.

BBB International Limited (Trading as Busy Bumble Bee)

Bernard Bumble has just completed 18 months of trading, starting in October 1992. He has discovered that his accounting year is nevertheless from 1st of April to 31st March because no other date was specified when the company was incorporated – 'Why didn't someone tell me I could choose?'. However he did very little actual business (but a lot of research and selling) in those first six months so there was not really any problem.

He really got going from April 1993 and did a lot of business up to the end of March 1994. He sold at an average mark up on cost of about two thirds which he guesses should guarantee a comfortable profit, and now the business looks like growing even better – except for the annoyance of that overdrawn bank account. According to the bank the overdraft on the 31st March 1994 stood at £4,700.

Bernard has designed and patented a small electro-mechanical metering device for the industry he has long been familiar with. He buys in the devices from the engineering firm making them and ships them to overseas markets. The device is small; less than a kilo including normal packaging so international post is feasible for single orders. Most of the other orders were passed to his freight forwarder who handled packing, paperwork and shipment.

On payments he has tried everything: open account to western Europe with some sales factored, but only accepted bills of exchange to Italy; mainly COD to North America, and a few bulk shipments to the US, Australia and New Zealand, again using accepted bills. On the factored sales he has refused to pay interest arising from immediate payment on shipment because he is quite happy (or was?) to wait for the money. In fact it has been a busy year.

As for accounting records he has discovered the ideal system; the cardboard box method. 'It's simple really! You just pile all the bits of paper – copy invoices, bank statements or whatever – into separate boxes and at the end of the year you take it all round to the accountant chappie. He does the accounts and sorts it all out with the tax people and with that fellow at Companies House while I get on with the business. Pity about that overdraft though; I wasn't expecting that.'

So the first step we must take in order to sort out Bernard Bumble's affairs for the year just ended is to add up all the relevant figures extracted from the 'vouchers' under suitable headings. so as to get totals according to the type of transaction involved. There were twenty of these totals covering the period April 1993 to March 1994, and the values (in £s) were:

1	Orders received from customers	488,000
2	Orders dispatched, invoiced at	360,000
3	Payments received	304,000
4	Bank fees and charges	12,000
5	Devices ordered worth	257,000
6	Devices delivered by manufacturer	229,000
7	Payments to manufacturer	191,000
8	Freight Forwarder's invoices	48,000
9	Payments to the Freight Forwarder	41,000
10	Office rent and services (Jan-Dec)	4,800
11	Insurances, quarterly in advance	11,200
12	Computer, purchased in April	5,000
13	Salaries (B.B. and secretary)	35,000
14	Miscellaneous office expenses	2,000
15	Sales travel expenses	3,400
16	Telephone bills (nine months to Dec)	900
17	Dispatches (Parcels, couriers etc.)	14,400
18	Promotional literature	3,000
19	Valuation of closing stock	13,000
20	Interest on bank loan	2,000

To make some sense of this list of miscellaneous transactions we will take the following five steps:

1 Take a look at the previous balance sheet to see where we are starting from.
2 Extract from the above list those transactions that did not have a **financial** implication.
3 List those transactions that refer to revenues and expenses, that is, those that either increased or decreased net asset value. From them we can prepare a profit and loss account for the period.
4 List the remaining transactions, which will be those that refer to changes in assets and liabilities without affecting net asset value. Some of these figures will have to be adjusted for

various reasons – 'the end of period' adjustments we mentioned a moment ago.

5 From the adjusted figures we can prepare an end of period balance sheet.

Step 1: The Last Balance Sheet

When we look at the financial performance of a company in any one year or accounting period, we must remember that the period does not start off with a clean sheet of paper. Any company that was in business in the previous year will end that year with a set of assets and liabilities, some short term, some long term, and these will be the basis of its operation during the new year. If the company is profitable it will increase the net asset value as we explained earlier. If those assets and liabilities include interest earning investments or loans on which interest must be paid then these will also have an obvious effect on the new period's profits.

Well, Bernard had already been in business for six months by the start of the period we are interested in. His accountant had prepared a P & L for the half year (October 1992 to March 1993), and a balance sheet for the 31st of March 1993. It showed a loss. 'Well of course it would! Can't get an export business going without spending money first.' So Bernard put these final statements in a drawer and got back to exporting. When we fished that balance sheet out of the drawer we got this:

BBB International Ltd
Balance Sheet for 31st March 1993

Fixed assets at cost
    Office furniture and fittings   4,000

Current assets
Stocks of devices for sale	3,000	
Trade debtors	2,000	
Prepayments (nine months' rent)	3,600	

Cash at bank	<u>17,000</u>	
total current assets	25,600	
Less trade creditors	<u>600</u>	
Net current assets		<u>25,000</u>
Total assets		29,000
less long term loan		<u>15,000</u>
Net assets		<u><u>14,000</u></u>
Capital and reserves		
Called up share capital		20,000
Balance on Profit & Loss account		(6,000)
Net shareholders' funds		<u><u>14,000</u></u>

From this we can see the following:

1 Bernard Bumble originally invested £20,00 in the company as share capital.
2 He also borrowed £15,000 from the bank, which makes a total investment in the business of £35,000.
3 The total assets at the end of the first six months (October to March) were worth only £29,000 implying a loss of £6,000. This is recognized in the reserves figure, which is labelled here 'the balance on the Profit & Loss account'.
4 Offset against that £29,000 set of assets is the £15,000 owed to the bank, so Bernard's own investment is now only valued at £14,000, again implying a £6,000 loss.
5 The company has done some trading and £2,000 of sales invoices remain unpaid – the 'Debtors' figure. He also has unsold stocks that cost £3,000 on which £600 is still owed.
6 Half way through those first six months he had to pay twelve months' rent for the office and services in advance. Only one quarter of the year's rent would have been added to the loss for the period, leaving three quarters or £3,600 as a prepayment of the rent for April to December 1993, in the next accounting period.
7 In spite of the loss the company was still pretty liquid with

£17,000 still in the bank. That provided working capital for the export business of the next twelve months.

Now we can turn our attention to the year just completed and see whether the business has started to grow from the foundations laid in those first six months.

Step 2: The Non-financial Transactions

There are just two of these, the total value of orders received from customers (1), and the total values of devices ordered from the manufacturer (5). Both these items refer to very important matters that stand at the core of the business, obtaining products and obtaining orders to supply them. But neither order changed the assets or the liabilities of the company. Although customers have ordered goods the company will have no claim on their money until it supplies them. Equally the company has no liability to the manufacturer until that company delivers the goods. Both transactions represent only the potential of profitable business, a potential that will only be crystallized by delivery and payment.

Step 3: The Revenues and Expenses of the Period

The single revenue item (2) is obvious. Some expense items are equally obviously, the things paid for; bank fees (4), insurances (11), salaries (13) and so on. But the expenses must also include things not yet paid for such as the manufactured devices just delivered (6) and unpaid invoices from the freight forwarder. The company has accepted these goods and services so it has a liability to pay for them in the near future.

There is another complication to consider. Not all these expenses relate, in a tidy fashion, exactly to the 1993/4 accounting period for which we are trying to calculate the profit.

Bernard Bumble paid a second £4,800 in January 1994 for the next twelve months' office rent (10) but only a quarter of that sum refers to the current, April 1993 to March 1994, accounting period and the balance must be regarded as a credit (technically a 'prepayment') to be carried over to the next period. In exactly the same way, a rent payment at the start of the business included a prepayment carried over to the current year. Fortunately in this case they balance out to give the rental expense for the year that is to be expected, £4,800. Nevertheless we will have to keep track of those prepayments.

There is a similar problem with the telephone expense. Bernard has received and paid three telephone bills amounting to £900 (16) which took him up to the end of December 1993. But he did not stop using the telephone then and he will get, in April 1994, another bill covering the months January to March. To correctly calculate the profit for the period we must take into consideration all the revenues and expenses relating to the period, as the **accrual principle** lays down. So we must therefore charge the profit and loss account with the full amount for the year, £1200, not just the £900 paid so far. The difference is, technically, an accrued expense and must be recorded as such – which we will do in a moment.

You will notice that we have not taken any notice of the £5,000 laid out in April 1993 on the computer. Bernard reasons that the computer will last five years before it will have to be scrapped as obsolete. So the cost ought to be spread over the five accounting periods because the company will benefit from the investment in all of the five. Remember that the objective of calculating a profit for a period is to record the effect of management decisions in the period. If the cost of the computer was 'charged against profit' either when it was first purchased or when it was scrapped there would be a meaningless dip in the profits in either the first or last of these five periods as compared with the other four. Instead we organize the accounting of fixed assets by the technique of depreciation, of which more later.

The Trading and Profit and Loss Account

We are almost ready to draw up the P & L. We will use the closing stock valuation figure of £13,000 (item 19) to calculate the cost of the goods shipped out to customers. There will also be a charge for the depreciation of the fixed assets, viz. the computer and the office furniture. This will total £1,400 and the details of that calculation we will explain in a moment. We will also change the format of the P & L slightly by splitting off the calculation of the gross profit as the 'trading account', and leaving the calculation of the net profit before tax as the 'profit and loss account'. Profits statements are not often split in this way but it does draw attention to the distinction between the cost of supplying goods or services (giving the gross profit) on the one hand, and the cost of running the business (which leaves only the net profit) on the other.

As before, we will calculate first the gross profit, then the operating profit and finally the net profit before tax.

BBB International Ltd
Trading Account for the year to 31st March 1994

Sales revenue		360,000
less cost of sales,		
Opening stock	3,000	
Purchases	229,000	
	232,000	
less closing stock,	13,000	
equals cost of goods sold		219,000
Gross profit, carried down		141,000

Profit and Loss Account for the year to 31st March

Gross profit, brought down			141,000
Selling expenses			
Promotional literature	3,000		
Sales travel	3,400		
		6,400	
Distribution expenses			
Dispatching	14,400		
Freight Forwarder	48,000		
Insurances	11,200		
Bank fees	12,000		
		85,600	
Administration expenses			
Office rent & services	4,800		
Salaries	35,000		
Miscellaneous expenses	2,000		
Telephone (12 months)	1,200		
		43,000	
Total overhead			135,000
Operating profit			6,000
less Depreciation of fixed assets		1,400	
Interest (Long term loan)		2,000	
			3,400
Net profit for the year before tax			2,600

Well, Bernard Bumble did in fact make a profit but not all that much, something which probably helps to explain the overdraft problem.

Step 4: Some End of Year Figures and Adjustments

In order to draw up the balance sheet we will need some figures from the ledger system and also make some adjustments.

Debtors

During the year customers were invoiced a total of £360,000 but only £304,000 was received (items 2 and 3 on our list). We also have to remember that the company was owed £2,000 at the end of March 1993. Inspection of the Debtors ledger showed a balance of £58,00. It is easy to check that:

Opening balance 1/4/93	2,000
New sales invoiced, 93/94	360,000
	362,000
Less payments received	304,000
Still outstanding	58,000

Trade creditors

This term refers to money owed to suppliers of goods for resale or materials for manufacture, or for services supplied. Again, the figure is available from the ledger accounts for the manufacturer and the freight forwarder, a total of £45,600. Checking, we see:

Manufacturer's account	
Opening balance 1/4/93	600
Invoiced by manufacturer	229,000
	229,600
Payments by BBB Ltd	191,000
Still to be paid	38,600

plus Freight Forwarder's account

Opening balance 1/4/93	0
Invoiced by Fr. Fwdr.	48,000
	48,000
Payments by BBB Ltd	41,000
Still to be paid	7,000

There are also three end of year adjustments, two of which we have already looked at.

Fixed assets

The computer is expected to last five years so the £5,000 cost should be spread evenly over that period, giving a depreciation charge of £1,000 each year. This means we shall this year reduce the 'book value' of the computer down from £5,000 to £4,000 in the balance sheet. Any reduction in assets is, by definition, an expense, a reduction of profit. There are, in fact, several different ways of calculating depreciation and we shall look at them in the next chapter.

The company's investment in office furniture and fittings should also be 'written down'. Their useful life is reckoned to be ten years so they will be depreciated by £400 down to £3,600.

Prepayments

The only prepayment was for the rent and that was quite simple to account for. Doing the job properly and starting from the balance sheet of 31st March 1993 we can see:

Opening amount prepaid	3,600
Paid in January 1994	4,800
total paid	8,400
Rent April 93 to March 94	4,800
Carried forward to 94/95	3,600

Accrued expenses

These arose from the fact that the company was running up telephone expenses during the first three months of 1994 but no paper work had been received so no record had been posted in the ledger. That ledger account showed, on the 31st of March 1994 only a total of £900, being the telephone bills received and paid by then. But we know that this is not going to be the cost for 93/94 and we therefore put the figure of £1,200 in the P & L. The difference must be accounted for; it will appear in the balance sheet as an 'accrued expense'. When the telephone bill does arrive it will be matched with the accrued figure and the two will cancel out.

We are now ready to draw up the balance sheet. You will notice that our calculations and adjustments refer to items 3, 7, 9 and 12 on the original list of transactions. Those figures and the closing stock figure, plus the unchanged figures brought forward from the previous balance sheet, give us:

BBB International Ltd
Balance Sheet for the 31st March 1994

Fixed assets	at cost		Depreciation	WDV
Computer	5,000		1,000	4,000
Fixtures & fittings	4,000		400	3,600
Total fixed assets				7,600
Current assets				
Stocks for resale		13,000		
Debtors		58,000		
Prepayments (rent)		3,600		
Cash at bank		0		
			74,600	
less current liabilities				
Trade creditors		45,600		
Accrued expenses		300		
Overdraft		4,700		
			50,600	

Net working capital		24,000
Total assets		31,600
less long term loan		15,000
Net assets		16,600

Capital and reserves		
paid up share capital		20,000
profit and loss account		
balance brought forward	(6,000)	
profit for the year	2,600	
balance carried forward		(3,400)
Total shareholders' funds		16,600

A Matter of Presentation

One of the difficulties we all face in assessing the significance of business data arises from the propensity of different managers, accountants or authors to present what is more or less the same story in differing ways using differing terminology. With experience this ceases to be a problem, but it is useful to become familiar with the 57 varieties of business presentations. In the case of this balance sheet the presentation may be summarized as:

Fixed assets	7,600
plus	
Net working capital	24,000
equals	
Total assets	31,600
less	
Long term loans	15,000
equals	
Net assets	16,600
Share capital	20,000
Reserves	(3,400)
Total shareholders' funds	16,600

This form of presentation looks at the company from the point of view of the shareholders. The value of their investment has been reduced to £16,600 and the top half of the balance sheet shows the present state of that investment. Alternatively, we could summarize it like this:

Fixed assets	7,600
Net working capital	24,000
Total assets	31,600
Financed by:	
Share capital and reserves	16,600
Loan capital	15,000
Total long term finance	31,600

This format looks at the company from the point of view of the management. A total of £31,600 is invested in the company and the management have applied those funds to £7,600 of fixed assets and the rest to working capital. But the working capital has also been additionally funded by the creditors, to the tune of £50,600 (the current liabilities) to give £74,600 of current assets.

Finally we could look at the company from the point of view of basic accounting principles, the viewpoint we used in chapter 5.

Sources of finance		Fixed Assets	
Share capital	20,000	Computer	4,000
Reserves	(3,400)	F and Fs	3,600
Loan capital	15,000		
Current liabilities		Current Assets	
Creditors	45,600	Stocks	13,000
Accrued exps	300	Debtors	58,000
Overdraft	4,700	Prepayments	3,600
Total liabilities	82,200	Total assets	82,200

This presentation shows the total amount of money put into the company including the money inadvertently put in by the unpaid creditors and the bank, set against the physical assets – what the money was used for. You will also notice that terms like 'net assets' or 'total assets' can be ambiguous.

But What Happened to the Cash During the Year?

We will examine the control of working capital and of cash flow in later chapters but we can, even at this stage, quite easily check that overdraft figure. Going back to that original list of transaction totals near the beginning of this chapter, we can list only those that referred to payments and to receipts of cash. Since everyone knows what it is to pay or get paid, only common sense is required to draw up a cash flow statement like the one below. Once again we will reference the transactions by the item numbers we originally used.

Sources of cash:

Opening cash balance, 1/4/93	17,000	
Receipts from customers	304,000	3
	321,000	
Overdraft at the bank	4,700	
Total cash in	325,700	

Applications of cash:

Bank fees deducted from a/c	12,000	4
Paid to manufacturer	191,000	7
Paid to Freight Forwarder	41,000	9
Office rent and services	4,800	10
Insurance premiums paid	11,200	11
Computer purchase	5,000	12
Salaries for B.B. and secretary	35,000	13
Miscellaneous office expenses	2,000	14
Sales travel	3,400	15
Telephone bills paid	900	16

Dispatch costs paid	14,400	17
Promotional literature purchased	3,000	18
Interest on loan deducted from a/c	2,000	20
Total cash out	325,700	

In preparing this cash flow statement we were not concerned with that 'accrual principle' because we did not aim to match expenses with the accounting periods that gave rise to them. We were only concerned with how much was paid out or paid in and when.

Could we not use cash flows instead of conventional accrual accounting to run the business? The answer is 'no' even though cash is a key asset of the business. The reasons why include:

1 Cash accounting ignores all the 'static' aspects of the business, particularly the semi-permanent fixed assets but also the longer term sources of finance. These change at infrequent intervals so they only appear in the cash accounts infrequently.

2 Because cash is just one asset amongst many, cash accounting cannot tell management whether the business as a whole is growing or shrinking.

3 Because the timing of cash receipts and payments do not synchronize with the activities that gave rise to them, management cannot judge the benefit of any particular decision or activity. A particular consignment may involve the shipment of goods purchased six months previously and the consignment financed with a 90-day bill. Was it profitable? Who can tell?

4 Cash balances can be a very misleading indicator of the current business success of a company. When trade is increasing the usual result is a temporary cash shortage. This can sometimes be severe, producing the undesirable condition known as **overtrading**. In contrast, when a business sees its markets contracting it should conserve cash by avoiding investment spending and by selling off peripheral assets. In such a case the company shrinks but, if well managed, preserves its cash balances.

5 Forward planning becomes very difficult if only cash records

are available. What will happen in the future will depend on decisions and events in the past that are mirrored only by conventional accrual accounting but on that basis a cash forecast can be made. A cash forecast is the result of forward planning so it cannot be the basis of it.

6 In general, cash is generated by profitable trading. Therefore forward planning implies forward planning of profitable sales. Without conventional accrual accounting it is impossible to plan profitability.

What We Have Learned from this Chapter

Knocking together a P & L is only one step in monitoring business success. The P & L and the balance sheet are direct summaries of the effects of management actions. To be of use those two final statements must be interpreted to form the base for future management decisions. They show what has happened in the past so that we can organize the future but they are only part of the management control system. This chapter has provided that control link between the past and the future.

So we must remember:

1 Some of the activities and transactions of a company may result in changes in the financial situation of a company and some may not. Those latter activities and transactions will not be recorded in the conventional financial reports though they should be recorded in other management reports covering things like stock levels, enquiry conversion rates, order processing times and so on.

2 Those activities and transactions that do have a financial significance can be divided into:
   (a) those that result in an exchange of one asset or liability for another. Such activities include paying bills, borrowing money and collecting cash from customers; and
   (b) those that result in a change in net assets, which implies either a profit or an expense.

3 The only way to earn a profit is to trade profitably, which means invoicing customers for more than the cost of the goods or services provided to them. This earns the gross profit.

4 The non-trading expenses of the business (wages, promotion, travel, interest, taxation and so on) whittle down that gross profit until, at the end, there is still a bit left for the shareholders, who were the people who got it all going in the first place.

5 The P & L tells us what happened during an accounting period. Once that period is over the details are largely past history except for the profit gained or the loss suffered. In contrast the balance sheet figures are essentially cumulative (up or down). The balance sheet shows the cumulative investment in or the cumulative borrowings of the company, the cumulative growth or decline in stocks or unpaid bills, the ups and downs of cash at the bank.

6 However to produce a meaningful set of accounts, that is to say a P & L and a balance sheet that all can understand, it is necessary to do two things.

(a) The accounts must relate to a specified accounting period. This causes some arithmetical problems in book-keeping as we have seen. The aim is to be sure that the calculated profit and other figures do genuinely relate to the period or date stated.

(b) The accounting records must comply with the generally accepted accounting principles and conventions.

7 The overall aim is to have a quantified record that can be relied on to tell management what were the effects of its decisions and, in particular, whether or not the company is growing and the business is expanding.

Questions for Discussion

1 There is a list of 'accounting concepts and conventions' in Colin Barrow's book (see the reading list in Appendix C) and a similar one in most other introductory books on business finance. Take eight of these and explain their relevance (or

perhaps their lack of it) to the management of an export business.

2 In traditional accounting practice only 'realized profits' are available for distribution. How relevant is this prudent concept to:

(a) The calculation, for purposes of management control, of the profit earned on an individual consignment invoiced on open account?

(b) The inclusion of the balance on the Debtors ledger account in the end-of-year balance sheet.

3 The financial record keeping process starts with a transaction producing a 'voucher' for entry into the company's books and ends with the preparation of the end-of-period balance sheet. Therefore any end of period adjustments at the trial balance stage are unnecessary. Discuss this statement.

8

Thinking About Costs

Why We Need to Think About Costs Before Doing the Sums

What is a 'cost' anyway? In the previous chapters we have seen that:

1 a successful business is a growing business;
2 a business grows if it trades profitably;
3 'profit' means supplying goods or services at a price which is greater then the cost; and
4 when that happens the net assets grow, so the business grows.

So what is the difference between an 'expense' and a 'cost'. An expense is any financially significant event that reduces the net assets of the company. A 'cost' is any expense that is associated with a particular activity, process or product so that it makes sense to ask, 'What is the cost of ...?'

In theory it is all quite simple. The cost of, for instance, a particular consignment to a particular overseas distributor can be arrived at by adding up all the expenses associated with the consignment in question. If a percentage is added for profit, and if that is done for every consignment, at the end of the year the year's profit will be that percentage of the year's sales revenue.

But we have all heard of the luxurious jargon of costing –

marginal costs, cost apportionment, sunk costs, job costing, holding costs, opportunity costs and so on. We also know that books on costing are fat and heavy, and that costing departments are usually bigger than one might expect. So why does it get so complicated, and is there a way through the maze? The answer to the second question is 'yes' and that is what this chapter is about. To answer the first question let us consider a not untypical situation.

Amalgamated Suck and Puff Limited, Known as 'ASAP' to the Trade

ASAP manufacture and distribute world wide, equipment for pressurising or evacuating particular categories of laboratory and medical equipment. One of their good markets is the whole Spanish speaking area from Barcelona to Los Angeles to Santiago. They are just planning the dispatch of a container to one of their South American distributors so they need to be able to set a price for each piece of equipment shipped, and in order to do that they need to know the 'cost' of each unit.

That cost will be made up of a large number of individual expenses which are related to supplying the goods to that particular distributor and, indirectly, to the end users. So let us list some of the expenses involved:

1 The manufactured cost. That is straightforward because the factory tells the export manager the ex-works cost is exactly and conveniently £1,000 per unit. We might pause there to ask how the factory arrived at that figure, but we won't because we will have problems enough downstream.

2 Packaging. That is also straightforward because the company's contract packers charge a unit price for packaging the individual pieces; there is no argument about that cost.

3 Every unit is supplied with a comprehensive technical manual for applications, for servicing and spares supplies, and for trouble shooting. It is in Spanish, standard Spanish but the customers seem to cope, even the Catalans. The cost of

preparing the manuals included payments to the technical author, the translator and the printer. The first of these expenses applied to all versions of the manual, the second only to the spanish edition but both these were 'one-off costs'. The printer's quote was for 'so much for 5,000 copies plus so much per 1,000 run on'. It is easy to see that the average cost of each manual depends on the quantity produced. Similarly, the authoring and translation expenses must be spread in some way over all the various language editions. When that has been done, we have the unit cost for each manual.

4 The shipment is CIP, carriage and insurance paid to the place of destination, the old 'CIF'. Unfortunately that container will hold a variety of products all with different manufactured costs, weights and cubes. The freight and insurance costs must be split sensibly across all of them in order to arrive at a cost for these items.

5 The main promotional expense in this market is exhibiting at a large biennial exhibition which attracts visitors not only from this distributor's territory but also across the border from the neighbouring country. The exhibition is a major expense involving not only the organizer's charges and the cost of the stand, but also the travel, accommodation and living and entertainment expenses of the exporter's own sales staff. This expense item is related to two sales territories, two years of sales effort, and a spread of individual products. So each unit of each type, sold in each market must carry an appropriate share of these costs. Local advertising, promotion and field sales are paid by the distributor so these are not costs to the exporter.

6 In addition, we must not forget the UK sales office, its manager and staff, its running expenses and, presumably a share of the company overheads. These company overheads include accounting, personnel and senior management functions, and there are in addition expenses for the heating, lighting, cleaning, security, insurance, rent and business rates to be allowed for. But once again we must decide how? How is the total to be split right down to the individual piece of equipment waiting to be packed?

Somehow or other all these expenses must be taken into account but the difficulties include:

1 There is no obvious, single way in which expenses related to several products, markets or activities can be apportioned to an individual product or unit of service being supplied to the customer.
2 The precise value of the expenses to be apportioned will not normally be known until after the prices need to be fixed. Therefore budgetary estimates must be used.
3 Because only some of the expenses are directly related to the unit to be costed, there is always a temptation to shave prices by ignoring some small part of the indirect expenses we have just described above. But is doing that bad policy? We need to be clear in our minds about that.
4 We cannot expect the accounting record system outlined in the previous chapters to help us resolve these problems. That system can only say what was the expense for any individual activity (the Sao Paulo exhibition, the trade mission to Venezuela, the 10,000 Spanish language leaflets and so on) either in the last period or what it is budgeted to be in the next.

We need a costing system to cope with these difficulties; in fact we need two systems, as we will now explain. But first we must ask an important question.

Why Do We Want to Calculate the Costs Any Way?

We don't necessarily have to calculate costs; we can simply find out what the customer is prepared to pay; to see 'what the market will bear' as an economist might put it, and let that set the price. There are many businesses which, for good or bad reasons, price their goods this way. In the case of quite new products, where technology is still developing and the potential market size can only be guessed at, there may be no better way.

Similarly for some providers of services, such as consultancy or project management, it is the expenses and the potential savings in the client's company that are the relevant price deciders. But even in these cases this market-led approach to pricing may not be the complete answer.

There are four reasons for wanting to be able to say 'the cost of this article is ...':

1 We need a basis for routine pricing. When estimating the costs of non-routine activities such as a major project it may be feasible to start off with a clean sheet of paper and write down all the relevant expenses. But most of the time we need a simple system to translate known expenses into a cost and then into a price. We need a simple system that can be delegated and can be applied efficiently and reliably to the setting of prices for, perhaps, 10,000 separate items.

2 We need cost figures for management control. As we saw in the last chapter the conventional accounting system will tell management, in arrears, what were the total expenses for any specified business unit. That is too slow for week by week management control. As each consignment is shipped it is necessary to be able to say that the cost, in relation to the invoiced amount, is indeed providing the gross margins necessary to the success of the business as a whole. If it does not, corrective action needs to be taken at once.

3 We need cost figures for strategic planning. If we are planning to supply a new market, to introduce a new product, to establish local manufacture, to change the balance of promotion to manufacturing expenses, we need to know the present costs of what is being done now. With those figures we can budget for the new costs, revenues and profits.

4 We need cost figures for tactical pricing. The danger of unthinking tactical pricing and a market-led approach to pricing, as described at the beginning of this section, is that it is a system for operating in the dark. Some of the company's products or markets, perhaps many of them, may be losing money if the relevant expenses (whatever they are) are greater than the revenues. This need to know our costs for tactical reasons has two aspects:

(a) It is vital to know when it is simply not worthwhile to chase a difficult order or to quote a silly price. On occasions management must have the self confidence to say: 'Let them have the business. They may bankrupt themselves. They may have a cost structure that we can't compete with. Either way we are better off without the business at that price.'

(b) It is strategically important to know, when developing a geographical market or entering a new market sector, that the inevitable costs of doing so make sense in the longer run. Our two scenarios, Aldine Activities and BBB International were in just such a situation, but they did, in broad terms, know their costs. They were therefore in a position to judge whether the business venture was going to be worthwhile in the longer term. In such cases, providing goods or services 'below cost' can make sense in the long run provided management knows what it is doing. That means knowing its costs.

If you think about it, these four needs suggest two different questions that need to be asked. For routine pricing and for management control the question to be asked is: 'What is the cost of …?'

In contrast, for strategic planning or for tactical pricing the question to be asked is: 'What happens if we were to …?'

The need to answer these two quite different questions implies two quite distinct ways of looking at the expenses of a business that we call costs. It means in turn two distinct ways of doing the calculations and of using the answers. But before we look at them in detail a few definitions might help to keep things clear.

Some Costing Definitions

Cost centre

The costs start when a business does something that implies an expense, something that implies a reduction in net assets. Such things include taking delivery of materials, the receipt of confirmation of an exhibition booking or a plane reservation, or making a forward foreign exchange contract. The costs of such decisions must be related to some aspect of the business, that is, to a cost centre. We will then be able to say that the materials cost or exhibition costs, or whatever it may be, for the period was so much. The cost centre tells us where the costs came from.

Cost unit

However we will not simply be interested in the accumulating costs of individual activities. For instance, we may be interested in field sales activity by UK staff in our Italian market. In that case some of the company's total hotel expenses must be apportioned to the Italian sales service costs. Cost units tell us where the costs end up.

The cost unit is usually expressed in some particular measure or cost rate. Thus we may get the cost per kilogram, per machine hour, per salesman, and for professional services, per chargeable client contact hour.

Direct costs

These are the costs that are clearly identifiable with a single cost unit.

Overhead costs or 'indirects'

These are costs that are identifiable with more than one cost unit.

Cost attribution

This is the name for the process of matching a particular cost with a particular cost unit. This involves cost allocation in the case of direct expenses that are clearly identifiable with a single cost unit, for instance the purchase expense of a particular spares item. When an expense involves two or more cost units we then have:

Cost apportionment

For example, attributing the cost of spares to a particular consignment presents no problem as far as the basic purchase cost paid to the original supplier is concerned. But the total spares cost for any consignment should also include the stock-holding overheads; the warehousing, the stores administration, the insurance, obsolescence and working capital financing. These overheads or indirects must be apportioned to the cost unit and then to the consignment.

Cost behaviour

This describes the way in which a cost may vary with different levels of activity. Sometimes the cost may be unaffected or sometimes it may vary in one of several different ways.

Variable cost

This denotes a cost that must vary in direct proportion to the level of activity. The packaging cost for ASAP Ltd, in the example at the beginning of the chapter, was such a variable cost. If the volume shipped increased by 20 per cent the packaging cost would also increase by 20 per cent.

However life is never quite that simple and we find that variable costs often do not vary in strict proportion to the level of activity. The printing cost of the Spanish leaflets would thus be a semi-variable cost, whilst the freight costs would be a stepped cost depending on whether one, two or more containers were needed.

Marginal costs

This denotes a more general idea than that of 'variable cost'. The marginal cost is any cost that changes as the result of a management decision or, more precisely, the marginal cost is the difference between what the cost was and what it will be. If ASAP Ltd introduced a new, much larger machine necessitating a larger stand at the next biennial exhibition, then that exhibition increase would be part of the marginal costs of introducing a new product.

Fixed costs

This term can be misleading. It refers to all those costs that are **not** variable costs; that is to say, fixed costs are all those costs that need not vary if the level of activity changes. If ASAP were to double their sales to South America it would not be necessary to double the expenditure on sales visits by UK based staff. The company may decide to do so; it may keep the expenditure the same; or it may even decide to leave the selling task to the distributor and so reduce its own expenditure.

Overhead costs

These are often taken to be the same as the fixed costs and often that is more or less true. Strictly speaking, overheads are all those costs that are not direct, that is, all those costs that are not specifically related to one particular cost unit.

Which are overheads and which are fixed costs? The total costs of a business may be split in two different ways: fixed costs and variable costs; or overhead costs and direct costs.

Most overheads are fixed costs, and most direct costs are variable. But licence to manufacture a proprietary, patented product may be a fixed amount irrespective of the quantity produced and sold. Such a licence would then be a fixed cost but one which is direct to that product only. In contrast, the telephone expense of a busy export office would be a variable expense. If the volume of trade doubles the volume of telephone traffic is also likely to double. But that variable expense is not direct, it must be apportioned in some way to all the products handled by that department during the year.

We Have Now Done Three Things. We Have:

1 identified the problem, or at least identified the problem facing ASAP Ltd in costing (and therefore pricing) an individual piece in a particular container shipment;
2 identified the four tasks for which we need usable and sensible cost figures, and the two sorts of questions that need to be answered; and
3 defined some of the terms used in the management of costing systems.

We must now look at the approaches to cost calculations. We must examine (briefly) how they are carried out, see what they are meant to achieve, and note any dangers in using the cost figures so generated for decision making.

Costs for Routine Pricing and Management Control

We need a system that can, in an efficient and routine way, gather together all the costs, from each cost centre relevant to a specified cost unit, so that management can say: 'The cost of that is so much'. In the case of ASAP Ltd's pricing problem, the required answer is of the form 'The cost of a single unit of Machine Type X, delivered to the place of destination under CIP terms is £Y', giving a figure which can then be turned into a selling price in local currency.

A rational, sensible calculation of costs for setting prices is needed to preserve the competitive situation of the company. Getting it wrong means setting prices either too high or too low. If too high, the company will lose business to more astute competitors who can make a profit at lower prices. If too low, the company gets the business but then risks going bust. It frequently happens.

The direct costs are not the problem. The factory delivered price and the packaging cost in our example were both 'per unit'. If the pieces of equipment had been shipped as singles, freight and insurance would also have been 'per unit', but that was not the case. Currency conversion charges, if handled consignment by consignment would have been 'per unit' but not otherwise. Other expenses however, like those for the technical manuals, the exhibitions and the other sales expenses, the expenses of the export department back home, not to mention many others like credit insurance, export financing, are relevant to many other products, to other distributors, to other markets, or to the export operation as a whole. They must be apportioned in some way over these activities in order to arrive at the cost of those individual activities or cost units.

This apportionment of indirect costs can be done either simply and crudely, or in a complicated and sophisticated manner. The simplest method is to have standard percentage mark-ups on direct costs that would cover all the indirects. In contrast the most interesting method under discussion at the time of writing is 'Activity Based Costing' or ABC for short. It is a method that attempts to identify each element of the indirect costs with some company activity that gave rise to it, and to use that as the basis of apportionment.

Whichever system is selected the overall aim is the same. It is a method of generating a sufficient amount of surplus earnings; those arising from the difference between what the customer pays and the direct costs of the goods or services supplied. That difference (which is greater than the gross profit) has to provide the revenue to pay for the indirect expenses, for the company overheads, for the cost of capital and also leave a bit over for profit.

Let us, just for the moment, concentrate our attention on the indirect expenses only. As the business of the company is carried on, shipment after shipment goes out, sales revenues are clocked up, but direct and indirect expenses are also incurred. It is obviously not practical to investigate the ledger accounts for the indirect expenses every time a price list or a quotation is prepared. But at the end of the year the company needs to be sure that the total amount credited towards, for instance, the promotion or insurance costs will be, more or less the amount which has actually been spent on these items during the year. If they are more or less the same the company should be able to hit its budgeted profit target.

Therefore the costing system must spread out or apportion the expected, budgeted indirect expenses to each cost unit in a rational way. It is the task of the Costing Department to establish and operate the system. Different circumstances dictate different bases of apportionment, by which individual indirect expenses are shared out; perhaps in proportion to the direct costs, or the salesman hours involved, or the departmental hours or whatever is deemed appropriate. That gives a cost unit rate or a predetermined overhead recovery rate. When a job is to be costed, the cost clerk applies the rate to the job in hand using the recorded hours or recorded direct costs as the case may be. If that is done for every job, product or consignment throughout the year the total apportioned costs will equal the equivalent total expenses. The 'overheads are fully recovered' to use the jargon. A simple example will show how this is done.

An exporter knows that the expenses of running its export

office can only be paid by recovering them from the monies received from sales. Therefore when costing any item or any consignment the exporter must add to the direct costs of what is to be supplied enough extra to pay for the expenses of the export office and for all the other company overheads as well. How much should be added to the direct costs to absorb the export office costs?

Step 1

Prepare a standard cost sheet for each cost unit (a single item, a consignment or whatever is appropriate) and on that sheet list all the expenses that need to be taken into account. In this example the relevant cost centre is the export office.

Step 2

Total the year's budgeted expenses for this cost centre. In this case the expenses were:

1 Staff, salaries, National Insurance contributions, company pension and employer's insurance.
2 General office expenses like stationery, materials and purchases of research material.
3 Depreciation of the office computer system and its software, plus data base access fees.
4 Training, for export practice, languages, research and computer usage
5 A share of the general building expenses – rent, rates, insurance, furniture and so on, telephone, power and building administration.

The amount budgeted for all these expenses in the coming year is £78,000. That money must come from somewhere.

Step 3

Decide on the basis of apportionment. This company has decided that the nature of the export operation is such that each consignment generates much the same amount of work. If orders are amalgamated in one shipment or split between several shipments it is still the number of consignments rather than the number of orders or the value of orders that generates the office workload.

Note 1

Selecting this particular basis of apportionment has the result that some other company expenses are excluded from this calculation. The export manager's work involves the whole export operation so his salary is not related so directly to individual shipments. It is a similar case with more general company overheads such as accounting services. These other expenses will be apportioned on some different basis.

Note 2

You can see that most of the relevant export office expenses would have been allocated to the cost centres in a straight forward way. The building expenses however are shared by all departments. In this company they would be totalled and then apportioned to each department on the basis of square footage occupied. So cost apportionment may need to be done in several stages.

Step 4

Calculate the pre-determined overhead recovery rate. To do that the company must look at the basis of apportionment and decided how many units of the basis are scheduled for the coming year. This company has decided that the export office is expected to handle 208 consignments – roughly four per week. Thus we get:

Budgeted overhead £78,000
Basis units 208 consignments
Recovery rate £375 per consignment

Step 5

When costing any consignment during the year, £375 must be added to help recover the expenses of running the export office. Other amounts must also be added to help recover other company overheads.

If, during the coming year, this is consistently done, and if the overhead expenses are as budgeted, and if the export office does handle 208 consignments then the relevant overheads will be 'fully recovered' from the monies received from the company's customers which is the only place they can be recovered from. If the 'actuals' are different from the budgeted figures, overheads will be either under or over recovered. That will mean an unplanned expense or an unplanned bonus.

Note 3

It would be possible to use the total consignment cost (direct costs plus total apportioned overheads) to arrive at the charge to the distributor. However it is more than likely that the agreement with the overseas distributor was made on the basis of an agreed price list. Therefore the charge to the distributor will be as the price list, but the company's own cost calculation will include the apportioned overheads as we have shown. The difference between the two is the profit on the consignment and that is obviously a figure that the export manager will be interested in.

You will also be able to see that if the customer is charged on the basis of a price list, the preparation of that price list must also involve calculations of overhead recovery but as budgeted figures rather than additional charges to be added to each invoice.

The Problem with Absorption Costing

Absorption costing aims to absorb all the indirect expenses into the calculated cost of any cost unit. If all the actuals work out more or less as budgeted the overheads will be recovered. 'Ay, there's the rub' as a Danish prince once said. What if the figures, the budgeted and the actuals, are not a close match? If the difference is relatively small there is an 'under-recovery' or an 'over-recovery' of the indirect expenses. With hindsight it may be said that our expectations about total costs, and therefore the prices charged, were either too low or too high.

On the other hand, if management is planning a significant change in its export operations, those volumes on which the cost calculations are based are also likely to change. The 'overhead recovery rates' will no longer apply. These considerations also apply to that ex-works cost of £1,000 for some of the units making up the container load. The factory had the same problem of 'absorbing' its overhead costs. Therefore if the export department could double the sales volume it would be reasonable to ask what change would that imply for the manufacturing cost per unit and for the quoted ex-works price.

We establish a costing system to enable us to say what the cost of any particular cost unit will be. In order to be able to use that figure for pricing or for management control, the costing system will only work if there is a steady, forecastable marketing environment. Big changes in volumes, whether planned or not, will invalidate the system. Absorption costing always implies a steady state for operating expenses.

This explains the dangers of marginal costing where attention is concentrated only on the incremental costs of doing something like shipping out an order. It is quite true that we may send a customer a consignment charged at a price that covers only the direct or the variable or the incremental or the marginal costs (which ever label you prefer). That policy will not produce a loss on its own because the value of net assets will not change. Sales revenue will equal the (marginal) cost of sales. But as we saw in the case of Aldine Activities, when the bills do come in later for those many overhead expenses then the company will in the end suffer a loss.

Costs for Strategic Planning and for Tactical Pricing

When we discussed the technique of using absorption costing for pricing and control we were primarily interested in distinguishing direct costs (which caused no problem) from overheads (which had to be apportioned over the individual, relevant cost units). We must now think about the distinction between variable and fixed costs. As we explained earlier in this chapter there is a tendency for direct and variable costs to be the same costs, and overheads and fixed costs to be the same. But not always and, in any case, we will be looking at them differently so it is necessary to be clear about the distinction.

Let us go back to the example of those exports by ASAP Ltd to the Spanish-speaking markets. Let us assume that the distributor, on the export manager's next visit, complains that it is the UK company that is holding back sales to this area. More specifically, the distributor suggests that if the exporter was prepared to invest significantly more in sales promotion or reduce his prices the volumes of goods shifted would increase substantially. The distributor is quick to suggest precise amounts of extra promotion and precise reductions in price but, when pressed, is less keen to be specific about the size of the resulting increase in sales. The export manager needs to be able to throw the argument back into the other's court by specifying: 'Sales must increase by X per cent to make it worthwhile. Will they, Señor Distribuidor?'

So how do we calculate that X per cent? It is easy to see what we cannot do.

If the company reduces its prices by, say, 10 per cent, that will reduce total sales turnover by 10 per cent at the same volume of goods shipped. An increase in volume shipped of

11 per cent would bring that sales turnover figure back to the previous one. But, because the volume had increased costs would also have increased. The same turnover, with increased costs means less profit. No deal!

If the company agrees to spend an extra £100,000 on boosting sales, that amount of money must come out of profits. If the net profit per unit shipped was £3,000, does that mean that the export manager must demand at least an increase of 34 units shipped? But we ought to suspect that shipping a higher volume will spread the exporter's costs over a larger number of units manufactured and sold. One would expect economies of scale to work in the exporter's favour. If so, an increase of something less than 34 units would probably leave profitability unchanged. But how much less than 34 before the company loses profit on the revised agreement?

It is clear that the cost and profit figures derived from absorption costing, however useful they may be for other purposes, cannot be used here. Since both parties to the discussion are considering changes in volumes the previously calculated unit costs and overhead recovery rates no longer apply. So let us take an example to see what the possibilities are.

Current annual sales to Señor Distribuidor

No. of units invoiced each year: 100 units

(Sterling values)	**Per unit**	**Total**
Direct costs	2,000	200,000
Indirect costs	5,000	500,000
Total costs	7,000	700,000
Net profit before tax	3,000	300,000
Invoiced	10,000	1,000,000

The company is selling to this agent at a 30 per cent net margin which looks pretty good, suggesting it might risk a price reduction if it could be shown to be worthwhile. On the other hand an extra £100,000 on sales promotion would knock one third off the profits unless it were compensated for by increased volumes.

In order to see the effect of any hypothetical change in volume the costs must be divided, not into direct and indirect but into fixed and variable costs. Remember that variable costs are defined as those that **must** vary if the quantities change. The manufacturing and packaging costs are clearly variable, assuming that a price reduction on the ex-works figure cannot be wrung out of the factory. On the other hand the apportioned cost of the export department would not change since the administration would be much the same as before. So that is a fixed cost. Some costs would have to be examined in detail. The printing costs of the manuals are a mix of fixed and variable, whilst the container related costs are a stepped cost, only changing when extra numbers demand an extra container.

You will notice that all the variable costs can be expressed as 'per unit'. Consequently, when the quantity changes, the variable cost per unit remains the same but the total variable cost changes in proportion to the quantity. The fixed costs, on the other hand, are not affected by the quantity shipped. As the quantity changes so those fixed costs will be spread over a greater or lesser number of units shipped. So we will avoid that complication by considering the total fixed costs simply as an unchanging total lump sum.

After making some assumptions the company decided that fixed costs amounted to £380,000. Of the £2,000 direct costs per unit £1,200 were variable and of the £5,000 indirect costs £2,000 were variable, making a total variable cost per unit of £3,200. The new breakdown of costs for a quantity of 100 units now became:

	Per unit	Total
Variable costs	3,200	320,000
Fixed costs		380,000
Total costs (as before)		700,000
Profit (as before)		300,000
Total revenue (as before)		1,000,000

You will notice that it makes no sense here to talk about 'fixed costs per unit'. The fixed costs are just that, fixed. The amount of fixed cost 'carried' by each unit will depend on the quantity sold and that is the figure we have yet to establish.

The export manager is now in a position to answer two different questions:

1 If the price were reduced by 10 per cent (from £10,000 each to £9,000 each) what increase in numbers of units sold would be necessary to keep the profit earned at the previous figure?

2 If £100,000 extra were spent on sales promotion, what increase in numbers of units sold would be necessary to keep the profit earned at the previous figure?

The Price Reduction Strategy

Since we regard total variable costs as increasing in direct proportion to numbers sold we can calculate the costs, revenues and profits for a range of possible quantities. The price remains, of course, at the new figure of £9,000 per unit. So starting the table at the current quantity we have:

Quantity sold	Variable costs	Fixed costs	Total costs	Revenue	Profit
100	320,000	380,000	700,000	900,000	200,000
105	336,000	380,000	716,000	945,000	229,000
110	352,000	380,000	732,000	990,000	258,000
115	368,000	380,000	748,000	1,035,000	287,000
120	384,000	380,000	764,000	1,080,000	316,000

From this table we can see that a volume increase of nearly 18 per cent is necessary to compensate for the 10 per cent decrease in unit price. If, in addition, the export manager thought that his own company ought to have some real share of the benefits of increased market penetration then he would be looking for a volume increase of 20 per cent or more. But he should also consider the situation of his distributor; after all, an exporting company and its distributors and agents are all partners in the same business. This distributor has his own mix of variable and fixed costs, and the balance between them would govern the net benefits received by his own company from any increase in volume.

The Sales Promotion Increase Strategy

If it were decided to increase promotion expenses by £100,000 per year this would be an increase in **fixed** costs, paradoxical though it may seem to talk about varying fixed costs! Remember that the term 'fixed costs' merely refers to all those costs that are not variable, the costs that need not change with a change in volume. This increase in the promotion expense is a discretionary one and, the decision having been made, that expense is then 'fixed' whatever the precise sales volume might turn out to be. So the new fixed cost figure is now £480,000 but, in this planning exercise, the unit price will remain the same as currently, at £10,000 per unit. That gives a new table of possibilities like this:

Quantity sold	Variable costs	Fixed costs	Total costs	Revenue	Profit
100	320,000	480,000	800,000	1,000,000	200,000
105	336,000	480,000	816,000	1,050,000	234,000
110	352,000	480,000	832,000	1,100,000	268,000
115	368,000	480,000	848,000	1,150,000	302,000
120	384,000	480,000	864,000	1,200,000	336,000

With this strategy, the required volume increase is a little less at 15 per cent.

We can now see that, if prices were reduced by 10 per cent, an 11 per cent increase in volume would be inadequate to preserve the current level of profit. We can also see that the unit profit of £3,000 when calculated on an absorption basis was a poor guide to the required volume increase to pay for the £100,000 additional promotion expense. Only an extra 15 units each year would be required.

However it would still be necessary for the distributor, using his knowledge of his own local market, to estimate the effect of the price reduction or of the promotion increase. It is he who has to make the promise of any budgeted volume increase, following a decision on prices or promotion.

The Idea of 'Contribution' Towards Fixed Costs

We will examine this very useful concept of 'contribution' in detail in chapter 12, but since it is both a very simple idea and a very useful one it is worthwhile to introduce it now.

When we did the calculations for the two strategies, using the distinction between fixed and variable costs for the purpose, you may have noticed the simple, regular way in which the profit figures changed with changes in volume. In the first case each five unit increase in volume produced a £29,000 increase in net profit, and in the second case it was a £34,000 increase for the same volume increase. This simplicity suggests that there must be a direct way of arriving at target volume figures for each strategy, as indeed there is.

The crucial quantity to watch is the difference between the price and the unit variable cost. It is the difference between the extra money coming in if one more unit is sold, and the extra money going out if one extra unit is manufactured and shipped. Because the other costs are fixed, that extra difference is pure profit; the other, non-variable costs having been already paid for.

To take the second strategy as an example, selling one more unit brought in an extra £10,000 but to produce and ship it cost the company an extra £3,200. Therefore each extra unit shipped netted an extra £6,800, or, with an extra five units, £34,000. Since an extra £100,000 of promotion had to be paid for, it is easy to see that the required number of extra units is £100,000 divided by £6,800, that is 14.7 units. This means in practical terms, 15 extra units which is what we found. Those margins of £6,800 on each unit **contributed** to that additional fixed promotion cost of £100,000. Hence the name of this way of looking at costs for planning purposes.

What we have not discussed in this chapter is the use of 'contribution' for tactical pricing. But to do that it is necessary to have a more comprehensive view of 'contribution' as a tool of strategic and tactical planning. Therefore we will leave that topic until chapter 12.

Accounting for the Cost of Fixed Assets

So far in this chapter most of the costs we have discussed have arisen from current expenses. But it is frequently the case that costing fixed assets sometimes leads to confusion. Sometimes it is asserted that items like machinery, computer systems, and especially freehold buildings are assets and assets are 'a good thing' in contrast to everyday expenditures which are just bad news. The feeling seems to be that expenditure on the fixed assets of a business ought, in some way, to be treated in an opposite manner to expenditure on materials, wages, transport and so on. Not so!

We have already noted in the last two chapters that the actual **purchase** of an asset that the company will hold and use for a considerable period does not **immediately** change the total of net assets of the company. Either one asset (cash) is exchanged for another of equal book value (the thing purchased), or the company assumes a liability to pay which balances the value of the asset acquired. Once acquired, the asset is recorded in the balance sheet 'at cost' and is now one of the things the company owns; one of the things the money (from the sources of finance) was used for. But fixed assets, with the exception of freehold land, do not last for ever. When the asset disappears from the balance sheet, net assets go down, so a loss must have been suffered. How is it to be accounted for?

We have already indicated that the depreciation technique by which fixed assets are written down is the method to use. The justification for the process is this:

1 Any fixed asset is a benefit to the company and to its business during the period of time (five years?, 10 years?) it is held and used.

2 There is a genuine cost. By the time the asset is finally scrapped the company no longer has it nor does it have the cash spent on the original purchase. There has been, between the time of the original purchase and the final scrapping a reduction in net assets, a loss, an expense. That must be shown somewhere.

3 It is reasonable to say that the profits earned over the life of the asset reflected the benefit arising from the company's possession of it. Therefore each accounting period should bear a share of the cost, though not necessarily an equal share.

4 The technique is therefore to charge the profit and loss account, in each period, with that share and that is the 'depreciation charge'. If, at the same time, the recorded, book value of the asset is reduced by the same amount the balance sheet still balances. The 'reserves' (one of the places the money came from) is reduced by the same amount as the fixed assets (one of the things the money was used for).

5 In the end, when the asset is finally written off, the total of depreciation charges from the date of purchase will equal the original purchase expense, and that makes sense.

6 The amount written off each period need not be the same. It depends on the arithmetical system preferred by the accountant. If an equal amount, a fixed percentage of the original cost, is written off each year; say one tenth of the original cost over a ten-year life, the book value of the asset declines

steadily and we get **straight line depreciation**.

Using an alternative system, the depreciation charge may be calculated as a fixed percentage of the written down value at the end of the previous period. This gives **reducing balance depreciation** which has the effect of shifting the depreciation expense more towards the earlier life of the asset.

There are other depreciation systems and the relative advantages are well explained in most books on business finance. All we need to remember is that:

1 The cost of the fixed asset works its way through into successive profit and loss accounts throughout the life of the asset.
2 The depreciation charge is an accounting book adjustment but it does refer to a genuine expense that has a real impact on the total value of the company.
3 Because the depreciation charge is a book adjustment, it does not affect the cash situation even though it does affect the profit situation of the company.
4 The purchase of a fixed asset does affect the cash situation of the company at the time the asset is paid for. Therefore the difference between the cash outlay and the depreciation charges is only one of timing. In the long run they come to the same total.
5 The depreciation charge is only there in the Profit & Loss account because the asset in question has a finite life. The charge is not a matter of putting money aside for replacement. If a company wants to do that then this will be a quite separate financial operation, normally known as a 'sinking fund'.

What We Have Learned from this Chapter

1 'Costs' are all those expenses that are related to some part or some activity of the business.

2 We can split the total costs of a business into direct costs and into overheads or 'indirects'. That is the basis of the absorption costing system.

3 Costs are collected together for each cost centre and must then be attributed to cost units. It is then possible to say: 'The cost of such and such a cost unit, last period, was £...'.

4 Direct costs are attributed, in a simple way, to one specific, relevant cost unit. Such costs are 'direct' to that unit.

5 Indirect costs must be apportioned, in a way which is both sensible, and easy to operate.

6 When that is done, management can say: 'The cost of that product/consignment/operation was so much last period.'

7 But the cost apportionment must be based on assumptions about volumes of business or of activities in the coming year. If these assumptions are wrong costs will be either over-recovered or under-recovered.

8 If management is planning changes in the way the business operates it will nullify the assumptions on which absorption is based. Instead it must base its planning on the distinction between variable costs and fixed costs.

9 Most direct costs are variable costs, and most overheads are fixed costs but for any planning exercise you must look at the details. When you have done that, a tabular layout or a computer spreadsheet will produce the answers.

10 But do not rely on variable and fixed costs to run your business. All that such an analysis will tell you is whether the changes you are planning will make the company's profit situation better or worse if you go ahead. It will not guarantee that there will actually be a profit at the end of the year.

Above all, remember two things:

1 Costing systems are complicated and books on costing are heavy going simply because businesses are complicated. Provided you have followed the arguments of this chapter you, as an exporter, should only be interested in the assumptions underlying any costing system and in the results produced by it. But you should be critically interested. As

Samuel Johnson put it: 'You may scold a carpenter who has made you a bad table, though you cannot make a table. It is not your trade to make tables'. Equally, it is not your trade, as an exporter, to operate costing systems.

2 To get useful answers to questions involving costs, you must be clear in your own mind exactly what you are asking and in what context.

Questions for Discussion

1 Explain the differences between and the usefulness of the terms 'cost centre', 'cost unit', 'cost apportionment' and 'cost absorption', mentioning the contexts in which they are relevant.

2 When discussing cost behaviour we often note that 'unit variable cost' is usually treated as fixed, whilst 'fixed cost per unit' varies in a most important way. Can you explain these apparent contradictions?

3 The salesmen said: 'If we let them have an extra three machines it will only cost the firm an extra £21,000. So if we invoice them to get in a net sterling of £22,000 we are not losing, and it keeps the customer happy.' Is this a good way of running a business? Discuss.

9

Cash, and How it
Flows In and Out

There is more to cash control than looking at bank statements. This chapter aims to get across to you three things:

1 The relationship between the 'profit and loss' view of a business and its cash flows. That relationship is closer than many might think at first. It is all about 'working capital'.
2 When managers talk about 'the control of working capital' they are aiming at a moving target. Not only is cash constantly moving in and out, the other elements of working capital are also continuously changing.
3 Since we will be talking about change, we will be making repeated reference to **time** in this chapter and also in chapter 14.

A Reminder About 'Working Capital'

In chapter 5 we introduced the idea of working capital. It was defined there as current assets less current liabilities, or, more concisely, as 'net current assets'. We also suggested there that working capital is sufficiently important to be clearly distinguished as such on the balance sheet.

Why is it so important? Consider what tools or levers the managers of the company have got in controlling an export business. They can direct staff and they can persuade suppliers and potential customers to do what is desired. But such actions usually imply spending money. In contrast the assets that management can more readily manipulate are the elements of working capital items. Materials can be converted into finished goods which can then be shipped to customers, money owed from customers factored if it cannot be brought in more quickly, supplies may be acquired or suppliers may be paid, and cash may be used for any necessary purpose. The business works by using its working capital – hence the name.

It is important to appreciate that working capital represents an investment, an essential investment, in the business. If we go back to our original, basic diagram of the balance sheet which we used in Chapter 5, but if, this time, we lump together the current assets with current liabilities, we get this :

LIABILITIES	ASSETS
Sources of finance	Fixed assets
	Working capital
Total liabilities	Total net assets

Using this diagram to look at the way the company has laid out its investment, we can see that the longer term invested funds can be put **either** into fixed assets, **or** into working capital. The fixed assets normally represent the money earning part of the business, whilst the working capital is what is necessary to make the business run but does not directly earn a profit. But the more that is invested in fixed assets the less that is available for working capital, and vice versa.

A company that has weighted its investment too heavily towards working capital will be easier to manage but will be a smaller company with a smaller profit earning potential. If the weighting is too much towards fixed assets the company will suffer chronically from shortages of stocks, consequent long delivery dates, shortages of cash with limitations on the financing of its export business, incessant pursuit of open account customers for their money, and bad relations with suppliers over delayed payments.

Obviously cash is the central element of working capital and also the most versatile. However in order to use cash efficiently we must first examine the way the ebb and flow of current assets is related to the profitability of the business as a whole.

Which is Important, Profits or Cash?

This bogus antithesis between business profits and business cash resources is often expressed or implied in discussions of corporate policy, and can have a malign effect on setting strategic targets. Therefore we need to clarify a few points before we go any further.

1 'Cash at the bank' as it appears on the balance sheet is just one asset amongst the many the company owns. But it is the most immediately usable and flexible asset.
2 A successful business is a growing business, and the measure of that growth is called 'profit'. A cash-rich but profitless business is not growing. There is no point to such a business.
3 A growing business is likely to show, on its balance sheet, a growth in working capital and that growth may be partly due to an accumulation of cash. But it need not.
4 Working capital, and cash resources in particular, are the assets which management uses to steer the business. If there is a shortage of working capital or of cash then there is likely to be a constraint on what management can do.
5 However, a temporary cash shortage can be met by further injections of cash in the form of loans or shareholders' investment. But that will only happen if the company is profitable or is very likely to be in the near future. In such a case the providers of that cash will be confident that they will be paid out of future earnings.
6 In the long run, profits imply the generation of cash inflows. So it follows that the **longer term** concern of management is profitability. If that is achieved, it is reasonable to hope

that the cash will look after itself. However, in the **short term**, management must monitor the cash situation. If profitability is lost management's attention will necessarily be concentrated on cash management, on the short term, on making the best of a limited range of possible courses of action. Long term aims will have to be put on one side.

Therefore we need, as managers, to pay due attention to cash flows. This is particularly true of an export business where the time span between producing goods for export and receiving the sterling payment can be embarrassingly long. The purpose of giving due attention to the cash flows is to stop cash problems dictating the day to day running of the business. A cash shortage so often means that the exporter must spend his time talking to his bank rather than to his agents and customers. An exporter, with his working capital under control, can concentrate on exporting.

The Working Capital Cycle

Remember Arthur Aldine when he started his little exporting business? He put his invested money into the company's bank account. He then put some of that into stocks of books. Of that stock he shipped £5,000's worth to Sweden on a 90-day bill. Later, we hope, that bill matured and the money went into the company's bank account, where it started from. The money had circulated around the company's working capital.

For a manufacturing exporter the circle is a bit larger. The money must first be put into materials and wages, which are then transformed temporarily into work in progress before becoming finished goods stock ready for shipment abroad.

There is also the complication that when materials or goods are bought from suppliers on credit the exporter is using the supplier's working capital in his own business. Consequently his working capital cycle meshes with that of his supplier. We shall see later in this chapter how, for any two companies in a commercial relationship, the working capital requirements of both are simultaneously involved together.

We therefore get this pattern of flows

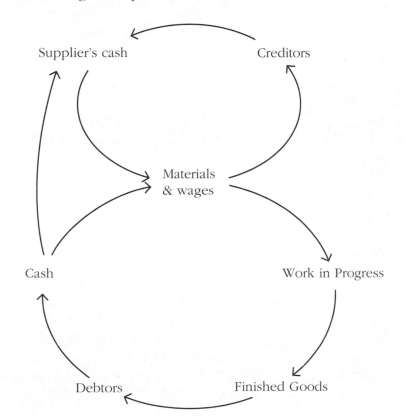

In this diagram, the term 'creditors' is used from the point of view of the exporter buying the materials. In the supplier's books the money owed would be a current asset, that is as a 'debtors' item. If the exporter always bought for cash the supplier's working capital would not be involved. If the exporter always bought on credit all the payments for materials would flow directly to the supplier.

It is easy to see why another name for working capital is the circulating capital of the business.

Our diagram is incomplete in one respect – it has no recognition that a profit is being earned. Therefore to complete it, and leaving out the supplier's working capital for simplicity, we now have:

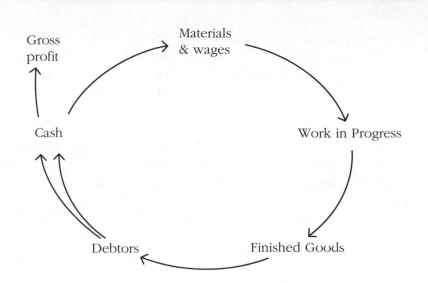

The cash that the exporter hopes to get from the customer is greater than the cash put into the goods shipped to him. That difference is the **gross profit**, the difference between the sales revenue (the invoiced amount) and the cost of goods sold. As we saw in chapter 7, the gross profit pays for the company overheads, the interest on loan capital, Corporation Tax and dividends, leaving a little over to plough back into reserves.

Three important ideas can be derived from this diagram.

1 The profit on trading emerges first in the working capital. That profit is not, at first, cash but will turn into cash in due course. That cash surplus can be left in the working capital (more stocks, more buyer credit, more cash in the bank) or it can be put elsewhere (more market research or sales pro-motion, or more fixed assets).

2 The circulation process takes **time**. Left to itself the cycle for some products or services and for some export markets may take four or five months. For those four or five months the exporting company must keep feeding in more and more cash into the cycle before the first lot flows back into the bank account. It is the role of export finance, in its widest sense, either to help augment these circulating flows or to short-circuit them by means of such devices as advances against bills or confirmed, irrevocable letters of credit.

3 As we have already explained, working capital represents an investment in part of the business that is not the profit earning part. Therefore that working capital investment should be the minimum amount necessary to make the business run. The amount involved is the sum of the investment in all those working capital items we have already discussed, that is, raw materials, work in progress, finished goods, debtors, buyer credits, prepayments or any other advances. Keep those down and you keep working capital down.

Keeping a Grip on Cash Flows

Seeing how the cash goes round and round is one thing, keeping control of the merry-go-round is quite another. In principle management can do it in two stages:

1 As part of the budgeting process, a cash flow forecast is drawn up which will spell out in sufficient detail how the cash will come in and how it will go out. It will also give a warning of any (temporary?) cash shortage during the budgeted period.
2 At regular intervals a cash flow statement will show the extent to which the budgeted cash flow is being adhered to.

In theory, the company's cash ledger, which records all payments and receipts, is a cash flow statement but the mass of detail contained in it means that it is effectively unreadable as a management report. In practice the cash flow statement is a summary report which shows not only what happened to the cash, but also what happened to the other, closely related items of working capital. In fact it is possible to derive a cash flow statement from the other two 'final statements', the P & L and the balance sheet.

To do that we will use the example of BBB International Ltd. In that company's first full year of trading it produced an unexpected cash deficit. In chapter 7 we suggested that Bernard Bumble's small profit for the year may have been one of the causes of the overdraft's sudden appearance. Let us see.

The Cash Flow Statement

Like the other final statements, cash flows can be presented in several differing ways but for the moment we will not use the layout suggested in FRS 1. Instead we will break down the relevant items into five groups like this:

1 Changes in working capital items
2 Cash flows arising from trading
3 Purchases or disposals of fixed assets
4 Changes in longer term financing
5 Anything else affecting the company's cash

Our cash flow statement will give a summary of what happened to BBB International's cash in the year up to the 31st March 1994. We will derive the information we need from both the P & L for the year, and the opening and closing balance sheets. You will have to refer back to chapter 7 to confirm the figures.
For each change, from the start of the year to the end, we will indicate whether the change represents a source of cash or an application of cash. For the majority of items this will be quite straightforward but there will also be a few that need explaining.

1 Changes in working capital

Item	Change	Source	Application
Stocks	3,000 to 13,000		10,000
Debtors	2,000 to 58,000		56,000
Prepayments	no change		
Cash	17,000 to (4,700)	21,700	
Creditors	600 to 45,600	45,000	
Accruals	0 to 300	300	
Total sources and applications		67,000	66,000
Net change in working capital		1,000	

2 Cash flow arising from trading

Profit for the year	2,600
Depreciation charge	1,400
Total inflow from trading	4,000

3 Purchases of fixed assets

Computer   5,000

4 Changes in longer term financing   – none

5 Other items   – none

Before we examine these figure from the point of view of the management of the business a little explanation of each item may help.

Stocks

These went up by £10,000 so they must have been paid for somehow, either by straight payment cash, or by running up debts which is allowed for under the creditors item. Either way it was an application of cash or its equivalent.

Debtors

Debtors increased from £2,000 to £58,000 which is an increase of £56,000. If you refer back to our diagram of 'the circulating capital of the business' you will see that what was happening was that £56,000 had been fed into and had flowed round the circuit until it came to a stop at the 'Debtors' stage. Another way of looking at it is to note that these slow-paying customers, the 'Debtors' were sitting on £56,000 of BBB's cash. So, another 'application'.

Pre-payments

There was no change here. Originally, in that first six months, Bernard Bumble had 'applied' £3,600 to paying his rent in advance and continued to do so each subsequent year. Having once primed that particular pump no further application of cash was required.

Cash at the bank

If a company wants cash quickly what better source than its current account at the bank? However BBB Ltd rather overdid it. Not only was the company's £17,000 nest egg raided for cash but a further £4,700 was extracted from the bank as an overdraft, giving a total source of cash of £21,700.

Creditors

This figure increased by £45,000 over the year. Just as an increase in 'Debtors' was an application of cash so an increase in 'Creditors' was a source. In practical terms, the company had an extra £45,000 to use by the simple expedient of not paying what it owed to the manufacturer of those devices being exported.

Accrued expenses

You will recall that 'accruals' such as the fourth quarter's telephone bill represent liabilities or potential debts being run up in advance of even getting the bill presented let alone paying it. So Bernard Bumble was using the telephone but keeping the £300 that it cost the company in the company's current account. So once again we have a source of cash.

Change in total working capital

The individual potential cash flows for working capital items added up to £66,000 of applications against £67,000 of sources. We see therefore that total working capital went **down** by £1,000. Since working capital is one of the two places in which a company invests its longer term funds, as we pointed out at the beginning of this chapter, then a reduction in working capital is a **release** of invested funds. Thus the net effect of the changes in the individual working capital items is a £1,000 source of cash.

You may also notice that this £1,000 cash source is immediately obvious if we compare the two balance sheets for 1993 and 1994. You can see that 'Net current assets' went down from £25,000 in March 1993 to £24,000 a year later.

Cash flow from trading

One would expect this to be quite straight forward. The company pays money in order to be able to ship goods abroad and in return gets money back from the customers and the difference is the profit or cash surplus. But not quite. We have already noted that timing differences cause a discrepancy between profit earning and collecting the money. However we have already allowed for those timing differences by noting changes in the debtors and creditors figures. So, subject to those adjustments, a profit should mean an equivalent cash surplus.

But not quite. If you refer back to the P & L for the year to 31st March 1994 you will see that all the items in that profit calculation referred to transactions that involved cash sooner or later; the work done by the freight forwarder for instance. But there is one exception, the depreciation charge which was a book adjustment but not a cash payment. It is true that it is related to the original cash payment but we have allowed for that separately in our cash calculations. The effect of the depreciation charge in the P & L is to **understate** the trading cash surplus from trading. Since we use the profit figure as a starting point we must **add back** that non-cash expense to get the true trading cash surplus.

Purchases and disposals of fixed assets

Towards the end of the previous chapter we showed how the expense aspect of acquiring fixed assets is fed into successive P & L accounts over the life of the asset, but the cash aspect is obviously recorded when the payment is made. For a manufacturing business the cash outlays on fixed assets (factories, machines, processing plant and so on) are a very significant application of the company's resources. For such companies forward looking cash planning is vital.

Disposals of fixed assets may also be very significant. During the UK recession at the beginning of the 1990s many struggling companies were forced to sell off subsidiaries (which count as 'fixed assets') to alleviate cash shortages due to a slump in sales.

Changes in longer term financing

You will remember that juggling current assets cannot earn a profit, but it may provide short term sources of cash. So a company may run down its stocks, chase customers for money or, if all else fails, stall on paying its suppliers. Longer term financing is a quite different category, one that includes both loans of all types – so-called debt capital – and further injections of share capital, the so-called 'equity' capital, as happened with Aldine Activities.

Other items?

Well this could include anything that the other four categories do not cover. Perhaps an investment in a joint venture should be separately distinguished in this way.

Analysing and Interpreting the Cash Flow Statement

We can summarize the cash flows of BBB Ltd even further, like this:

Sources of cash :

Decrease in working capital	1,000	
Cash surplus from trading	4,000	
Total sources		5,000

Applications of cash :

Purchase of fixed assets	5,000

Incidentally, a cash flow statement laid out as a list of sources and a list of applications should always balance exactly, like this one.

So what can we say about Bernard Bumble's performance as a manager of his company's cash resources? We can see that the (small) profit almost paid for the computer system but it was necessary to raid the working capital for the difference. But BBB Ltd's business was expanding and expansion requires **more** working capital not less. In this particular case more working capital was required to finance increased stocks and increased debtors, so how did BBB Ltd manage? We need to examine what went on **within** working capital.

The situation was:

Changes in working capital

Item	Change	Source	Application
Stocks	3,000 to 13,000		10,000
Debtors	2,000 to 58,000		56,000
Prepayments	no change		
Cash	17,000 to (4,700)	21,700	
Creditors	600 to 45,600	45,000	
Accruals	0 to 300	300	
Total sources and applications		67,000	66,000

Because of the increased volume of business BBB Ltd needed an extra £66,000 to finance stocks and to be able to afford to wait for monies to arrive from abroad. In order to finance those extra stocks and debtors the company used all the cash it had available (plus some of the bank's), the rest coming from its supplier's working capital. The suppliers had financed deliveries of manufactured devices with £45,00 of their own cash which had **not** been made up by payments from BBB Ltd.

Remember what we said about the inter-linking of a supplier's working capital with that of its customer's. Exporting can involve long chains of supply from raw material purchases in the UK to retail sales abroad. At each stage somebody's working capital is being used to fill that part of the supply chain. Negotiations about payment terms are often negotiations about whose working capital is to be used.

So what might Bernard Bumble have done if he had prepared his cash flow forecasts and planned his cash flows a bit better. His options would have been:

1 Keep a grip on stocks of devices for sale. By close liaison with the manufacturer and adopting a 'Just-in-Time' policy it may have been possible to reduce stocks by, perhaps?, £10,000. But there is always a catch. It would mean either:
   (a) improved sales forecasting, so the manufacturer could plan **his** production to deliver 'Just-in-Time'; or
   (b) the manufacturer holding stocks for BBB Ltd which would then be called off as required as export orders came in. In that case the manufacturer's cost (and prices) would increase because of the cost of holding these stocks.
2 Reduce the debtors figure by changing the payments terms. It is in cases like this one that the attractions of 'cash with order' as compared with non-discounted 90-day bills becomes very obvious. Once again there's a catch. The banks or other advisers will always proffer a wide variety of solutions but each solution will fall into one or other of two categories, either:
   (a) it will be a solution that puts the onus onto the buyer. Cash with order is the worst from the buyer's point of

view, but any method of payment on shipment also involves the buyer investing his own working capital in the deal. If an exporter's marketing strategy includes buyer credits in any form this is obviously not the way to go; or

(b) it will be a solution that costs the exporter. Whether or not it is simple advances against bills, or the discounting of bills, or factoring of sales invoices, or forfaiting, or general revolving credit or what ever device the bank comes up with, there will be an interest charge. This is even true for the exporter who, unlike Bernard Bumble, has organized enough of his own cash resources to provide his own export finance. In that case the cost is the **opportunity cost** of losing the interest the money might have earned elsewhere.

So a policy of keeping down the debtors figure carries either a **marketing cost** or a **financing cost**.

3 Obtain an additional source of cash. The techniques we have just mentioned do just that but on a consignment by consignment basis. In other words we were talking about short term financing but a financing that is usually automatically secured, either on invoices, accepted bills, or similar. Longer term financing of working capital for export is likely to involve two aspects whatever its precise nature.

(a) It is secured more on the company than on the consignment. Taking out longer term finance requires confidence both on the part of the lenders and on the management borrowing that the prospects for export business are sufficiently assured to make the financing both affordable and prudent.

(b) Like 'consignment' finance, there is an interest charge but the longer the term of the borrowing the longer the term of the commitment to pay those interest charges. So the forecasting task becomes not so much cash flow forecasting as market forecasting.

What We Have Learned from this Chapter

1 Investment in working capital is a pump-priming exercise. The company must invest in stocks and (effectively) buyer credit before the exported goods and services earn the profits that were the original point of it all.

2 The resources invested in working capital take time to circulate and it is the task of day to day management to keep them flowing as quickly as possible with no stagnant accumulation of resources anywhere.

3 Export finance is primarily about the provision or management of working capital. That is also true when exports are financed from a company's own resources.

4 The elements of working capital are continually changing from one form to another. Astute management will ensure that there is an optimum mix of these elements.

5 Working capital always carries a cost. It may be the potential need to pay good dividends on share capital invested in a company's working capital. It may be the premium paid on using hire purchase for the acquisition of fixed assets. It may be a marketing cost when we get the buyer to use his working capital to finance the trade.

6 Control of working capital is inescapably involved with forecasting; forecasting production, forecasting sales, forecasting cash flows.

Therefore we now need to look at the technique of cash flow forecasting which we will do in the next chapter.

Questions for Discussion

1 During one year a company recorded a gross profit of £305,000, a net loss before tax of £145,000 and an increase in 'cash at the bank' of £125,000. Name three possible sources of this apparent anomaly between profit and cash movements.

2 Your company has increased its overdraft but has just reported

a profit for the last quarter. When discussing the overdraft situation with your bank manager what aspects of your business might you emphasize to reassure him that the overdraft situation was not going to get worse.

3 The salesman for Universal Factors Plc has shown you the way his company will provide instant cash against invoices. What are the possible advantages and disadvantages of using the factor's service?

10

The 'Why' and 'How' of Cash Flow Forecasting

All businesses, whether sole traders, partnerships, small or big companies, should prepare forecasts of their future cash situations. However, export businesses have a greater need to take these forecasts seriously. The reason for that is **time**; export strategies, because they take a global view, must work to a longer time-scale. With that fact in mind, we will now start to look at cash movements and consider the time value of money. This very important idea will be covered in chapter 14 but we will need to have a preliminary idea of its implications in this chapter.

Therefore, in this chapter, we will examine:

1 How cash movements and 'the time value of money' in particular affect both the management and the profitability of the exporter's business.
2 How to incorporate the all-important time aspect of our budgeting into the cash flow forecast.
3 A systematic approach to organising the planning and cash budgeting processes.
4 The production of forecasts that are readable; that are of practical use to managers who need them but who did not prepare them.
5 Why cash forecasting is quite a different activity from profit planning so that we do not get them muddled up.

Cash or Profits – What's the Difference?

In previous chapters we have already indicated one strategic difference between the 'cash' and the 'profit' view of managing a business. In the long run a successful business is one that grows, which implies a growth of net assets, which is by definition a profitable growth. Such a growth should either generate cash surpluses or make borrowing feasible and prudent. But cash is just one of the assets of a business, one that can be mis-managed even in a profitable business. Losing control of the cash means immediate, unnecessary and distracting problems for the managers of that business.

You will remember that the monies invested in a business can be used to fund either fixed assets or working capital. The money put into working capital can be used (or misused) to fund any of the assets comprising working capital. So we can see that a cash crisis can arise from one or more of the following mistakes:

1 The business is not profitable so that working capital, as a whole, shrinks.
2 Too much has been invested in fixed assets which may often include investment in the take-over of other companies. Either way working capital is starved.
3 Too much has been invested in stocks. This may happen through a combination of adverse trading conditions and slow management reactions, producing a situation where materials are still being purchased and goods produced even though customer demand has fallen off.
4 Too much has been invested in 'debtors'. Profitable sales may have been achieved but the money is too slow coming in. This can result from a too aggressive marketing policy offering too generous terms to customers, or may simply be the result of inadequate use of available facilities for export finance.

Shortage of cash is the one business problem that cannot be

hidden from view. At the very least your bank will know the situation. In addition the inability to offer the usual credits to customers, slowness in paying suppliers, or sudden cut-price sales campaigns may all indicate to the market place that your business has problems. This can easily produce the vicious circle of a cash shortage undermining sales which, in turn, aggravates the cash problem. Ferranti Plc, when it ran into serious difficulties in the early 1990s, was in exactly this situation. Declining liquidity made potential customers doubt the company's ability to finance the big projects it was seeking – projects that it was then desperate to get in order to survive.

To put it briefly, avoiding cash problems enables management to concentrate on profits.

Cash, Profits and the 'Time Value of Money'

In chapters 3 to 8 we identified 'profit' as the growth of net assets. We looked at that statement of assets and liabilities called 'The Balance Sheet', and we also saw how the profit and loss account explained how, over one accounting period, the business moved from one balance sheet to the next.

What we also did in those chapters, but did not say so, was to assume that, as Gertrude Stein might have put it, a pound is a pound is a pound. Not so!

Anyone, on being told that he is to get a gift of £1,000, would be a trifle disappointed to then be told that the gift will arrive in exactly three years time. Even the least financially sophisticated of us would suspect that £1,000 three years ahead is not as valuable as the immediate gift of the same amount.

It is easy to put a precise figure on that difference. Getting the money now would enable us to invest it for those three years and so end up better off than we would have been merely collecting the money on that future date. The difference is the interest that may be earned by that sum of money over that time span. We will develop that idea in chapter 14 but it will be sufficient for the time being just to see that **time** is important, and that interest rates make it so.

So, why did we not bother about this time factor before if it is so important? The reason was the relatively short time scale involved; an accounting period of perhaps one or three months. When deciding how well we were doing by calculating the business's profits on its operations, any adjustment for time alone would not have made a significant difference.

What will make a difference to profits will be the interest payable on short-term borrowings, particularly if the 'short-term' was not so short as is so often the case when a business is deciding how to finance its export sales. That interest charge will be a charge against profits. When a business is borrowing cash or failing to invest surplus cash, the interest paid or foregone will be a charge against profits. So we need to know the effect on our budgeting and profit planning. In order to know that we need a cash flow forecast.

The Essential Features of Cash Flow Forecasting

The four essential features can be summed up as:

1 time;
2 payments;
3 receipts; and
4 cash balances.

The time aspect

When budgeting for cash not only do we have to decide what will happen but when. That means not when it should happen, not when we would like it to happen, but when, realistically, it will happen. We may plan to finance our exports by advances against accepted bills but the buyer may be slow in accepting them, leaving our consignment sitting on some dockside collecting demurrage charges. Perhaps we might get a sudden, last minute request for extra credit or delayed shipments.

It is not possible to prevent such things happening. However it is possible to forecast when such events will produce a serious problem if for instance the company was already going to be tight for cash. It is also possible to be able to warn the bank of impending difficulties before the bank warns the company.

The payments aspect

Good management implies, amongst many other things, running the business on a minimum level of working capital. There should not be a cushion of unused money held 'just in case'. That in turn means careful planning and monitoring of cash outlays. Yes, the new production machine will be a good investment but when precisely will the supplier expect to see his money? Armed with a cash flow forecast management is in a better position to juggle a variety of expenditures, all of which may be perfectly sensible individually.

The receipts aspect

An exporter cannot make a delinquent buyer or a slow moving foreign bank keep to the exporter's planned schedule. But if there is one thing that will encourage such delinquency it is for the other parties to spot that the exporter does not notice when the cash comes in late. A budgeted schedule for monitoring receipts should be a standard tool of any exporter.

The cash balances

What matters in the end is not so much what came in or how much went out. What matters is the cumulative effect of those cash movements on the liquidity of the company as a whole. So the last line in the forecasts which we are now going to prepare will be the closing cash balance for each budget period.

A Small Service Company and its Cash

ConCon Ltd is a very small engineering consultancy specializing in supervizing aspects of the commissioning of power plants being installed worldwide, but mostly in North America and the 'Old Dominions'. Their forecasting is made easier by the fact that the work comes towards the end of long construction schedules. Provided the schedules are adhered to and, of course, provided the main contractor subcontracts the project to ConCon Ltd the company can forecast its cash flows.

At the start of January 1995 the consultancy did not have any jobs on hand but five were due to start during the first half of 1995 and a couple more were fixed for an August start. Therefore cash looked like getting tight before the payments flowed in round about April, and again before the autumn. So they needed a cash flow forecast.

A convenient way to lay out such a forecast is to display it in four sections corresponding to the four essential features we listed above; events, payments, receipts and bank balances.

Step 1: What is planned to happen

Before the company can consider the cash inflows and outflows it must, as with any budgeting exercise, consider the activities that will give rise to those flows. As a very first step the company must also decide the budget time periods, weekly, monthly, quarterly or for a whole year. ConCon Ltd do their planning on a monthly basis. At the start of 1994 the five prospective consultancy contracts were:

Contract	Duration	Scheduled
No. 1	3 months	January to March
No. 2	2 months	February and March
No. 3	4 months	March to June
No. 4	1 month	March only
No. 5	4 months	May to August

The contract work is charged to the client at an all-inclusive rate of £22,500 per month, payable on completion which means, effectively, the cash is received the month after completion.

The company was also looking forward to receiving cash for work done in 1993. These outstanding payments amounted to £87,000 expected in January and £44,000 in February.

The costs for each contract were budgeted as:

Initial set-up expense	£1,450
Operating expenses	£8,700 per month
Reporting and presentation	£1,600

The initial and the operating expenses are actually paid during the relevant months, as the consultancy work proceeds. The final reporting and presentation expenses, mostly for work done by outside suppliers, are paid in the month following completion of each contract.

In addition to the direct expenses of the contract work, the company has an annual overhead expense (covering salaries and administration) of £380,000 involving continuing payments throughout the year. Building expenses; rent, rates, insurance, power, security and so on, amount to £60,000 a year but the related cash payments are scheduled as quarterly payments in January, April and so on.

Step 2: A schedule of payments

It is important to remember that we are not preparing a schedule of costs. In many cases the monthly expense to be charged against profit will be the same as the cash payments; salaries are an obvious example. But some, like the report preparation expenses for work done by outside contractors, will be paid in the month after they were incurred. There will also be expenses that do not involve cash outlays at all, the principal one being the depreciation expense for the company's computer system and its bespoke software which all have a relatively short life. These non-cash expenses amounted to £32,000 a year which meant that the annual cash payments for the overheads were

£348,000 or an average of £29,000 each month.

These payments were then scheduled, together with the schedule of work, and this is shown, with the rest of the forecast, on page 167.

Step 3: A schedule of receipts

This is usually a simpler part of a cash flow forecast since most businesses have fewer sources of cash than outflows. ConCon Ltd presents its bills to clients in the last month of each contract and is fortunate in that it almost always sees the cash arrive in its UK sterling account before the end of the following month. In that respect it is luckier than most; many other companies see their cash dribbling in over several months, especially where open account invoicing is the rule. In other cases cash may be received on shipment or, in the case of service companies like this one, as progress payments. In all cases the cash flow forecast must be based on a realistic estimate of both times and amounts.

Step 4: A forecast of bank balances

Using the totals of payments and receipts already worked out, the closing bank balances for each period can now be estimated. The arithmetic can be expressed either as so much out and so much in, or by combining the two flows to give net cash flow for the period (as below). This net figure can obviously be either negative or positive.

However ConCon Ltd has an agreement with their bank by which they can earn three per cent (at an annual rate) on their credit current account balances. Because the forecast is calculated on a monthly basis the interest calculation must incorporate the equivalent rate which works out at 0.25 per cent per month.

To start these last calculations it is necessary to have the first opening cash balance. In this case the balance in ConCon's current account on the 1st of January was £45,000. From that figure all the subsequent balances follow naturally.

Step 5: Put the figures together and see the consequences

As with any planning exercise, the primary requirement is to be tidy and logical. Applying the figures the company has already collected together, the final, six-month forecast was therefore:

Construction Consultancy Ltd
Cash Flow Forecast: January-June 1994

Month	Jan	Feb	March	April	May	Jun
Contracts						
No. 1	Start	.....	Finish			
No. 2		Start	Finish			
No. 3			Start	......	......	Finish
No. 4			S.& F.			
No. 5					Start	......
Payments						
For contract work						
Set-up	1,450	1,450	2,900	0	1,450	0
Operating	8,700	17,400	34,800	8,700	17,400	17,400
Final	0	0	0	4,800	0	0
On overheads						
Salaries etc	29,000	29,000	29,000	29,000	29,000	29,000
Buildings etc	15,000	0	0	15,000	0	0
Total payments	54,150	47,850	66,700	57,500	47,850	46,400
Receipts	87,000	44,000	0	135,000	0	0
Bank balances						
Opening balance	45,000	77,963	74,308	7,794	85,313	37,676
Net cash flow	32,850	(3,850)	(66,700)	77,500	(47,850)	(46,400)
Interest	113	195	186	19	213	94
Closing balance	77,963	74,308	7,794	85,313	37,676	(8,630)

Step 6: Drawing the conclusions

In the case of a simple forecast exercise like this one, the conclusions are clear.

1 The company needed to warn its bankers about likely problems in June, and also in the following two months. It would be September before the cash situation recovered. The size of the budgeted shortfall (£8,630) implies that minor adjustments would not be enough to eliminate it.

2 Cash would be rather short in March. If all went as planned there would not have been a problem, but the figures did warn the management to watch both payments and receipts rather more closely than usual until the cash from Contracts 1, 2 and 4 was safely banked.

3 Because the company was in the fortunate position of having clients who paid up reliably and quickly, short term export finance techniques, such as advances against bills, would not make any difference. Consequently, longer term financing might well be a point to raise when the company spoke to its bankers. Possibilities might include short term loans, financing any capital expenditure by hire purchase or leasing, or an agreement on revolving credit given the expected regularity of the company's contract work.

4 The three per cent interest received on the company's current account balances is really neither here nor there as it amounted to less than £1,000 over the six month period. This could be another subject of discussion with the company's bankers.

5 Payment of UK Corporation Tax has been left out of these calculations since the precise figure would depend on a number of other factors. The date of payment, which is nine months after the end of the company's last accounting period, might well have fallen in this six month period and so aggravated the situation in June.

6 Quite apart from anything else, the next Board meeting could have discussed longer term capital and revenue expenditures, and the longer term financing of the company as a whole. Was the company being extravagant? Was it under capitalized?

The Mill in South East Asia

Pretty Polly Plantations Plc are exploiting the economic potential of the 'Pacific Rim' and of south east Asia in particular. They are planning to build and operate a processing mill, taking in plantation products as raw material and supplying the processed product worldwide. They have obtained the co-operation of the local government authority subject to limitations on remittances to the UK. Therefore PPP Plc will borrow locally to finance the project and use the cash flows to pay off the debt as quickly as possible before reopening negotiations with the authorities about repatriation of funds. The local currency loan will be secured by sterling guarantees. The company is interested in how quickly the loan will be paid off and cash starts to flow back to the company either in the UK or to their other subsidiaries elsewhere in the world.

A cash flow forecast for this capital investment will cover a much longer time span than that for ConCon Ltd; at least seven years. It will also be a much more complex operation. As a consequence the cash flow forecast will be rather more of a summary document as compared with the previous example and it will not be possible to show individual payments. In order to be sure that the whole forecast makes sense it will be necessary to use what we have already learned about the financing of a business. It will also be necessary to list the relevant activities before we attempt, as we did in the last example, to schedule them in the first of the four sections of the forecast.

The plan for the overseas mill

PPP Plc will base its budgets, and therefore its cash flow forecasts, on the following costs and policies:

	$	
Cost of freehold land	200,000	
Buildings and basic services	300,000	
Investment in plant:		
3 processors at $400,000 each	1,200,000	
Other equipment	150,000	
Total capital investment	1,850,000	
Operating expenses		
Direct and indirect wages	600,000	pa
Variable production overhead	150,000	pa
Sales and administration expenses	200,000	pa
Management salaries and services	160,000	pa
Depreciation, straight-line, based on:		
Buildings 50-year life		
Plant 10-year life		

Each processor has an output capacity with a sales value of $900,000 but the planned sales turnover of $2,700,000 is not expected to be reached until the fourth year of production. It is therefore planned to install one processor per year over three years. The annual expense figures refer to the situation where the mill is fully equipped with the three processors.

Other budgetary items are: Purchase of the land, erection of buildings and installation of the plant which will take one year. The land and buildings must be paid for during that year but the plant will be paid for on installation.

Although each processor is capable of producing processed material with a sales value of $900,000 in a full year, it is expected that training and the inevitable teething troubles will give operating efficiencies of only 70, 80 and 90 per cent in the first three years of production.

It is proposed to hold an average level of raw material stock equal to one and a half month's consumption. Work in progress stocks are expected to be negligible, whilst finished processed stock will represent one month's sales.

The cost of raw material consumed will be equal to 20 per cent of the sales value of the finished processed output.

The growers are to paid for their raw materials on delivery so there will be no outstanding 'Trade creditors' figure. All the operating expenses will be paid for as they are incurred with the exception of the variable production overhead. Those expenses will be paid in the following month, that is, one month's credit on average. Debtors are expected to be given two month's credit.

The three (identical) processors will be purchased as production and sales build up, that is, one per year. However all the 'other equipment' will be needed from the start of production. Similarly the direct and indirect labour force are budgeted to expand in steps, in proportion to capacity, that is, the number of processors. The sales and administration expenses will be incurred in full from the start of production. The management and services expenses will be incurred from the start of the project, as soon as the land purchase is negotiated.

The parent company will obtain a $2,000,000 loan in local currency, backed by its Sterling denominated guarantees, bearing an interest charge of 12 per cent per annum. Should an overdraft be needed this will be available at an interest charge of 18 per cent per annum. For planning purposes, the budgeted overdraft interest will be calculated on the previous year's closing overdrawn balance – if there is one.

As part of the deal with the country's government, it is intended that the subsidiary will initially devote its cash surpluses to repaying the loan rather than repatriating them to the UK. PPP Plc hopes that this can be done in order to reduce borrowings to $1,000,000 or less as quickly as possible. Local company taxation is not included in this forecast.

Drawing up the cash flow forecast

The completed forecast is shown in table 10.1. Note that it does not extend beyond Year 7 but that is only for reasons of space. Also note that the cash figures are rounded to the nearest $100. Anyone interested should have no difficulty in extending it to Year 10. When reading the rest of this section you should make continual reference to the figures in the forecast.

Table 10.1: A cash flow forecast

Pretty Polly Plantations Plc. The Planned S.E. Asia mill
Note: All financial figures are in thousands of local dollars

YEAR	One	Two	Three	Four	Five	Six	Seven
No. of processors	0	1	2	3	3	3	3
Cumulative capital investment							
Buildings	500	500	500	500	500	500	500
Processors	0	400	800	1,200	1,200	1,200	1,200
Other equipment	0	150	150	150	150	150	150
= total inv.	500	1,050	1,450	1,850	1,850	1,850	1,850
Var. production O/H	0.0	50.0	100.0	150.0	150.0	150.0	150.0
Op'g efficiency	0%	70%	80%	90%	100%	100%	100%
Sales invoiced	0.0	630.0	1,440.0	2,430.00	2,700.0	2,700.0	2,700.0
Raw material							
Consumption	0	126	288	486	540	540	540
Stock values							
Raw material	0.0	15.8	36.0	60.8	67.5	67.5	67.5
Processed	0.0	52.5	120.0	202.5	225.0	225.0	225.0
Purchases							
Raw material	0.0	141.8	308.3	510.8	546.8	540.0	540.0
Creditors	0.0	4.2	8.3	12.5	12.5	12.5	12.5
Debtors	0.0	105.0	240.0	405.0	450.0	450.0	450.0

SEVEN YEAR CASH FLOW FORECAST

	One	Two	Three	Four	Five	Six	Seven
RECEIPTS							
From sales	0.0	525.0	1,305.0	2,265.0	2,655.0	2,700.0	2,700.0
Loans received	2,000.0						
= total	2,000.0	525.0	1,305.0	2,265.0	2,655.0	2,700.0	2,700.0
PAYMENTS							
On fixed assets							
Buildings	500.0	0.0	0.0	0.0	0.0	0.0	0.0
Plant	0.0	550.0	400.0	400.0	0.0	0.0	0.0
For operating expenses							
Raw material	0.0	141.8	308.3	510.8	546.8	540.0	540.0
Dir & ind wages	0.0	200.0	400.0	600.0	600.0	600.0	600.0
Var Prod O/H	0.0	45.8	95.8	145.8	150.0	150.0	150.0
Sales & admin	0.0	200.0	200.0	200.0	200.0	200.0	200.0
Management etc.	160.0	160.0	160.0	160.0	160.0	160.0	160.0
Loans repaid						500.0	1,000.0
Total payments	660.0	1,297.6	1,564.1	2,016.6	1,656.8	2,150.0	2,650.0
Loans outstanding	2,000.0	2,000.0	2,000.0	2,000.0	2,000.0	1,500.0	500.0
Cash balances							
Balance B/Forward	0.0	1,100.0	87.4	(411.7)	(477.3)	195.0	565.0
Total receipts	2.000.0	525.0	1,305.0	2,265.0	2,655.0	2,700.0	2,700.0
	2,000.0	1,625.0	1,392.4	1,853.3	2,177.7	2,895.0	3,265.0
Total payments	660.0	1,297.6	1,564.1	2,016.6	1,656.8	2,150.0	2,650.0
Interest @ 12%	240.0	240.0	240.0	240.0	240.0	180.0	60.0
Interest @ 18%	0.0	0.0	0.0	74.1	85.9	0.0	0.0
Balance C/Forward	1,100.0	87.4	(411.7)	(477.3)	195.0	565.0	555.0

Step 1: Scheduling the events

We must first fix the timescale for the forecast. It will be at least six to eight years before the loans are paid off. We will therefore construct the cash flow forecast on a year-by-year basis.

Year One will be devoted to buying the land and constructing the buildings and the necessary infrastructure. Cash outlays in that year will be limited to these activities and management salaries and services.

In Year Two the first of the processors will be installed and commence production. Sales will now be made but that also requires production staff to be employed. In addition sales will be limited by the prospective 70 per cent efficiency level.

Years Three and Four will see the other two processors installed, but full production and sales will not be achieved until Year Five. During these first five years the level of raw material purchases and stocks, processed stocks, creditors and debtors can be calculated from the annual sales figures.

Note that:

1 It will be necessary to consider the level of investment in fixed assets in order to get a figure for the related cash outlays. The planned investment in land, buildings and plant, and the planned levels of stocks, debtors and creditors will enable us to calculate how much **cash** was spent or received during each year. Effectively we will use what are balance sheet figures to calculate the related cash flows.

2 Because of the extended time scale chosen for the forecast we will not attempt to detail the delays in payments and receipts as we did in the last example. Such delays will all be shorter than the 12-month time span in each step of the forecast. The 'timing' aspect will be taken care of by noting the changes in these creditor and debtor figures from one year to the next.

For these reasons it is useful to spell out in some detail what will be happening over those seven years. Therefore we have calculated the variable production overhead, sales, raw material consumption, stocks and purchases, and the creditors and debtors figures. That gives us the basis of the actual cash forecast.

Step 2: Scheduling the receipts

The first item will be the receipt of the $2,000,000 loan in Year One. Sales start in Year Two and from then on the cash receipts will be: the previous year's (closing) debtors plus the current year's sales less the current year's closing debtors. That gives the actual amount of cash received from customers during the year.

Step 3: Scheduling the payments

The outlays of cash will be of three types:

1 Payments for the fixed assets; land, buildings and plant.
2 The cash required for purchases of materials and for the operating expenses.
3 Repayment of loans, and interest on the loan and on any overdraft.

The first of these is straightforward, being the difference from one year to the next of the cumulative capital investment in the mill.

Payments for raw materials will be equal to what is consumed plus the change in stock from one year to the next. Similarly, payments for the variable production overhead will be the cost plus previous year's unpaid bills (that is, creditors) less this year's unpaid bills. The other operating expenses are paid as they go so they are straightforward.

The repayment of loans is something that cannot be decided until the forecast is nearly complete. In this case PPP Plc noticed that the mill would be able to start repaying the loan in Year 6 and clear it in Year 8. That decision affects the interest payable which is something more conveniently shown in the last section of the forecast.

Step 4: Forecasting the closing bank balances

As in the ConCon Ltd forecast this part is more straightforward. For a change, we will lay it out as: Opening bank balance, plus Total Receipts, less Total Payments, less Interest Paid, to give the closing bank balances to be carried forward to the next year. The loan interest is based on the 'loans outstanding' figure, whilst the overdraft interest is based on the previous year's closing bank balance as we explained earlier.

Step 5: Drawing the conclusions

By Year Six, the mill will have obtained a steady, positive operating cash flow of $1,050,000 (sales receipts of $2,700,000 less cash operating expenses of $1,650,000). There remain interest payments of $180,000 but this will decline, being reduced to zero in Year 8 when the loan can be entirely cleared.

This is not as satisfactory a situation as it looks. By early Year 8, the plant will have been operating for over six years and replacement will have to be considered. The cash flow forecast does not show this aspect of the mill's operations. The depreciation charges which, quite correctly, did not appear there, would appear in the profit and loss account. These depreciation charges would record the decline in net assets caused by the wearing out of $1,850,000's worth of fixed assets.

The mill would be profitable in Year Four even though it would still operating at only 90% efficiency (but with three processors). Given a 50-year life for the buildings and a ten-year life for the plant, all depreciated on a straight-line basis, a summary P & L for the year works out as:

Sales revenue		2,430,000
less:		
Materials	486,000	
Wages	600,000	
Variable overhead	150,000	
Sales and Admin.	200,000	
Management etc.	160,000	

Depreciation		
Buildings @ 2%	10,000	
Plant @ 10%	135,000	
Interest	314,100	
Total expenses		2,055,100
		————
Net profit		374,900
		————

The fact that it would be profitable by Year Four merely means that would be the point at which the mill **started** to reduce its overdraft and then, later, its borrowings.

One of the factors contributing to the positive cash flows after Year Five would be that it would no longer be necessary to invest further cash in working capital. It can be seen that stocks and debtors cease to grow. That, in turn would be because sales would be static at $2,700,000 per year. Expanding trading always requires an investment in additional working capital.

The fact that, in the end PPP Plc paid off the loans and overdraft and pulled in some cash, does not necessarily imply that their longer term financial strategy was satisfactory. The UK parent company accepted the sterling equivalent of a $2,000,000 liability and would be exposed to this for over seven years. Could they not have borrowed that money for some other purpose and got a higher return? What was the company's return, assuming that no replacement investment in plant would be commissioned after ten years? These are questions that we will look at in chapter 14.

What We Have Learned from this Chapter

1 Cash flow forecasting is one particular, but very important, aspect of business planning and budgeting. It is particularly important for exporting businesses.
2 It is essential that the cash flow forecast is prepared carefully and methodically, producing a layout that is easy (as far as that is possible) for management to read, analyse and criticize.

3 Cash forecasting is all about payments and receipts spaced over time. All these elements must be realistic, but it is the timing schedules that are most liable to suffer from undue optimism, and such optimism can be dangerous.

4 Cash flow forecasts are **not** about profits, losses, costs or revenues although the figures must be closely related to those in the budgeted P & L account. This means that capital expenditures are in, but depreciation charges are left out. Also left out are items like stock write-offs and provisions for bad debts.

5 The forecast cash flows are also closely related to but not the same as the figures that appear in the balance sheet. As we pointed out in preparing this second example, it was the **changes** in items like fixed assets, stocks, loans and so on that show the related cash flows in and out.

6 Some of the figures in the cash flow forecast cannot be finally decided until at least a draft of the forecast is prepared. Such 'contingent' items include interest payments and decisions about borrowing or repayment of loans. Therefore it will be necessary to repeatedly amend and adjust the forecast until it looks both feasible and acceptable. The tool for doing that is the conventional computer based spreadsheet and that is one of the things we will look at in the next chapter.

Questions for Discussion

1 Patrick Pragmatic says: 'If I fail to make a profit it doesn't worry me. It's only a book-keeper's calculation after all and, in any case, I pay less Corporation Tax. But if I run out of cash I can't pay the bills and the bank would close me down. So I run my business strictly on cash flow forecasts.' Discuss the advantages and disadvantages of this corporate strategy.

2 Canny Corporation has, on the 1st of September, £32,500 in the bank. After the summer lull it has no outstanding debtors except one for £23,000 and this money has been promised, 'without fail', before the end of the month.

The company has budgeted sales of £15,000, £25,000, £30,000 and £10,000 for the four months, September to December.

The company has also budgeted for cash payments of £23,000 for each of those four months.

It knows by experience that it will receive from customers 40 per cent of invoiced amounts in the month following, 30 per cent the following month, 20 per cent the next and the balance in the next month.

How much cash should it expect to have on the last day of each month?

3 A software design house has just landed a very profitable contract to supply a complete production control system to an existing New Zealand plant. It is estimated that, after system analysis, it will take six months to write the program, and a further three months to install and test it.

What are the cash flow implications for this success story?

11

Cash, Stock and Working Capital

A Review of What We Discovered in the Last Few Chapters

During 1993, when the UK economy was slowly pulling itself out of recession, some public attention was directed to the UK statistics on company insolvencies. This was partly an expression of concern about the effects of the recession itself, but partly an attempt to use those statistics as a measure of the rate of economic recovery. This led to debates as to the extent to which levels of reported insolvencies or receiverships were a 'lagging indicator'.

For any individual, struggling company, there is likely to be a period of many months between a fall-off in orders leading to an adverse cash flow, producing an unsupportable debt to the banks or to suppliers, and the formal completion of negotiations with the banks leading to a final decision to appoint a Receiver. Given that possibly protracted sequence of events the official statistics could be said to indicate the adverse market conditions of perhaps 18 months previous to the demise of the company. The statistics would be a lagging indicator of economic conditions.

The contrary argument could have been that, as soon as any particular UK market sector showed signs of recovery the banks and other creditors would take a different, more optimistic and supportive view, thus leading to a quicker fall in the reported statistics of business failures. A high rate of reported insolvencies would, on this theory, merely indicate that 'no light could be seen at the end of the tunnel', not yet at any rate. The statistics would indicate the contemporary economic climate; they would be a concurrent indicator.

However, some financial analysts at the time took a view quite different from these two, one that is particularly relevant to any manager budgeting his working capital and cash needs over the short to medium term. This alternative view was that the level of business failures was not a function of the level of the economy, whether lagged or not, whether UK only or European generally. Rather it was a function of **changes** in the level of the economy.

Most people can easily see that a declining economy leads to diminishing confidence, to a fall in orders and ultimately to cash problems for individual businesses. But why should economic **growth** also lead to increased numbers of business failures, as some analysts feared in the autumn of 1993? Their fears were based on two facts:

1 Any expansion of business requires an immediate expansion in working capital, long before the profits arising from that expansion feed back into the company's working capital, thereby producing, rather late in the day, the required growth. But if the working capital as a whole does not expand, the growth in stocks and debtors must mean a decline in cash, as there is nothing else to take the strain.
2 This first fact of business life would not be a problem if the financing of expansion was properly planned. But the second fact giving rise to concern was that UK businesses, whether exporting or not, were regarded as notoriously poor at planning working capital in general and cash needs in particular. In short, could many UK businesses actually cope with commercial success?

In theory we have covered all that is necessary to forecast cash flows. Nevertheless, it will be useful to have a summary of the ways in which **changes** in the level of a company's business activities affect its working capital and the friendliness of its relations with its bankers.

We will therefore look at how an expansion of orders will affect both an exporter of manufactured goods and an exporter of services. We will finish by commenting on some aspects of this and cash flow forecasting.

A Manufacturing Explosion

Multitudinous Machinery Manufacturing Ltd, a Yorkshire engineering firm, have quietly built a limited export business to European markets over the last fifteen years on a very simple basis. Established relations with regional continental distributors have enabled MMM Ltd to stick to open account invoicing (just as with their fewer UK customers) and that means effectively DDU. Four office secretaries each with a language ability handle sales and orders exclusively by telephone, and a local RoRo carrier delivers via Humber ferries to Rotterdam. It has never really been quite that simple, what with constant changes in technical barriers, SAD forms, then Intrastats, continuous changes in the way the bank handled things, never a dull moment in fact. But George Multitude 'runs a tight ship' and even with a very small engineering firm he does a respectable level of export business.

But he is currently facing a more difficult problem; his Munich distributor has threatened to quadruple his rate of ordering from MMM Ltd. George Multitude was not born yesterday so he knows that he has the prospect of paying out a lot of extra money and then having to wait quite a while before it starts to flow back into the company's current account. George Multitude went to see the bank manager who said, in effect, 'No problem Mr Multitude! Just give me the details of what extra working capital is required and also details of how you can pay for it!'

The answer to the second question (how is it to be paid for?) will be revealed by his accountant's profit projections on the extra business. But that matter is very much for the future so we will not look at it in this chapter.

But what extra working capital is required? Let us take the relevant working capital items one by one to see the effect of a large increase in business on each of them.

181

Raw materials

More manufacturing means, for a start, more orders for materials. The advice at the 19th hole of the local golf club was: 'Apply JIT principles, George and keep everything to a minimum.' Unfortunately George's suppliers have an equal and opposite problem to his. If George wants immediate call-off on small deliveries they must hold extra stock in order to be able to do that. George's 'raw material stock' figure will only go down if their finished goods stock goes up. Quite apart from physical stock holding, the really crucial question is when will payment actually be made? If George's cash flow is helped by delaying payments and increasing his 'trade creditors', their cash flow is hindered by the related increase in their 'trade debtors'.

In theory, both problems could be solved by both companies, jointly practising 'Just-in-Time' working, which means tight scheduling throughout the whole supply chain. Unfortunately that chain will also involve the distributor in Munich and, possibly, his customers as well. In practice, reductions in physical stock need to be organized for the whole supply and distribution chain. That in turn implies tight management control by all the companies involved, almost certainly using EDI links. We will look at the possibilities arising from the application of EDI in a later chapter.

Work in progress

MMM Ltd takes a bit of time to make the machines it supplies to its European customers. Even if the company can organize the manufacturing process so that the time required per machine manufactured remains the same (not that easy if the through-put has grown) the total amount of money locked up in part finished work will increase proportionately and inevitably in line with the volume of sales.

The 'work-in-progress' item that appears in every manufacturer's balance sheet is not just an accounting abstraction; it is something to be seen on the factory floor, in the materials paid for but not yet saleable, in the related timesheets and wage dockets, in the necessary power and consumable materials which have yet to be paid for.

Finished goods stock

Again, the physical reality is there to see. It is the steady build up of packed goods ready to complete each consignment. Once again, in theory, JIT principles indicate a way of minimizing the money locked up in finished stock. But the requirements of economical consignments for the RoRo carrier, the Humber-Rotterdam ferry schedules and uncertainty about the distributor's precise delivery requirements make a difference between theory and practice.

An unavoidable difficulty at this stage is the conflict between the advantage of steady production in the factory to keep manufacturing costs down, and the disadvantage of frequent small consignments which are not only visibly more expensive (packer's and carrier's charges) but carry a less visible administration cost.

Goods in transit

The relevance of this part of 'working capital' will depend on whose working capital it is part of, and that in turn will depend on the terms of the contract or other payment arrangements. If the contract ensures that the exporter is paid against documents then it is the buyer who is providing the working capital to finance the final delivery, the part covered by transit from the port or airport of shipment to final delivery to the final customer, wherever that might be. But it still takes time for the documents to progress from the exporter's bank to that of the buyer and then for the buyer to be notified and for the funds to reach the exporter's account. If the deal is 'documents against acceptance' on a term bill then that extends the period so much longer.

The significance for any exporter's cash flow of the 'goods in transit' figure does depend on when title passes. Is the deal 'completed' when the goods are shipped or at some later stage? However, in many cases, this may not be such a significant difference since what ever is in the contract about transfer of title, the importance to the exporter's cash flow is 'when does he see his money'? The practical difference may only be the difference of the outstanding sum appearing as 'debtors' instead of 'goods in transit'

As a last point, if the exporter is shipping to a wholly owned distributor then the exporter is as much concerned with financing his distributor's increased working capital as that of the UK parent company.

So where does this leave MMM Ltd and George Multitude's discussions with the bank? Because he is shipping on his own responsibility the distinction between 'goods in transit' and 'debtors' is less significant than the total time from carrier collection in Yorkshire to receipt of the cash into his sterling current account. Whether he should be pestering the carrier, the customer or the bank is only a question of which produces the greatest reduction in the overall working capital requirement.

Debtors, and bank reconciliation

Controlling the cash flow by minimizing the wait for payment is, to a large extent, what export finance (as opposed to credit insurance) is all about. There are four elements involved: working capital; security; cost; and marketing policy. At one extreme there is the possibility of insisting on payment in advance or on cash with order. Much of the working capital problem is thereby solved, the security problem is totally solved and there are no visible costs to be paid. The whole burden is on the marketing aspect of the exporter's business because the whole financial burden is carried by the buyer. But if you can do all your export business that easily you don't need to be reading this book.

For ordinary mortals like the average exporter it is always necessary to balance the trade offs between these four elements: liquidity; security; cost; and marketing. To strike a sensible balance between them it is necessary for the exporter to know the cost (and all export finance carries a cost) and then to set it against the less visible costs of the company's self-financed working capital and that of the 'expected cost' of a (low?) risk of default and a bad debt write off. 'Expected costs' or 'Expected Monetary Values' (EMVs) will be looked at in chapter 13 when we consider uncertainty in more detail.

One final point about 'bank reconciliation'. As we all know, the amount of money **we** think that we have in our bank never seems to be quite the same as what the bank prints on the bank statements because of delays in debiting or crediting payments. For a company, reconciling the latest bank statement with its own cash ledger is just one of those regular chores that must be performed 'just to be sure'. The delays that make the reconciliation necessary should not normally be of significance. But in dealing with foreign transactions, delays in transmission or in currency conversion may become significant. When planning or monitoring cash flows, it is the date at which the company's sterling account is actually credited that marks the completion of the sale, not when the company was 'paid'.

Software and Hard Bargaining

Super Streamlined Systems Ltd is a software house specializing in production control systems. They believe that they are just about to break into the big time with a turnkey project in New Zealand which will increase turnover by about 40 per cent from this one new order alone. The company will design the system, develop the software, test it and implement it in the customer's plant.

The management of the company is happy about the technicalities, given their previous experience on very similar but smaller projects elsewhere. Nor is there a problem with capacity, since SSS Ltd normally subcontract the bulk of the software development to freelance programmers. Furthermore, because they are a 'service' supplier they are not concerned with those unavoidable problems of financing physical stocks or work in progress. Or should they be?

The names may be different and the payment arrangements will certainly be different but the problem of financing an expansion of business by financing the necessary expansion of 'work in progress' will be much the same as for MMM Ltd.

Even if SSS Ltd can negotiate progress payments against bench-marked 'milestones', the client cannot be expected to release the greater part of the payment until the system has been proved by live-running for an agreed period. That is likely to be a long time after SSS Ltd start to spend money (their money) on the development work.

System design

Bespoke software implies tailored systems designed, at least initially, on the customer's premises. The system design staff working in New Zealand must be supported and their travel and expenses paid for as long as it takes to produce an agreed system specification to allow the detailed development work to go ahead in the UK. There is no question here of shipping out a standard machine in a container and posting the documents to a UK bank.

Internal fixed costs

In theory the company would be paying the salaries, the office expenses and computing expenses of its permanent staff irre-spective of whether it got the commission or not. Nevertheless these expenses will represent an outflow of cash that cannot be scaled down if the project is to be completed (and paid for) as quickly as possible. So cash is flowing out from the beginning.

Sub-contracting

A company like SSS Ltd survives by its ability to manage over-seas projects like this one and it does it by tapping the skills and knowledge of a wide variety of individuals and small businesses in the UK. It cannot afford to choke off this basic supply of expertise. But these individuals and small companies will be even more concerned about their short-term cash flows than the main contractor SSS Ltd. As the individual jobs are commissioned and delivered so a continuous stream of payments must be made to them.

Testing and installation

If this is done, as is usually necessary, on the customer's premises, the company has once again to pay out cash to meet all the costs of arranging for its UK staff to carry out testing and installation at many thousands of miles distance.

Approval and Payment

For a project of this nature, the cash flow forecaster can be pretty sure of three things:

1 The project will, sooner or later, to a greater or lesser extent, slip behind schedule.
2 The system development will throw up unexpected snags not foreseen in the original approved design such that, even if everything else went according to plan, there would still be a delay in completion.
3 Even when all these wrinkles have been ironed out, the customer's own internal strategic planning committee will be slower to approve actual payment than the main contractor, SSS Ltd, would like or even would reasonably expect.

The Difference Between Expansion and Just Being Big

The difference is that fundamental hazard for a manager attempting to control cash flows, namely **time**. If MMM Ltd were already dispatching the larger volumes of machines to Munich or elsewhere the larger volumes of cash receipts would also be flowing in regularly. Instead it will take time for the cash flows, in and out, to settle down to an acceptable balance.

In fact any management, having taken the company to such a plateau, can too easily become complacent. Having overcome the immediate cash flow problem it is easy to forget that the now affordable investment in working capital is costing the company money. That cost may be visible as interest paid on overdrafts or on short-term export finance. It may be invisible, the opportunity cost of **not** using that investment money on directly profit generating investments.

Similarly with SSS Ltd, it was the expansion of business that will cause cash flow problems. Later on, perhaps, when they may have the prospect of a steady stream of major projects there would be several possibilities for financing the increased working capital. These possibilities could include anything from joint ventures with local investors (thus tapping a local source of non-interest bearing equity finance), through forfaiting on favourable terms to, perhaps, unsecured loan stock issued in the UK.

Spreadsheets and Planning

It may be assumed that anyone involved in an export business is familiar with computer based spreadsheets, and will be using one for at least some part of their daily work. Nevertheless it is worthwhile considering some relevant aspects that may affect their usefulness to export planners, particularly when fore-casting cash.

Is the spreadsheet flexible enough?

A spreadsheet is a **dynamic** tool. If the user is not making frequent changes to the figures contained in it then he or she is not using it effectively. The most obvious dynamic use is the 'What if?' technique of exploring possibilities. Break-even figures, optimising, and probing constraints are others.

Flexibility is obviously achieved by the maximum use of formulae which in turn implies an absolute minimum of cells containing input numbers, preferably less than one per cent of the total. Input numbers, whether parameters or other data, should never need to be repeatedly entered across the sheet; repeats should copy themselves automatically so that changes do the same. Where specific parameters are needed these should be held in one place only, preferably in a look up table. By such means, changes to even the basic assumptions of the sheet can be done with a single entry.

How reliable is it?

The flexibility of a spreadsheet can be a serious disadvantage, particularly if there is more than one user. Generous use of locked cells combined with passwords are obviously a help but all these can, in practice be circumvented by someone else. The difficulty then is can the original user spot that a change has been made?

With small sheets, perhaps. With sheets of a practical size, containing many formulae 30 to 40 characters long in many hundreds of cells, random checking is, at best, a feeble defence.

How well structured is the sheet, or sheets?

The logical structuring of a spreadsheet is as essential as in any other form of programming. A comprehensible structure is the basis of a coherently logical design, it makes reliability checking rather more feasible, and it facilitates major modifications. It also enables output functions for printing or graph production to be better designed by 'blocking' these as separate elements. Above all, a structured design enables several sheets to be linked together to feed data from one to another or to build a hierarchy of detailed and summary sheets.

How suitable is it for the business?

Spreadsheets are essentially a planning rather than an operational tool. Their basic simplicity and flexibility means that they are quick to set up and adapt, and this is the main reason for their popularity. But those characteristics are also the source of danger when using a spreadsheet as a permanent operating business tool. For such a use the export manager should seriously consider at least a data base of some kind or, better still, dedicated application software specifically designed for the job to be done.

Such job-specific software, unlike a spreadsheet, has the following advantages:

1 Data and functions are not all mixed up as they are in a spreadsheet where neighbouring cells can contain text, parameters, live data, and the programmed instructions controlling them. At least with a data base and certainly with a program using defined data files the user knows the information base of any output.
2 With properly designed data files, data input, data up-dates and data consistency and integrity are that much easier to manage. The contrast here is between a spreadsheet and a relational data base (howsoever accessed).
3 User-interfaces can be designed quite separately from the structure of either the programming or the data files. Validation routines can also be designed separately.
4 The programming, the way the software runs, when done in a conventional way with a programming language (like 'C' for instance) can be kept out of the reach of the enthusiastic user. Such a user may have the desire to adapt your spreadsheet for a particular one-off job and not tell you about the changes. A program running compiled code is proof against that.

It is true that many of these deficiencies in spreadsheets can be partly overcome by use of multiple sheets and the use of well planned macros. But it will still be a spreadsheet.

Questions for Discussion

1 Explain, in simple terms that anyone in business can under-

stand, what is meant by the term 'overtrading' and why it may be important.

2 A company has established, at some cost, EDI links with its major suppliers in order to implement its 'Just-in-Time' purchasing policy. Explain exactly how the implementation of JIT will produce a beneficial effect on the 'bottom line' of its annual Trading and Profit and Loss Account.

3 An exporter distributes, mostly using seafreight, its products through wholly owned distributors in a number of developed countries. Should it hold stocks locally or centrally in the UK? Should it repatriate earnings to its UK sterling account as quickly as possible or not? Should the UK parent company charge minimum or maximum prices to the subsidiaries?

What are the cash planning considerations relevant to the making of these decisions?

12

Prices and Costs (And Some Other Things As Well)

What this Chapter is All About

In the previous chapters we looked at the elements that make up a profitable export business. We looked at the structure of the business, how we measured its financial progress, and the significance of profit figures, of cost figures, of cash flows and stock levels. Chapter 4 also introduced the idea of the business as a machine, as an integrated, interlocking set of processes where any part may be affected by any other.

In this chapter we will look at the way in which some of the financial elements interact with one another. We will consider volumes, costs, prices, revenues and profits and argue that it is unwise for management to consider any of these in isolation. This is a real danger in any business arising from the necessary divisions, by departmental responsibilities, within the organization.

Therefore you should, by now, be clear about the significance of costs in calculating profit, about unit prices as distinct from sales turnover, about direct costs and overheads, and about variable costs and fixed costs.

After reading this chapter you will be able to calculate breakeven volumes of sales in both simple and more complicated situations, apply the very useful idea of 'contribution' to pricing decisions, cope with varying market response to different levels of price, and to formulate an overall profitable pricing strategy.

193

A Problem Involving Pricing and Profits

The Expo Enterprises Co. Ltd have identified a new market for one particular product in a south east Asian country and are preparing to negotiate with a potential distributor. So EEC Ltd must do some financial calculations. The price charged to the distributor will affect the revenue arising from this new business but this price is also likely to affect the volume that can be sold and therefore the volume EEC Ltd will ship. The volume shipped will determine the total costs involved but not in direct proportion because, as we saw in chapter 8, some of these will be fixed. Both of these uncertain figures, the volumes and the total costs, will determine the profit EEC Ltd will earn from this new venture.

Undoubtedly there will be other uncertainties; for example the distributor might ask EEC Ltd to carry the cost of any specially prepared technical and promotional material, or of holding minimum levels of stock in that country; another uncertainty is a possible change in exchange rates if, for instance, it was agreed to transact business in US dollars rather than sterling.

What management needs, therefore, is some simple method of looking at the interaction of all these factors taken together, a method that will also enable management to quickly calculate (or at least make a good guess about) the effect of a change in any one of them. To be able to do that should be an advantage when it comes to face-to-face negotiations.

The methods that we will discuss in this chapter will cover:

1 the idea of 'break-even' volumes;
2 the 'break-even chart';
3 some techniques for calculating break-even volumes;
4 the idea of 'contribution to fixed costs';
5 coping with a mix of products and prices; and
6 the possible relationship of demand and price.

Break-even Volumes

If the sales of any product or service increase we naturally expect the business to be more profitable, but by how much? The costs will increase but not in proportion to the volume of business because some of those costs are 'fixed'. Sales revenue, on the other hand, will normally increase in proportion, as long as prices are not changed. Consequently, profit will increase rapidly – we will get 'economies of scale' to borrow a term from the economists.

We saw in chapter 8 that all the thousands of costs involved in running a business can be usefully grouped into just two categories; direct costs or overheads. Alternatively the two groups can be variable costs or fixed costs. Fortunately, as we showed then, overheads are usually fixed costs and in a similar way, direct costs are usually variable ones. From now on we will treat all costs as split between fixed and variable, but the methods we will employ can be easily adapted to the alternative view.

Unfortunately, 'economies of scale' also mean that profits will decline rapidly and possibly become a loss if the volume of business declines. This is because some of the costs are fixed. This situation is normally described as an inability to 'cover the fixed costs' or, more often, an inability to 'cover the overheads'.

However, before we start applying these ideas to EEC's new venture we should first define our terms more exactly. By 'variable costs' we mean those items of cost that **must** change with a change in volume. Examples would be materials consumed, freight and insurance, and so on. All other costs can be referred to as 'fixed' simply because they do not **have** to change. Management may decide to change them for some other reason. It may decide to increase, decrease or hold promotional expenditure quite independently of changes in the volume of goods or services being supplied but it does not have to. So, for the moment, promotion costs would be included in the 'fixed' category.

We should also be clear about the terms 'variable costs' and 'marginal costs'. We introduced the latter term in chapter 8 and defined it then as 'the cost of producing one more item'. In practice it is best to restrict the term 'variable cost' to the extra cost of producing one more item where no large changes are required in the way the goods or services are produced. That way 'marginal cost' can be reserved for those cases where we refer to all the possible changes in cost from whatever cause.

Nevertheless, we often get into the habit of assuming that 'variable cost' and 'marginal cost' mean the same thing. In practice, when applying such terms, we need to take into account the management decision-making context. In our example, Expo Enterprises are only considering one projected market in isolation. Thus, the 'fixed costs' will be those costs that the company will be committed to if it decides to go ahead. The 'variable costs' will be only those marginal costs arising directly from supplying that market in greater or lesser volumes.

Calculating the Break-even Volume

To calculate the break even volume we need to know before we start:

1 the net sales revenue per item;
2 the total variable costs of producing one item; and
3 the total relevant fixed costs.

For UK sales, the net sales revenue is normally the price charged. For exporters it will be the net sterling received after all deductions, for example by the transmitting banks. In this example we will just use 'price' for net revenue per unit.

In doing break-even calculations we normally assume that the total variable costs per item remain the same at different volumes. However some things, for instance volume discounts received for materials purchased, may complicate calculations in practice. Another complication is that the total relevant fixed costs to be considered will depend on whether we are considering the company as a whole, or a division, or a product, or perhaps (as in the example we are going to look at) just one overseas market.

Well, EEC Ltd have done the costings and have decided to base their break-even calculations on:

1 a net revenue per item of £100, sterling. (the 'price');
2 a total variable cost per unit of £30; and
3 total relevant fixed costs of £50,000 per year.

These 'relevant fixed costs' might include such things as the promotions and exhibition expenses for this market, sales force expenses covering salaries and travel there, financial assistance to the local distributor and so on. We may call them 'fixed costs' because they will be much the same whether we sell a lot or a little in that market.

The task is now to calculate the 'break-even volume' per year. We define break-even volume as: 'that volume of sales such that total costs equal total revenue, so that no profit is earned but no loss suffered'. This would obviously be a starting point for any negotiations with the prospective distributor.

There are four ways to calculate this break-even volume:

1 drawing a break-even chart;
2 using a spreadsheet and a 'trial and error' method;
3 performing a simple algebraic calculation; or
4 calculating the 'contribution per unit'.

The Break-even Chart

A break-even chart is the graphical representation of the marketing situation the company is faced with. From the chart we will be able to see that at such and such a volume the business is just not big enough but perhaps at some higher level we will be making satisfactory profits. Figure 12.1 shows how it works for this market and this company.

Break-even charts are drawn up in standard way. The horizontal, 'x-axis' is the scale of possible volumes running from zero on the left to the maximum worth considering on the right. The vertical, 'y-axis' is a scale measuring money (revenues or costs).

First we plot the 'total costs' line. The total costs line obviously starts at £50,000 because the company is committed to that expenditure even if sales prove to be zero. It then goes up by

£30 for each additional item supplied giving a straight line across the graph.

Figure 12.1: A break-even chart

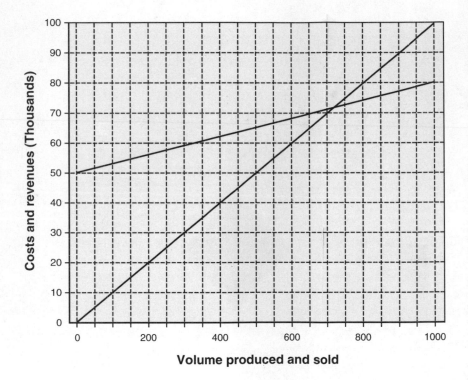

Volume produced and sold

Now we plot the 'sales revenue' line and this sales revenue, at any one point, is simply the net revenue of £100 per unit multiplied by the volume. The revenue line starts at zero but climbs more steeply than the cost line. Where it crosses the total cost line clearly costs equal revenues and at that volume the project breaks even. You can see from the chart that this happens at a volume of about 714 units per year. With higher volumes, the divergence of the two line indicates increasing profit.

We can check the accuracy of that calculation by doing a little quick budgeting. Taking that volume figure of 714 units per year as a basis:

Sales revenue: 714 units at £100 each   £71,400
Variable costs: 714 units at £30 each   £21,420
Fixed costs per year: £50,000

                       Total costs: £71,420

                     Loss for the year: £20

which is as near to zero as anyone would want!

Going back to figure 12.1, you can see that the slopes of the two lines are proportional to the unit variable cost of £30 and to the unit revenue of £100. It should also be obvious that the profit increases, proportionally, faster than sales revenue or volume once break-even volume has been achieved. The area between the lines represents loss (to the left of break-even) or profit (to the right).

We can also see some other things from such a chart. If the actual volume of sales (either planned or achieved) is only just above the break-even volume then the company is risking that a small change in sales will turn a small profit into a loss. We should also note the angle between the lines – whether it is large or small. If it is small, that is if the difference between the unit variable cost and the price is small, then it should be obvious that any small change in any one of these basic values may produce big changes in the forecast break-even volume or profit.

Using a Computer Spreadsheet

If you are not good at drawing graphs or dislike doing calculations, a computer spreadsheet can easily be made to show the break-even volume.

The spreadsheet should be set up with a series of columns showing, successively:

1 the range of possible volumes of sales arranged in suitable steps, so that we have a manageable run of figures;
2 the variable costs for each of these volumes, using the unit variable cost; £30 in our example;

3 the total costs for each volume, which simply means adding the fixed costs of £50,000 to each of the total variable cost figures;
4 the sales revenue, which is, of course, the volume multiplied by the price of £100; and
5 the profit for each level of volume, that is the sales revenue minus the total cost.

Provided the initial run of volume figures was properly chosen, we will then see the column of profit figures passing from negative to positive. The point at which this happens is the one closest to our break-even volume. Table 12.1 shows how this is done.

Table 12.1: A break-even calculation for Expo Enterprises

Units sold	Variable costs	Total costs	Revenue	Profit (loss)
0	£0	£50,00	£0	(£50,000)
50	£1,500	£51,500	£5,000	(£46,500)
100	£3,000	£53,000	£10,000	(£43,000)
150	£4,500	£54,500	£15,000	(£39,500)
200	£6,000	£56,000	£20,000	(£36,000)
250	£7,500	£57,500	£25,000	(£32,500)
300	£9,000	£59,000	£30,000	(£29,000)
350	£10,500	£60,500	£35,000	(£25,500)
400	£12,000	£62,000	£40,000	(£22,000)
450	£13,500	£63,500	£45,000	(£18,500)
500	£15,000	£65,000	£50,000	(£15,000)
550	£16,500	£66,500	£55,000	£11,500
600	£18,000	£68,000	£60,000	(£8,000)
650	£19,500	£69,500	£65,000	(£4,500)
700	£21,000	£71,000	£70,000	(£1,000)
750	£22,500	£72,500	£75,000	£2,500
800	£24,000	£74,000	£80,000	£6,000
850	£25,500	£75,500	£85,000	£9,500
900	£27,000	£77,000	£90,000	£13,000
950	£28,500	£78,500	£95,000	£16,500
1000	£30,000	£80,000	£100,000	£20,000

By refining the steps in the values in the first column we can make our reading of the table more precise. An example of this is shown in table 12.2.

Table 12.2: A closer look at the break-even calculation

Units sold	Variable costs	Total costs	Revenue	Profit (loss)
710	£21,300	£71,300	£71,000	(£300)
711	£21,330	£71,330	£71,100	(£230)
712	£21,360	£71,360	£71,200	(£160)
713	£21,390	£71,390	£71,300	(£90)
714	£21,420	£71,420	£71,400	(£20)
715	£21,450	£71,450	£71,500	£50
716	£21,480	£71,480	£71,600	£120
717	£21,510	£71,510	£71,700	£190
718	£21,540	£71,540	£71,800	£260
719	£21,570	£71,570	£71,900	£330
720	£21,600	£71,600	£72,000	£400

You can see from the second table that the minimum quantity that will enable the company to break-even in this market is 715 units a year. You can also see that for each additional unit sold the profit increases by exactly £70. We will be looking at that figure a little more closely in a moment.

There are two advantages in using a spreadsheet in this way. The first is that, having set it up, we can quickly see the effect on the break-even volume of changes in the three basic figures that the calculation started from. We are making use of the 'what if' facility that any spreadsheet can offer.

The second advantage of the spreadsheet is that we can now get it to draw the break-even chart for us using the graphic facilities that all spreadsheets possess. We can produce different charts for any combination of price, unit variable cost or fixed costs that we may wish to consider.

Using Simple Algebra to Calculate Break-even Volumes

This method is the quickest of all, provided one is happy about using algebraic symbols for the variables involved. In the case of Expo Enterprises we have:

Q = the annual quantity of goods sold or services provided
V = the variable cost per item or unit of service
F = total fixed costs per year
P = the price per item or unit of service

The total sales revenue at any volume of business will be the price times the volume, that is:

$$\text{Total revenue} = Q \times P$$

The total costs at any volume of business will be the total variable costs plus the fixed costs, that is:

$$\text{Total costs} = (Q \times V) + F$$

At break-even volume we make no profit because total costs will (by definition) equal total revenue, that is:

$$(Q \times P) = (Q \times V) + F$$

Solving this equation for Q, we get:

$$(Q \times P) - (Q \times V) = F$$
$$Q \times (P - V) = F$$
$$\text{Thus} \qquad Q = F/(P - V)$$

If we now apply this formula (which, if you think about it, is only common sense) to the situation of Expo Enterprises we can see that:

$$Q = £50,000/(£100 - £30)$$
$$= £50,000/£70$$
$$= 714.3 \text{ units sold each year}$$

which was the result that we got from either of the two methods we used before. In practice, of course, this means 715 units since none of our customers wants to buy three-tenths of whatever we are selling!

Take another look at the formula we have just derived: $Q = F/(P - V)$. The expression 'P - V' indicates, for any situation, that we are using in our calculations a particular value: Price minus variable cost. This is a very significant number, and we will now use it to show you the fourth way to calculate a break-even volume.

Contribution to Fixed Costs

The idea of 'contribution' is such a useful one for maximizing profitability that it is worthwhile spending a little time explaining what it involves before we get down to applying it to our task of calculating the break-even volume for Expo Enterprise's new market.

When a company engages in any kind of commercial activity it will be doing two things: it will be committing itself to certain expenses and will be looking forward to some amount of revenue. If the latter is greater than the former, then there is the prospect (but not the certainty) of earning a profit.

Now this simple view of business activity is true of the company as a whole, true of each and every profit centre or product, and is also true of any single activity about which management might decide to engage the company in. The very simple question that is being asked is: 'Does the company get more out of this (whatever the activity is) than it puts in?'

Even when the answer to the question is 'yes' it does not follow automatically that this activity will make the company profitable. The reason is that there are those ever present 'fixed costs' that must also be paid for. If there is anything left over after paying them, there will be a profit. Therefore what management must also ask is: 'Is the difference between what we put in and what we get out of doing this thing going to contribute enough to paying our fixed costs, so that there will, in the end, still be some profit left?'

This need to pay those fixed costs is something that is ever present in any commercial business; it is what keeps managers awake at nights; it is the inability to pay those fixed costs that puts a company, even when it is still busily trading, into receivership. So therefore management should look at each part of its business and ask: 'What contribution is that part of the business making to our fixed costs?'

Definitions of 'contribution'

The simplest definition, and the one that we shall use, is: 'Contribution to fixed costs is equal to unit price minus the unit variable cost.'

To go back to the example of Expo Enterprises we can see that, in the new market under consideration, the contribution to fixed costs per item sold is:

£100 minus £30, which is equal to £70 per unit

It is worthwhile pausing for a moment to look at the implications of this little piece of arithmetic. It tells us that for each unit produced and sold the company must pay out £30 (it must do so in order to have the item to sell) but it receives £100. This leaves a surplus of £70 from each unit sold. But, in this example, the company must have enough £70s each year to pay those fixed costs of £50,000. If there are not enough then this market will produce a loss; if there are indeed enough this market will be generating a profit.

Two important facts follow from what we have observed. First, once the fixed costs have been paid for, every additional £70 is pure profit. Secondly, it follows from this that the contribution we have calculated is not just a contribution to fixed costs but is a contribution to fixed costs **and to profit** – once the fixed costs have been covered.

Using 'Contribution' to Calculate the Break-even Volume

If we think in terms of unit contribution to fixed costs we can proceed directly to the calculation of the break-even volume. The procedure, starting from scratch, is:

1 Identify the net receipts (often simply the price) per item or unit of service sold, as we did using the other methods.
2 Add up all the variable costs per item or unit of service, again as before.
3 Subtract the variable costs from the receipts to get the unit contribution.
4 Divide the unit contribution into the annual total of fixed costs to get the break-even volume.

Applying this procedure to the case of Expo Enterprises' new market, we have:

Receipts = £100, and total variable costs = £30.
So contribution to fixed costs = £70 per unit sold.
Break-even volume = 50,000/70 = 714.3 = 715 units per year.

You will notice that this last little bit of arithmetic was exactly the same as for the algebraic method, and there is nothing very surprising about that. Either way, we are analysing the market situation by observing the interaction of volumes, prices, variable costs and fixed costs. But the concept of 'contribution' directs our attention to a most important aspect of the finances of a company's marketing activities.

A little later on we will see how this idea of contribution can be applied to a wider variety of situations. But before we do that we must first enlarge the definition of contribution.

Different Ways of Looking At Contribution

In the definition of contribution that we have used so far, we considered only a single item or unit of service, and we considered only the way each item contributed to paying the fixed costs. Sometimes, instead, we may wish to look at the total contribution achieved in aggregate by one or by several products. Sometimes we may be concerned about paying our 'overheads', the indirect costs of the business activity, which are not quite the same as the fixed costs. If you are not clear about this, go back to chapter 8 to remind yourself of the (small) difference.

It is convenient, in practice to be able to select one out of four possible definitions of contribution according to the details of the situation. The four definitions are:

1 Unit contribution to fixed costs = price less unit variable cost.
2 Total contribution to fixed costs = sales revenue less total variable costs.
3 Unit contribution to overheads = price less unit direct costs.
4 Total contribution to overheads = sales revenue less total direct costs.

When doing any calculations involving contribution it is only necessary, before you start, to make up your mind as to whether you are going to do the calculations for contribution per unit or for total contribution, and to meet fixed costs or to meet overheads and then stick to your choice and don't get into a muddle!

Developing the Idea of Contribution

Before we can extend the idea of contribution to fixed costs we must first recognize that, so far, our decision-making model is quite limited in its applications. A break-even chart like the one shown in figure 12.1 or illustrated in many books on management finance, is based on several assumptions. These include:

1 that we are concerned about break-even rather than profit;
2 the chart is for one product in one market only; and
3 we assume constant prices at differing volumes.

In the final three sections of this chapter on prices and costs we will take these points one by one to discover ways of overcoming them so as to get a practical decision-making technique.

Incorporating a Profit Target

There are many ways of expressing a profit target but on most occasions it is likely to be in one of two forms:

1 a specific profit figure in pounds sterling; or
2 profit as a specific percentage of sales turnover.

In the first case, incorporating the profit target into our calculations is easy. We simply add the target profit to the fixed costs and then proceed as if we were calculating a break-even volume as before. But in this case the answer we get will be a volume that will not only pay for the fixed costs but will also produce the required profit figure.

Let us go back to Expo Enterprises and assume that senior management has decreed that this new market must produce a profit of £25,000 each year. Using the contribution method for our calculations, we have:

Contribution per unit	£70	(as before)
Annual fixed costs	£50,000	(as before)
plus profit	£25,000	
equals	£75,000	

So this market must now generate this new total contribution. The volume that will achieve that is:

Volume = 75,000/70 = 1,071.4 = 1,072 units each year

Checking that we have got it right at that volume:

Sales revenue: 1,072 units at £100 each		£107,200
Variable costs: 1,072 at £30 each	£32,160	
Fixed costs:	£50,000	
Total costs:		£82,160
Profit per year		£25,040

The profit figure does not quite match because we rounded up the volume of sales. Selling one less (that is, 1,071) would reduce the profit by exactly the unit contribution of £70, down to £24,970.

Now let us tackle the problem of incorporating the second type of profit target into our arithmetic. Let's assume that Expo Enterprises has a corporate policy that each export market must produce a profit to the parent company of at least 20 per cent of net sterling receipts. Once again the arithmetic is familiar and easy but, first, a little reflection on what that target implies. A 20 per cent profit margin on sales means that for every £1 received in the UK, 20 pence is already earmarked for profit. That leaves 80 pence to help pay for the variable and the fixed costs, but only those costs. So we perform an adjusted break-even calculation based on a 'price' of £80 per unit, which is equal to the net receipts less 20 per cent.

Using the contribution method again, we have:

Unit 'price'	£80
Unit variable costs	£30
Unit contribution	£50
Fixed costs per year	£50,000 (as before)

Required volume = 50,000/50 = 1,000 units per year

We can check that result just as we did last time:

Sales revenue: 1,000 units at £100 each		£100,000
Variable costs: 1,000 units at £30 each	£30,000	
Fixed costs per year:	£50,000	
Total costs		£80,000
Profit per year		£20,000

Does this profit figure meet the company's target? Calculating the profit as a percentage of sales, we get 20 per cent.

In doing these two profit calculations we used the contribution method, but we might have used any of the other three methods instead. However the contribution idea is quite simple and versatile, and is to be recommended in most cases.

Several Products and Markets: A New Problem and a Simple Approach

Now we must tackle the second sort of the three complicating factors that we listed above. What do we do if we are considering several products together? Perhaps we may only have available to us the aggregate figures for these several products but we still need to decide what aggregate level of business is required to break-even or to produce a specified level of profit.

In the first break-even chart (figure 12.1) Expo Enterprises Ltd were planning for just one market and for one product to be sold there. However the company is also concerned about the worldwide performance of Division D which is selling a variety of products to a variety of markets. The company is concerned because for the last two years the Division has only broken even; no profits but no losses. Can they use a break-even chart to discover what volume increase would produce a target profit for next year?

The relevant figures for Division D for last year, are:

Total net revenue received   £8,400,000
Total variable costs   £6,300,000
Total fixed costs   £2,100,000

Profit target   £800,000

Table 12.3: A profit for Division D?

Net revenue	Variable costs	Total costs	Profit (loss)
0	0	2,100	(2,100)
1,000	750	2,850	(1,850)
2,000	1,500	3,600	(1,600)
3,000	2,250	4,350	(1,350)
4,000	3,000	5,100	(1,100)
5,000	3,750	5,850	(850)
6,000	4,500	6,600	(600)
7,000	5,250	7,350	(350)
8,000	6,000	8,100	(100)
9,000	6,750	8,850	150
10,000	7,500	9,600	400
11,000	8,250	10,350	650
12,000	9,000	11,100	900

We can use a break-even chart or any of our other three techniques to show the required sales revenue increase. We note that the variable costs are, on average, 75 per cent of sales revenue or, in other words, an extra £1,000 of net sales revenue will imply an extra £750 in variable costs. We will assume no change in the balance of the quantities of the products sold by Division D and that the mark-up on variable costs is much the same for all those products.

Given these assumptions, we can draw a break-even chart even though we have no details of the volumes of the individual products. You will see from figure 12.2 that a break-even chart, showing what is required, has both axes scaled in money values and the sales revenue line is at 45 degrees to the axes. We can plot the total costs line because we know that this will be £2,100,00 (the fixed costs) plus 75 per cent of the sales revenue (the variable costs). We can see that the division needs a sales revenue next year of £11,600,000. At that level, the variable costs will be £8,700,000 (75 per cent of the sales revenue) and total costs will be £10,800,000, giving the required profit.

Figure 12.2: A profit for Division D?

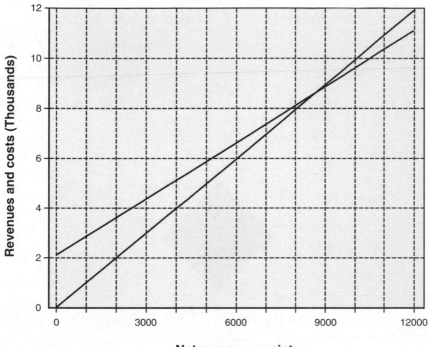

We could employ the contribution concept instead of a chart. Because we are dealing with an aggregate of products and lack the details for each one we cannot calculate the contribution per item sold. In any case this may vary from one individual product to another. But we do know that the variable costs are, on average, 75 per cent of the sales value. Therefore the contribution per £1,000 of sales is:

Sales revenue	£1,000
Variable costs	£750
Contribution	£250 per £1,000 of sales

Total contribution to fixed costs and profit required is:

Fixed costs	£2,100,000
Profit target	£800,000
Total contribution	£2,900,000

Required sales level = (2,900,000/250) x £1,000

= £11,600,000 (as before)

We can get to this answer even more quickly if we remember that, once volume has passed beyond the break-even point the contribution goes straight into profit. In this case we need a profit of £800,000 and we get a contribution of £250 for each £1,000 of sales revenue. So, we then get:

Additional contribution = (800,000/250) x £1,000

= £3,200,000 additional sales

Plus existing sales of £8,400,000

New sales target of = £11,600,000 (as before)

Several Products and Markets: A More Detailed Approach

If we know the contribution to fixed costs (or to overheads) per unit sold for each of a range of products we can refine our marketing policies still further. When budgeting, we can use the figures for budgeted prices and the variable costs for each individual product to calculate individual unit contribution figures.

Multiplying them by the budgeted sales volume we get the total contribution earned by each product and the total earned by all these products taken together. That latter total should cover the fixed costs and also provide the budgeted profit we want.

From these figure we will be able to see two things. First, we will see which products earn the greatest contribution either because of larger volumes sold or from greater margins. We will then see the way in which our marketing strategy, our product mix, supports our financial strategy.

The second thing to be derived from these contribution figures is the marketing policy for each product taken individually. We can see the effect of a price or a cost change on individual product contribution and therefore on total contribution. We should then remember that any change to the total contribution automatically changes the overall profit figure by exactly the same amount. We can also see whether any product has a negative contribution which means that that product is reducing our overall profit by the amount of this negative contribution.

Optimizing the Volumes and Prices

We now come to the last of our techniques involving break-even charts and contribution to fixed costs. Expo Enterprises have so far done all their profit estimates using only internal data, internal to the firm. Given the company's cost structure they can prepare budgets based on net unit revenues ('prices') and on the estimates of the quantities that they hope to sell. Unfortunately the customer may have different ideas about these sales figures as Expo Enterprises discovered when they discussed a possible sales agreement with their overseas distributor.

The conversation went something like this, with Expo Enterprises opening the batting:

'We are looking for a net £100 sterling per unit and we would like you to take at least 1,200 units a year.'
'I am afraid your price is rather high. The most we could shift at that sort of price would be 1,000 maximum.'
'That is getting too near our break-even volume. In any case our accountants were originally asking for a net £120 per unit.'
'Quite impossible! That would halve the volume we could sell; no more than 500 a year. Why don't you reduce your prices to, say, £60 net? I could quadruple that volume to 2,000 a year.'
'That sort of money would more than halve the unit contribution and there wouldn't be any profit in it for us. Nevertheless

we think that we should be able to agree on prices and the annual quantities to be shipped to you.'

The reason why Expo Enterprises think that a deal can be struck is that they have entered the figures quoted by the distributor onto their lap-top computer. Taking the distributor at his word, the unit net receipts and quantities shipped would go like this:

Net receipts	Quantity shipped
£60	2,000
£100	1,000
£120	500

If we were to plot those figures on a graph it would be easy to interpolate the quantities that the distributor ought to be able to take at any other price within a reasonable range of prices. The more mathematically minded will easily see that the quantity is a simple, linear function of price: Q = 3,500 - (25 x P).

Table 12.4: Varying the prices

Unit Price	Quantity Sold	Net Revenue	Variable Costs	Total Costs	Profit (Loss)
10	3,250	£32,500	£97,500	£147,500	(£115,000)
20	3,000	£60,000	£90,000	£140,000	(£80,000)
30	2,750	£82,500	£82,500	£132,500	(£50,000)
40	2,500	£100,000	£75,000	£125,000	(£25,000)
50	2,250	£112,500	£67,500	£117,500	(£5,000)
60	2,000	£120,000	£60,000	£110,000	£10,000
70	1,750	£122,500	£52,500	£102,500	£20,000
80	1,500	£120,000	£45,000	£95,000	£25,000
90	1,250	£112,500	£37,500	£87,500	£25,000
100	1,000	£100,000	£30,000	£80,000	£20,000
110	750	£82,500	£22,500	£72,500	£10,000
120	500	£60,000	£15,000	£65,000	(£5,000)
130	250	£32,500	£7,500	£57,500	£25,000)
140	0	£0	£0	£50,000	(£50,000)

This function is what Expo Enterprises used to set up a simple spreadsheet to do the calculations. The results are in table 12.4, but the graph in figure 12.3 will make things clearer.

Figure 12.3: Bargaining over the price

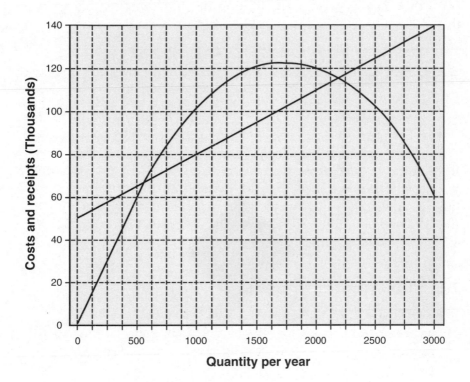

Quantity per year

Unlike our original, simple break-even chart, which assumed a fixed £100 net receipts, this chart shows how much the sales revenue can vary. If the price is too high revenue drops to nothing because we don't sell anything. If we give them away the revenue is also nothing. In between there is an optimum price but we must also take into consideration the costs. Because the costs increase with volume, revenue and profit do not reach a maximum at the same point. If the company merely wished to maximize receipts it should aim for a net £70 per unit with an annual volume of 1,750 units a year.

But Expo Enterprises would rather maximize profit so they asked the distributor to sign an agreement to take 1,375 units a year at a price giving net receipts of £85 a unit or £116,875 in total. This he agreed to do, still wondering why the exporter turned down an opportunity to sell half as much again. Equally puzzled was the Chief Accountant who wanted an explanation for this '15 per cent discount'.

What We Have Learned from this Chapter

1 There is always likely to be some trade off between prices and volumes for any product or service except in the case of fashion or luxury products.
2 Therefore sales revenue will be maximized at some volume, but that volume does not usually maximize profit.
3 The point at which profit is maximized will depend on the mix of fixed and variable costs (or overheads and direct costs, if you prefer).
4 However, if yours is a small company competing against larger ones then you are likely to be a 'price taker'; your prices will be effectively set by the competition. In that case our simpler break-even charts would apply.
5 There are four ways to calculate a break-even volume or the volume required to hit a profit target. However the 'contribution' approach is usually the best.
6 We can apply these methods even in cases where we have only aggregate financial figures but where we wish to estimate the effects of changes in the volume of business done.
7 By looking at the contribution of individual products or services we can see at once the extent to which each contributes to the overall profit of the division or company.

Questions for Discussion

1 One division of an exporting company is manufacturing and shipping a single product. The variable production cost per unit manufactured is £2,250, there are fixed divisional

overheads of £400,000 per year to be recovered, and the company requires each division to achieve a divisional profit equal to 17 per cent of net sales receipts. The current selling price, net of remittance expenses and credit insurance, brings in £3,400 per unit shipped.

How many units per year must the division ship in order to hit the profit target?

Try to answer this question in the four different ways described in this chapter.

2 Explain in simple terms why the concept of contribution may be useful to an exporter shipping twelve different products to seven very different overseas markets, all seven exhibiting different degrees of price/demand elasticity.

3 For what type of price/demand relationship would it be true that the price which maximized sales revenue also maximized profit?

Part 3

Putting it Together

Running an export business, however small, is a complex and hazardous activity. Knowing where you want to get to and knowing, in principle, what is involved in getting there is not enough.

Whatever the company and whatever the market, the export manager must skilfully balance all the relevant elements of the job, including ever-present uncertainty about the whole environment in which he operates. He or she must be able to distinguish the less important from the vital elements, and then put it all together as an action plan.

So we will be looking, in broad terms, at the planning and information handling process and the evaluation of the plans that those activities produce.

13

Coping with the Uncertainties

What this Chapter is All About and Why it is Here At All)

This chapter is different from all the previous ones in this book. Let's have the bad news first. There are few facts here to pass on to you, and there is little that might be called 'information'. But before you hurry on to chapter 14 we will give the good news. Because this chapter deals with 'uncertainties' it deals with something fundamental that faces every business, export or not, manufacturing, construction, distribution, service, extraction – any business in fact.

So if this topic is so basic, why wasn't it chapter 1; why leave it till now? The reason for that is quite simple: until you know what you want from your business, until you have decided how 'success' is to be defined and measured, it is impossible to think clearly about the uncertainty of achieving those aims. If you don't know what the target is you will never be able to assess the likelihood of missing it.

So that, basically, is why this chapter is here. Now let us explain why we think it is important in spite of there being few 'facts' and little 'information'.

1 All businesses face uncertainty to a greater or lesser extent. An export business faces uncertainty to a much greater extent

than one that cautiously restricts itself to the home, UK market. Exporting is the more complicated operation so there is more to go wrong, there are more markets to deal with, dealing with them involves more outsiders from that translation agency for your sales literature to some remote end user known only to your local distributor.

2 Whether you know it or not, you are already coping with this uncertainty, usually by paying out good money. The money you spend on credit references, on preparing letters of credit, on credit guarantees, on forward exchange premiums, are all in one way or another the costs that uncertainty imposes on our business.

3 'But!' you will say, 'they don't go on about it like this in the other management books I've read. Why now?' Well, exporting is rather special in spite of our claim in chapter 1 that it is the non-export business that should be regarded as odd. If you restrict your business to the home market you reduce the variety of risks that you face. Because of the (usually) shorter time scale of operations it should then be easier to repair the damage arising from one's mistakes. The home businessman can (usually) muddle along. Exporters are more exposed.

4 So we, as exporters, need to think rather more clearly about 'risk' and how to cope with it, because cope with it we must. But to cope with risk means being able to think clearly about what is involved, about devising a suitable course of action, about explaining it to colleagues when getting their support, and (this is the really difficult bit) making sense of that post-mortem when things do not work out quite the way we planned. Did they ever!

After reading this chapter you will:

1 have a clearer idea of what is meant by those familiar but ill-defined terms: 'uncertainty' and 'risk';
2 see the need to define more precisely than is usual those situations involving uncertainty and risk;
3 be able to select some appropriate techniques to simplify the more complicated type of situation;
4 be in a position to decide on suitable decision strategies

which suit your existing competitive situation;

5 be able to quantify the elements of such a situation to achieve an objective justification for your strategy; and

6 know and be able to explain to others the limitations and hidden assumptions underlying your decision strategy.

We will start by defining some terms and considering some simple situations in order to clarify some basic ideas. We will then be able to analyse situations in greater depth and see the relevance of them to the decisions that management must make. But the overall aim of this chapter is to enable you to think clearly, logically and confidently about uncertain situations.

What Do We Mean By Uncertainty or Risk?

The reason why many people have difficulty in coming to grips with this aspect of business decision making often arises from a failure to see the logical gulf between what has actually happened on the one hand and, on the other, what **might** happen in the future and how more likely or less likely it is to happen. This is the difference between 'facts' and an abstract idea. But it is also the difference between the past and the future.

To put what we are now going to tackle into context let us glance back to the first three chapters of this book where we discussed what business is all about and what constitutes a successful business. The value of the business that we have built up or intend to build up is the **future** value of the earnings of that business. You may have noticed that all the topics covered in chapters 5 to 9 concerned what **has happened** in the immediate or more remote past. As managers we use past records to plan the future, but the future is uncertain, it is theoretical, it is abstract – until it happens!

So what does it mean when we talk about uncertain future events? What it means is this:

We simply don't know, we are making decisions from a basis of partial or near total ignorance!

But nevertheless we have to make the right decisions now, today. So what do we mean by the 'right decisions'? Let us start defining some terms.

The first step is to note the source of the uncertainty. Because there are so many unknown factors influencing what might happen, effectively any one possibility may be regarded as a random event. Alternatively, the uncertainty may arise from the unpredictable decisions of a competitor, decisions that may be influenced by what the competitor guesses about our decision? In that latter case we would be involved in so-called game strategies.

If we are uncertain this must mean that we are faced with more than one possibility. So, at the start of the assessment of any situation, we must define the possibilities.

Next, we must decide whether or not these possibilities are mutually exclusive. If one possibility actually happens does that mean all the others will not? Our analysis will be simplified if we can reduce all the possibilities to a mutually exclusive set.

We must now check that our set of possibilities is exhaustive. Are any left any out? At this initial stage of analysis we include even the most unlikely ones – we can discard them later.

Can we evaluate each of these possibilities; the value, the profit or the loss, if that possibility actually happens?

Do we have any information as to how likely it is that any one of those possibilities will happen. Can we quantify the probabilities? Sometimes we can, sometimes we can guess and sometimes we simply don't know.

Finally, having established the nature of the uncertainty facing us we can think about the risk. This last word is rarely defined in everyday speech but we shall use it to denote the probability of an unacceptable possibility. This is often called the 'downside risk'.

We can now apply these basic ideas to two simple situations.

Scenario 1

We are supplying six overseas markets in all of which price is a major factor in achieving sales. Consequently, changes in the exchange rates will, in the medium or longer term affect our competitive position and therefore our sales. However we do read the economic forecasts and we think we have a reasonable idea of the spread of possible future rates, and we also think that changes in one rate will not affect the likelihood of changes in the others.

The actual rates that we will ultimately get in the event will not be affected by any thing we can do. Therefore each rate for each market may be regarded, as far as our company is concerned, as a random variable.

We can guess the spread of each possible rate so we can then enumerate the spread of possible rates and, by extension, the possible sales volumes. Because such possible volumes constitute a continuous variable we would divide them up into 'chunks' (for example $200,000 to $299,000, and so on) to make the analysis manageable.

For each individual overseas market the possibilities are mutually exclusive, unless we are dealing with one of those economies with a both a 'commercial' (or 'official') rate and an open market rate. Let us forget about that complication! The final, forecast sales figures, each based on a possible exchange rate, are also mutually exclusive – we will in any one future accounting period get just one or other of the possible figures.

Bearing in mind the uncertainties of economic forecasting we cannot be sure that the spread of rates in each market covers all the possibilities. Therefore, on practical grounds, we will do any analysis as if we had an exhaustive list of possibilities. But we will remember, as we read the Financial Times over breakfast, to look out for the unexpected in any one of these markets or in the value of sterling itself. We would then need to quickly revise our analysis to accommodate the new spread of possibilities.

Do we know anything about the relative likelihood of any particular rate for any particular currency? Probably not, so we will probably have to make some intelligent guesses about that. However, in practice, intelligent guesses can be revealing about the spread of reasonably likely overall sales figures. Thus we quantify the probabilities which are the basis of any analysis, in order to quantify the probabilities of the final outcomes.

Finally we look at the spread of possible sales figures to note the ones that are unattractive or quite unacceptable. We also note how probable such figures are. This step tells us what the 'downside risk' is.

That completes the situation analysis but management must now use that analysis for decision making. To do that management needs a decision strategy, something which we will look at in the penultimate section of this chapter.

However, before we do that let us apply these basic ideas to a very different but much simpler situation.

Scenario 2

It is the first day of the big 10-day international exhibition. The stand is up (more or less), the sales promotion literature did actually arrive on time, and the last of the exhibits have been promised for tomorrow. The question now is: how many visitors will step on to the stand today, tomorrow and during all the rest of the show?

We can now look at this situation in the same way as we did with the first.

The causes of any individual exhibition visitor stepping onto the stand will depend on so many unknown factors that it may be treated as a random event.

What are the possibilities? By defining each possibility as a specified number of visitors during the course of one hour, we get a range of numbers starting from zero (yes! there might be a very quiet spell) up to some large number. But how large? Perhaps we can specify that – with too many people already on the stand passers by will do just that – they pass by. We could instead do our calculations without arbitrarily assigning a maximum number. Whichever way we choose, the numbers of visitors that are possible will be, of course, whole numbers, or 'integers' if you prefer.

Therefore this spread of possible numbers of visitors will be a set of mutually exclusive possibilities but not an exhaustive set unless we set an arbitrary top limit.

We need no separate evaluation of the possibilities because at this stage of the exhibition we are only concerned with the level of interest. No doubt orders will come later.

What are the probabilities? Do we have any evidence on which to base our calculations? Well we can use our experience from last year but that only gives an average rate of visitors arriving. Sometimes it will be more, sometimes it will be less. Therefore we need to be able to calculate how much more and how much less, and in that way discover the downside risk of getting too many all at once.

Finally we can use our analysis for the management of the stand. If we have a quiet period does this imply that the forecast average rate was too optimistic? If we get a very busy hour does this imply that we are going to run out of brochures and enquiry forms? We can calculate the probability of either.

Now that we have introduced some essential concepts we will introduce some basic and simple technicalities.

Quantifying Probabilities

Whatever the uncertain situation there will one or more points in time when something may or may not happen. An 'open account' customer may or may not post the cheque, there may or may not be an error in the next letter of credit going to the bank, our agent in Milan may or may not get that order he promised for this month, our freight forwarder may or may not get the consignment on the plane in time. Each of these crucial points we call a **trial**.

In the examples quoted, each 'trial' had just two outcomes, the answer in each case was of the 'yes/no' variety. But a trial may have several outcomes: will the distributor send us an order for one, two, three or four machines? So we then have a trial with four outcomes. Sometimes there may be a very large number of outcomes: this quarter's figures for shipments by value will be one of a range of many possible values.

The probability of any outcome of any trial can be expressed as a number between zero (implying no possibility at all) and one (implying something is bound to happen). You can if you like express probabilities as percentages – a probability of 0.25 is the same as a 25 per cent chance of it happening. However, when doing calculations, stick to decimals rather than percentage figures; it makes it easier to do the calculations.

The basis of this system is the 'frequency concept' of probability. This means that if something has happened in the past on 10 per cent of the occasions on which it might have happened then we may say that there is a probability of 0.1 (or 10 per cent) that it will happen the next possible time. This frequency concept is useful and practical but there are qualifications which we will discuss in the last two sections of this chapter.

We are often interested not in the probability of a single outcome of a single trial but groups or sets of outcomes. We are not interested in the probability of having exactly five visitors to our stand in the next hour but in the joint probability of any number from zero to five as any one of these figures would be bad news. In such a case there are six different, individual possibilities. We need to know how to combine the probabilities.

There are two basic rules to learn:

Rule 1 For mutually exclusive events the probability of A **or** B is the probability of A plus the probability of B:
$$P(A \text{ or } B) = P(A) + P(B).$$
Rule 2 For independent events (ie. arising from independent trials) the probability of A **and** B is the probability of A multiplied by the probability of B:
$$P(A \text{ and } B) = P(A) \times P(B).$$

If you have any difficulty in remembering these two basic rules just remember that probability figures are **always** less than one. Therefore when we add two or more probabilities we get a larger number which implies a higher probability. This makes sense. The chance of getting either A or B (we are not bothered which) must be greater than the chance of getting one of them. When we multiply probabilities we get a smaller number – a half times a quarter equals one eighth. Again this makes sense. If both A and B are individually uncertain the chance of getting both happening is bound to be more uncertain still.

Textbooks that deal with these statistical ideas more deeply will add two more basic rules covering non-mutually exclusive events and conditional probabilities. Both these additional rules can be derived from our two basic ones, but if you want to take it further the books in the reading list will help with that.

It is useful to remember that if we spell out all the outcomes of one particular trial the probabilities must add up to one. We are certain that we will get either the first or the second or the third etc. because our exhaustive list includes all the possibilities. The joint probability is the sum of all the individual probabilities which must then add up to one. If it does not there is a logical error somewhere.

The other point to remember is that the answer to any specific calculation of the probabilities of a particular outcome or event must produce an answer that is less than one. There is no meaning to a probability figure greater than one, or to a negative figure for that matter. In a similar way, a figure of exactly one implies certainty which we never get if uncertainty is involved.

We now have the concepts and the basic technique for tackling some real problems. When we have done that we will see how the answers can be used to develop a decision strategy, and how decision strategies can be employed in making management decisions in the widest sense.

The Contracts Problem

A company has made 'sealed bids' for four separate contracts and the management must think about its prospects whilst waiting to hear from the four (unconnected) principals. It knows what profit it will make on each contract if it gets it, and has a fair idea of its chances in each case. The details are:

Contract	Profit	Probability
A	$20,000	0.5
B	$30,000	0.2
C	$50,000	0.1
D	$50,000	0.1

Before we do anything else, let us clear away some sources of confusion. Each sealed bid is, technically speaking, a 'trial' and in this situation there are four trials each with just two outcomes. If there is a 0.2 probability of a successful bid this also implies there is a 0.8 probability of not getting it.

It might also be asked at this stage why the quoted probabilities do not add up to one. This is because each quoted figure refers to a separate and distinct trial. For each individual trial they must add up to one.

The first step in analysing this type of situation is to ask ourselves what exactly is it that we wish to know. Several different questions might be asked, such as:

1 What possible total profit figures are in prospect?
2 How likely are these figures, individually?
3 What is the downside risk of earning, say, less than $50,000?
4 Are the prospective (and uncertain) rewards from this bidding process worthwhile in view of the very certain costs that the company has incurred in gearing itself up as a credible contractor?

What are the possibilities?

There are quite a lot. The company, because the individual principals are independent of one another, could obtain anything from four contracts to none at all. But that does not mean that there are only five possibilities. For instance, getting A and C, or getting C and D both produce two contracts but with different total profit figures and with different probabilities. We need to examine every combination of successes and disappointments.

In fact there are 16 possible combinations. You can check this at once by noting that there are two outcomes from each trial or bid, and there are four trials which gives 4^2 distinct possibilities.

If we now also calculate the probability of each of these 16 we can answer both the second and the third questions on our list above.

To calculate any one of these probabilities we will use Rule 2, the one for independent events. For example, the probability of getting contracts A, B and D but not C will be the product of the individual probabilities of getting or not getting each as the case may be. So altogether we get for this possibility:

0.5 x 0.2 x 0.9 x 0.1 which equals 0.009

The full list of possibilities (with the profits in thousands of dollars) is provided in table 13.1:

Table 13.1: Possibilities and profits earned

Contracts obtained	Profit earned	Probability
A B C D	150	0.001
A B C	100	0.009
A B D	100	0.009
A B	50	0.081
A C D	120	0.004
A C	70	0.036
A D	70	0.036
A	20	0.324
B C D	130	0.001
B C	80	0.009
B D	80	0.009
B	30	0.081
C D	100	0.004
C	50	0.036
D	50	0.036
None	0	0.324

So much for the arithmetic. In analysing situations of uncertainty the arithmetic is often quite easy – it is the thinking that most people find difficult, so this is what we must now tackle.

The first thing is to check that the calculated probabilities add up to one. They should do because we should have an exhaustive list of all the possibilities with none left out. Consequently we are certain that one or other of them will happen. So this list answers questions 1 and 2.

The next thing to note is the variation in the magnitude of the probabilities. For example this company is over three hundred times more likely to get Contract A on its own than Contracts B, C and D jointly. More to the point, there is approximately a one-in-three chance that the company will get no contracts at all in spite of bidding for all four.

We can also answer question 3. From the list of possibilities we can see that there are three sets of circumstances which will produce a total profit figure of less than $50,000. What is the probability of this happening? That is to say, what is the probability of either getting A on its own, **or** B on its own, **or** none at all? Note the 'ors'. We are dealing with mutually exclusive events and Rule 1 for joint probabilities applies. The joint probability is therefore:

$$0.324 + 0.081 + 0.324 \text{ which equals } 0.729$$

So the downside risk of getting a poor profit figure is nearly three chances in four! Even if the original estimates of the probability of getting any one particular contract were a bit wrong, the chances of a zero profit are still likely to be high.

The last of the four questions posed earlier asked about the financial implications of this uncertain situation. To answer that question requires us to tie together what we were told about the varying profitability of these contracts with what we have discovered about the probable outcomes of the bidding process. The technique required to answer that is something that we will leave until later in this chapter.

The Successful(?) Distributor Problem

A company has launched a hand-held gadget incorporating the latest electronic wizardry, and the planned marketing technique will be for distributors in each country to visit senior managers of retail chains introducing the gadget with on-the-spot presentations. Initially the export manager will accompany each distributor to ensure that all goes smoothly and to explain the technology.

The company's distributor covering five New England states (Maine is excluded for the moment) has arranged a programme of presentations and has forecast, on the basis of his previous experience of the trade and the area, that one in four presentations will produce an agreement to stock the product.

Obviously, on this basis, there will be more disappointments than agreements and there will be, in any case, a random pattern of successful presentations even though the company is confident in the longer term about the distributor's claimed 25 per cent success rate. So what **might** happen from the first three calls?

We could tackle this problem in the same way as we used for the contracts problem by listing all the possibilities and investigating them individually. A more versatile alternative is to present the situation as a **probability tree**. In such a probability tree each trial is represented by a branching point. The individual branches emanating from that point represent the outcomes of that particular trial. Successive trials are represented by successive branching points so that the whole tree represents all the possibilities. Any individual 'route' through the tree from the base to the ends of the branches represents one particular possible sequence of events. Plotting the probabilities of individual outcomes in the tree makes it easy to calculate the overall probability of any and every sequence. It is also easy to see the financial or physical implications of any sequence.

Trees are very useful and versatile devices for modelling simple and complicated situations, whether they are probability trees, decision tress or more sophisticated devices. The recommended reading will give you an insight into these wider possibilities. However there is just one very odd feature about all these 'logic' trees: as drawn in textbooks they very rarely 'grow' from the ground upwards, more often from left to right as shown here, sometimes even from the top of the page downwards! Figure 13.1 shows how this situation is represented.

It is best to construct such a tree in five separate and easy stages.

1 Forget about probabilities or profits or costs for the moment. Instead, start by identifying the trials and the outcomes from each trial. In this problem each presentation is technically a trial, and each trial has just two possible outcomes: the retailer says either yes or no to an invitation to stock the product.

Figure 13.1: A probability tree

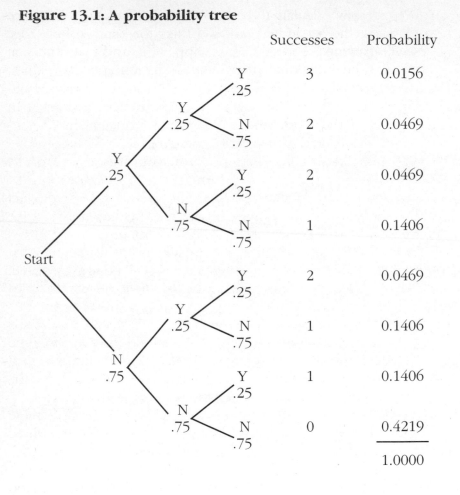

	Successes	Probability
Y .25	3	0.0156
N .75	2	0.0469
Y .25	2	0.0469
N .75	1	0.1406
Y .25	2	0.0469
N .75	1	0.1406
Y .25	1	0.1406
N .75	0	0.4219
		1.0000

2 Now we draw the tree, trial by trial, putting in the correct numbers of branches emanating from each branching point. The completed tree, at this stage, shows the **logic** of the situation.

3 Since each 'route' through the tree represents a particular sequence of possible events, we can calculate any relevant profit, cost or success scores that would be achieved by such a sequence of events. For this example, at the end of each branch ending, we show the number of retail outlets stocking the product.

4 We now write in, for each trial, on each branch, the probabilities of each outcome.

5 We can now calculate the overall probability of each sequence by using the second of our two rules for joint probabilities. Each sequence represents 'this happening, **and** that, **and** that ...', so the individual probabilities are multiplied together. These overall probabilities may now be written down the right-hand side against the end of each sequence of events. In figure 13.1 they have been rounded to four decimal places.

From a tree like this the UK export manager can see:

1 The tree is a complete representation as indicated by the fact that the probabilities add up to one – we have an exhaustive set of possibilities.
2 There is a 42 per cent chance that these first three presentations will all be fruitless. Therefore it would be unreasonable, at this stage, were this to happen, to start to doubt the sales abilities of the distributor or the reliability of his promises.
3 The chance that all three targeted retailers will sign up is only 1.5 per cent or one chance in 64. Therefore it would be most unreasonable, on the basis of the distributor's original forecast, to expect quick results. It will be the usual marketing long haul requiring persistence and patience.
4 There is just over an even chance (0.5625 in fact) that the distributor will get one or two successes out of the three presentations.

Once again, as with the previous example, we need not put too much faith in the precision of the distributor's 25 per cent claim because we can see that, even if it were only approximately correct, the broad conclusions to be drawn by the export manager would be much the same.

Furthermore, although conclusions of this kind might be guessed at, an analysis of this kind has three advantages over guesswork:

1 We can see that the export manager's conclusions have a sound, logical basis. We can be confident about them.
2 Guessing would be easy in a situation where only three presentations are involved. It would not be easy at all to assess

the progress of this sales mission if we were talking about 30 or 130 presentations. But, unlike guesswork, our quantitative analysis can be easily extended to cope with larger numbers as we will show in the next example.

3   All the time, during his New England trip, the export manager will be assessing the abilities of his distributor to shift the product. In theory, in the long run, 25 per cent of presentations would show a success. But common sense tells him not to expect exactly 25 per cent but only something round about it. But how much round about before the export manager has to conclude that this distributor is better than or not so good as he claimed? That question is answered by the technique of sampling theory, which involves the assessment of sample data and the significance of its accordance or discordance with our marketing expectations. That topic is founded on the type of analysis that we have just made but, unfortunately, is outside the scope of a small book like this. The reading list will help you.

Some Points to Remember About Probability Trees

Probability trees, and other types of logic trees, are very useful tools for getting to grips with complicated or confusing situations. The fundamental idea is a diagram where we start at the beginning (always the best place to start!) and, step by step, we draw an expanding pattern of branches on the basis of 'if this, then that, and then follows these, and so on …'.

Whenever one attempts, by drawing a logic tree of some kind, to get down on paper a comprehensible representation of a confused pattern of possible events or decisions, there are three possible results:

1   One realizes that it was not so complicated after all, now that the whole picture is clear and on paper. The sketch of the tree is thrown away having served its purpose.

2   One realizes that it is indeed quite complicated but the tree will make it possible to do some necessary calculations or

draw some useful conclusions. We keep the sketch of the tree to show other people what it is all about.

3   One realizes that it is even more complicated than first suspected but at least the incomplete sketch can show us:
   (a) exactly why it was so much more complicated than we thought at first, which indicates in turn:
   (b) what further assistance or more advanced techniques will be necessary to complete the analysis.

Logic trees come in all sorts of shapes and sizes according to the peculiarities of the task in hand. Probability trees are just one type but they have the special virtue of being a practical first step in the analysis of a situation of uncertainty, particularly in those confusing circumstances where one does not know how to begin. If in doubt, try a tree and see what happens!

The Successful(?) Distributor Problem, Continued

If our fictional export manager really wanted to assess the abilities of his New England distributor he would now know that he needed a larger sample of his distributor's sales technique before coming to any conclusions. For any larger number of sales presentations he would still hope for a 25 per cent success rate or better. He would also know that it would be too much to expect exactly 25 per cent but only something round about that. So we still have the question to answer: 'How much round about?'

With increasing numbers of presentations (increasing numbers of trials) any probability tree technique quickly becomes unmanageable. If we have 'n' trials with only two outcomes to each trial, the number of end points in the tree will be 2^n. Thirty presentations would give us a tree with approximately one billion branch ends. It looks as though we need another technique to solve this!

Fortunately the technique is ready to hand: it is called the Binomial Probability Distribution. The arithmetical calculations are given in Mathematical Note 1 at the end of this chapter, and fuller accounts can be found in the books on the reading list. We shall be interested here only in the management implications.

There are three requirements if we want to apply this technique. The first is that we must know the number of trials. Let us assume that the export manager will report back to his UK company after 30 presentations, which means 30 trials, or as the statisticians would express it, 'n = 30'. The second requirement is that each trial should have just two possible outcomes. In those cases where each trial has more than two we can get round this restriction by defining our questions in terms of 'one particular thing happening or not happening'. The latter possibility covers all the other, less interesting possibilities. The third requirement is that the probability of the thing we are interested in is the same for all trials. Assuming that our distributor does not fall sick or lose his enthusiasm we will base our calculations on the promised 25 per cent success rate being constant.

To work out the probability of any specified number of successful presentations out of the 30 possible we fill in the formula given in Mathematical Note 1 using the following values for the three **parameters**

$$n = 30 \qquad p = 0.25 \qquad q = (1 - p) = 0.75.$$

The 'x' value is the number of successful presentations that we wish to know the probability of. The 'q' value is the probability of **not** getting a success in any one presentation, So we get:

Table 13.2: The successful(?) distributor?

n = 30 p = 0.25

x	^nCr	p^x	$q^{(n-x)}$	P(x)
0	1	1.000	0.000	0.000
1	30	0.250	0.000	0.002
2	435	0.063	0.000	0.009
3	4,060	0.016	0.000	0.027
4	27,405	0.004	0.001	0.060
5	142,506	0.001	0.001	0.105
6	593,775	0.000	0.001	0.145
7	2,035,800	0.000	0.001	0.166
8	5,852,925	0.000	0.002	0.159
9	14,307,150	0.000	0.002	0.130
10	30,045,015	0.000	0.003	0.091
11	54,627,300	0.000	0.004	0.055
12	86,493,225	0.000	0.006	0.029
13	119,759,850	0.000	0.008	0.013
14	145,422,680	0.000	0.010	0.005
15	155,117,520	0.000	0.013	0.002
16	145,422,680	0.000	0.018	0.001
17	119,759,850	0.000	0.024	0.000
18	86,493,225	0.000	0.032	0.000
19	54,627,300	0.000	0.042	0.000
20	30,045,015	0.000	0.056	0.000
21	14,307,150	0.000	0.075	0.000
22	5,852,925	0.000	0.100	0.000
23	2,035,800	0.000	0.133	0.000
24	593,775	0.000	0.178	0.000
25	142,506	0.000	0.237	0.000
26	27,405	0.000	0.316	0.000
27	4,060	0.000	0.422	0.000
28	435	0.000	0.563	0.000
29	30	0.000	0.750	0.000
30	1	0.000	1.000	0.000
			Total =	1.000

Table 13.3: Number of successful presentations

No. of successful presentations	Probability of that number
0	0
1	0.002
2	0.009
3	0.027
4	0.060
5	0.105
6	0.146
7	0.166
8	0.159
9	0.130
10	0.091
11	0.055
12	0.029
13	0.013
14	0.005
15	0.002
16	0.001
17	0
Total =	1.000

It is easy enough to calculate a table like this but it is less easy to interpret it and to make use of it. That is what we, and the export manager must now do. To help comprehension we can present the spread of probabilities as a bar chart – figure 13.2.

1 The first thing to remember is not to succumb to number blindness even though there are lots of digits. Common sense tells us any figure less than 0.02 implies a one in a hundred chance or less. Therefore the only real possibilities in these circumstance are some number of successful presentations between three and twelve. Any thing else is so unlikely not to be worth considering.

Figure 13.2: The 30 presentations – how many will succeed?

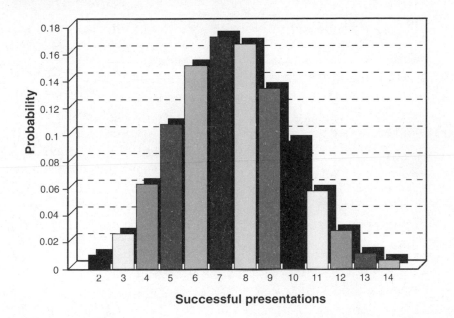

2 If you look at the column of probabilities or look at the chart you will see that they rise to a peak and fall off again. This spread of probabilities is clustered around the expected average of 25 per cent of thirty; that is around seven or eight. So our export manager now knows the spread of genuine possibilities.

3 A little mental arithmetic tells us that the probabilities of between four and 11 successes add up to approximately 0.9. This means that, if the distributor does indeed have an average 25 per cent success rate **in the long run**, then for these 30 presentations there is a 90 per cent chance that he will record somewhere between four and eleven successes. That quantifies our expectation of '25 per cent more or less' for sales performance.

4 In the view of any manager, concerned about sales performance, this is a pretty wide spread of possibilities. Nevertheless it is the simple logical consequence of two facts or alleged facts: that there will be 30 presentations and that the distributor averages a 25 per cent success rate in the long run. The

consequence of all this is that sales budgets must be flexible and that sales figures must be continually monitored to see if, in the longer run, the 25 per cent target will be met in spite of the ups and downs of individual monthly or quarterly figures.

5 What can we conclude if, after 30 presentations, the score is outside the expected 90 per cent probability range, that is, if the score is less than four or more than eleven? Perhaps it might be just a run of bad luck. There is indeed a small chance of this happening and we have already calculated that probability. However that probability is very small and our export manager is more likely to accept this very small risk of being misled by a freak result and conclude instead that the basic 25 per cent figure was wrong – either too low or high depending on the actual number of successes achieved.

Before we leave this problem of the New England distributor we must face up to the computational problem that would seem to arise if it were not 30 but 60, or even 100 sales presentations. The arithmetic that produced the table above was not difficult but it may be reasonably regarded as tedious. For larger numbers of trials it gets worse but, as is usually the case, a technique is available to simplify that task.

If you look at the **shape** of the probabilities distributed across the range of possible success scores you can see that it is close to a neat 'bell-shaped' pattern. Calculations involving larger numbers of trials would produce an even neater and ultimately unchanging pattern. We would get what is technically known as a 'Normal Distribution'. Because such a distribution has a fixed 'shape' a simple table can be used to derive any probabilities we need with only the absolute minimum of calculation. The details and applications of this technique can be found in the reading list, or in most textbooks on business statistics.

The Exhibition Stand Problem Re-visited

When we described scenario 2 we were interested in the inevitable variability of the numbers of visitors stepping on to the exhibition stand in any one period, even though we were fairly confident about the average rate over the ten days of the exhibition. We can calculate the probabilities of receiving in any one hour or in any one minute, any specified number of visitors over or under the expected average.

How can we represent the situation? Clearly we cannot draw a probability tree because we do not know how many branching points to put in – we do not know the number of trials. For the same reason we cannot use the Binomial Probability Distribution – there is no value to give for 'n' in the formula. All we do know (or think we know) is the average rate at which visitors are expected to arrive. Once again there is a way out, and the technique is to use, as a model of the situation, another theoretical probability distribution called the 'Poisson Probability Distribution' named after its French inventor.

The details of the calculation are given in Mathematical Note 2 at the end of this chapter for those readers who want more detail. However the practical application is easy to follow. Let the assumption be that an average of two visitors per minute are expected to step on the stand. Basing our calculations on that single parameter we get these probabilities:

Table 13.4: Numbers of visitors in any one minute

Number	Probability
0	0.135
1	0.271
2	0.271
3	0.181
4	0.090
5	0.036
6	0.012
7	0.003
8	0.001
Total	1.000

What conclusions can be drawn from this?

1 The chance of getting more than four visitors in one minute, given this average rate, seems really very small. Adding the probabilities (Rule 1 again) the total is 0.052 or just one chance in twenty. But we are working to a 1-minute time unit and if the exhibition is busy for eight hours during the day there are 480 1-minute periods. We would expect therefore to have more than four visitors arriving in one minute on 25 occasions (480 x 0.052) during the day. Similarly, we would expect to get more than five in one minute on seven or eight occasions a day. Will the sales staff be able to cope – or will the coffee machine?

2 The probability of nobody arriving during a one minute period is 0.135 or roughly one chance in seven. This could therefore be expected to happen 65 times during one day (480 x 0.135). But will the sales staff get two successive minutes free? We can use Rule 2 to see the probabilities of getting two, three, four and so on, successive minutes free. The logic is this: the probability of three (to take an example) successive minutes is the probability that the first, **and** the second, **and** the third will all be free. Using Rule 2 we get:

$$0.135 \times 0.135 \times 0.135 = 0.002$$

or, in other words one fifth of one per cent, or putting it another way, one chance in 500. Given the fact there are 480 minutes in the busy period this implies it will, on average, only happen about once a day.

3 All these calculations were based on an average rate of two visitors per minute. That is the same rate as 120 per hour and that latter figure could be used to calculate the relative probabilities of any given number of arrivals **in any one hour**. In fact any time unit could be used provided it was used both for the average rate (which was the basis of the arithmetic) and in the answers produced.

4 Because we can calculate the relative probabilities of different arrival rates per minute, we now have a means of checking that basic parameter of 'two per minute, average'. If the actual numbers differed markedly from these calculated probability figures then we would have grounds for altering our estimate of that average rate, hopefully, altering it upwards!

Selecting a Decision Strategy

What we have done so far is to offer some guidance on how to think about situations of uncertainty, how to quantify that uncertainty, and how to apply some standard techniques to get useful answers to questions about that situation.

Having got answers to questions, the next step is to decide what to do about those answers. It is necessary to have a decision strategy. It is important to realise at the outset that the choice of any particular decision strategy must depend on the circumstances of the person making the decision, whatever decision that might be. It is not possible to get a computer to make the choice for you.

One essential element of any decision strategy is the criterion of choice, which is some quantity that will determine which way the final decision will go.

We will now look at some possible strategies and the factors influencing a choice.

Expected Monetary Value – or 'EMV'

This can be applied in those cases where we have quantified probabilities and quantified payoffs from any decision that might be taken. In spite of its name, this strategy need not be confined to financial value; it is applicable to costs or to any quantified target that a manager might wish to maximize or minimize.

We can apply this strategy to the contract bidding example for which we have already calculated the probabilities. But first, a definition and an explanation.

$$EMV = \text{Probability} \times \text{intrinsic value of an event}$$

The intrinsic value of an event is the value (profit, cost, score and so on) that would be obtained if the event actually happened; it is the value leaving out the uncertainty. Therefore the EMV is the criterion of choice. The justification of the EMV strategy is that, in the long run, it does measure the potential benefits or costs of applying the decision strategy. Applying it to the contracts example we get:

Table 13.5: EMV strategy

Contracts obtained	Profit ($000)	Prob.	EMV ($)
A B C D	150	0.001	150
A B C	100	0.009	900
A B D	100	0.009	900
A B	50	0.081	4,050
A C D	120	0.004	480
A C	70	0.036	2,520
A D	70	0.036	2,520
A	20	0.324	6,480
B C D	130	0.001	130
B C	80	0.009	720
B D	80	0.009	720
B	30	0.081	2,430
C D	100	0.004	400
C	50	0.036	1,800
D	50	0.036	1,800
None	0	0.324	0
Totals:		1.000	26,000

What can the management make of this additional information? It can now answer the fourth question that was asked about this opportunity to bid – is the whole bidding process worthwhile?

When the 'EMV strategy' is used management's aim is to maximize total expected monetary value or minimize total expected monetary cost. In this case the EMV of $26,000 must be set against the costs of the bidding procedure. If these costs were known for certain, the EMV of the costs would be the actual cost because in this case the 'probability' is equal to one exactly. Therefore, applying the strategy, it can be said that the maximum acceptable cost is the same $26,000 at which level the whole project would have a net EMV of zero. If the cost were some other amount, the EMV, which is the criterion of choice, would be negative or positive and would thereby indicate the decision to be made.

When the contracts were placed the actual profit or loss would, of course, depend on what actually happened. The profit earned could be any one figure from $150,000 to nothing, as table 13.5 shows, less the costs.

The advantage of using EMV as a criterion of choice is that it is simple to calculate, simple to explain and makes sense in the long run. So it is a sensible strategy to apply for repeated situations of uncertainty. But for the 'one-off' situation another strategy may be preferred.

The 'minimax' strategy

This strategy is often adopted unconsciously. Therefore we should define it in order to know what precisely it is that we are doing. The strategy is to **minimize the maximum loss**. This normally implies management has several possible courses of action and needs some criterion to choose between them. If we use this same example, we can say that the management has a choice between bidding on the one hand or doing nothing on the other. If it decides to make the four bids and the relevant costs amount to, say, $10,000 then the possible net profits range from $140,000 down to a loss of $10,000.

On the other hand, by doing nothing, the company would be sure of losing nothing. The maximum loss, which would otherwise be $10,000, is minimized to zero by doing nothing.

The minimax strategy is essentially a 'play for safety' approach and is the one likely to be adopted by the risk-averse manager. But it is also the strategy adopted when we take out an insurance policy, sell foreign currency forward, buy cover from the ECGD or from NCM Ltd, or pay for a credit reference. In all such cases the exporter is incurring a certain cost in preference to an un-certain but large loss. He thus minimizes the maximum loss to which he is exposed. The minimax strategy has the advantage that it can be applied when the probabilities are unknown, provided all the possibilities are defined.

The 'minimax regret' or 'least regret' strategy

The disadvantage of the cautious, minimax strategy can be seen in our example. The risk-averse manager applying the minimax strategy to the bidding opportunity is throwing away a chance of earning $100,000 or more merely to avoid the risk of losing $10,000 (or whatever the cost might be).

For most practical business situations it is too pessimistic to assume that the worst will always happen. If the minimax strategy were adopted (as above) the manager would look with regret on the lost opportunities. By 'regret' we mean the difference between the maximum payoff and the cost of taking, in this case, no action at all. The 'least regret' strategy is most useful where the manager's choices involve a range of costs with each one associated with a particular payoff. The selected choice is then the one that minimizes the maximum regret.

This strategy can also be applied where probabilities are unknown or unreliably estimated. It is the strategy for the more enterprising business strategist.

There are other strategies described in textbooks on more advanced statistical methods and, in particular, in those on game theory. However these brief descriptions should give some idea of the possible management approaches to tackling uncertainty. It should also make you more self-consciously aware of what you are doing when taking decisions in the face of uncertainty. In practice decision makers will use some subconscious mental processes which substitutes for a formal and explicit strategy, but whether it is 'optimal' who knows!

Decision Making in the (Uncertain) Management Context

All that we have dealt with so far has treated the decision maker in isolation; as though it was always a matter of a sole-trader thinking through his or her dilemmas all alone in the office. In practice, as we are well aware, uncertain situations and the need to make difficult choices are much more likely to involve protracted meetings and very many people. So how can the ideas covered in this chapter help in that situation.

1 Uncertain situations require clear thinking. The basic, fundamental ideas of sets of possibilities, of the conflict between possibilities and actuality, the applicability of quantified probabilities and so on should help to get those thinking processes going.

2 The discipline of identifying all the possibilities, at least initially, provides a foundation to any process of logical analysis. It should also inhibit the common tendency to leap straight from the identification of a few possibilities to a final, snap decision.

3 Quantification of probabilities, and in particular joint probabilities often throws up relative differences that are not intuitively obvious. To go back to the contracts problem, how many would guess correctly that the chance of getting nothing was one in three?

4 There is an observable psychological tendency, in the face of uncertainty, to over-estimate low probabilities (who's afraid of flying?) and under-estimate high ones (so we get knocked down crossing the road). Quantification provides an objective way of avoiding this.

5 Probabilities are, in practice, just estimates so we need to know how to take that fact into consideration before making any decisions. By quantifying the uncertainty we can calculate whether probable errors will make or not make a significant difference to any final management decision.

6 Awareness of what is involved encourages the manager to be explicit both about the decision strategy and the criterion of choice adopted. If these are explicit they can be explained to colleagues whose support or criticism is needed.

7 The end result must, in all cases, be management action whether it is the preparation of flexible budgets (how flexible?) or performance assessment (was it just bad luck?). If the action is to be justified to either junior or to senior staff there should be a logical basis that can be communicated persuasively. And that was what this chapter was all about.

Mathematical Note 1

The Binomial Probability Distribution

This probability distribution provides a model of those situations where there is a known number of trials, where each trial has just two outcomes (a 'success' and a 'non-success), and where the probability of a 'success' in any one trial is constant. The formula below gives the probability of any specified number of successes. The values used, in the formula, to calculate the probabilities are:

n The number of trials
p The probability of a 'success' in any one trial
q (1 - p), which is the probability of a 'non-success'
x The particular number of successes we need to know the probability of. Alternatively this is often denoted by 'r'.

The calculations for all the possible values of 'x' are made using:

$$P(x) = \frac{n!}{x!(n-x)!} \quad x \quad p^x \quad x \quad q^{n-x}$$

The first part of the formula calculates the number of combinations of trial outcomes that will produce the specified total 'x'. If your calculator has a 'combinations' function, the formula now becomes:

$$^nCr \quad x \quad p^x \quad x \quad q^{n-x}$$

For example, with five trials (n = 5) and with a probability of a 'success' in any one trial of 20 per cent (p = 0.2), then the probability of a total of three successes is:

$$10 \times 0.008 \times 0.64 = 0.0512$$

Note that the total of possible different values of 'x' is always (n + 1).

Mathematical Note 2

The Poisson Probability Distribution

This probability distribution provides a model of those situations where the average number of events (denoted by λ) occurring in a specified time period or similar unit is known or can be estimated. The formula then gives the probability of any number of events occurring in that time period. The values used in the formula are:

λ The average number of events in one period. This is sometimes denoted as 'the mean'.

e A constant value, equal to 2.71828, which should normally be given on your calculator

x The particular number of events in the time period, we need to know the probability of

The calculations for all possible values of 'x' are made using

$$P(x) = \frac{\lambda^x \times e^{-\lambda}}{x!}$$

In theory there is no maximum value for 'x' but in practice the probabilities will decline to zero when 'x' becomes large.

Note that when large numbers are involved both the Binomial and the Poisson distributions become difficult to calculate, but the Normal Distribution will then be a good or very good approximation to either.

Questions for Discussion

1 In one particular overseas market a company has been invited to take a stand in a special 'one-off' exhibition. Any sales generated would be in addition to existing business in that part of the world but would not necessarily lead to continuing business from that area.

The marginal cost of taking the stand would be only $40,000. The profit on any sales would be 15 per cent. The level of sales that might be achieved is uncertain and the range of estimates is:

Sales of	$500,000:	10% probability
	$400,000:	20%
	$300,000:	30%
	$200,000:	25%
	$100,000:	10%
No sales at all:		5% probability

On the basis of these figures, would you recommend incurring the cost of taking a stand at this exhibition?

2 Your local distributor has arranged for you and himself to give five presentations to five different prospective customers during the week of your visit. He assures you: 'They are all good people, I know them well. I get an order about every third visit. You will see, we shall get some good business for you before you go back to England!'

If the distributor was accurate about his ability to get orders what are the likely outcomes of your one-week visit in terms of the possible total number of orders from these five customers?

Calculate the prospects in two ways, using a probability tree and than by using the method shown in Mathematical Note 1. The answers should be the same.

3 The overseas sales enquiry desks of several different divisions

have been amalgamated to achieve greater efficiency. It is known that in the past, for all the divisions together, telephone enquiries came in at an average rate of one every forty minutes and it normally takes about an hour for the Customer Service staff to sort out the details and complete the quotation.

On that basis the export manager considers that two members of staff will be able to cope with the incoming calls. Is that reasonable? How would you decide?

14

The Planning Process: Performance and Budgeting

The Three Main Topics Covered in this Chapter

In theory this book should stop at this point. We know what we want our export business to achieve. That is profitable growth. We also know how to measure that growth by monitoring the growth of the excess of assets over liabilities. We know how to monitor the features of every business that will continually pull it down, namely costs. We also know the relative importance of the company's assets in general (which gives us the measure of profitable success) and at the same time that so vital asset, cash at the bank. This particular asset is the life blood of the business. If cash can, through good planning and control, be taken for granted, management can concentrate on managing. To do that requires the cash planning we looked at in chapters 9 to 11.

To put these ideas into practice we will examine three specific management techniques:

1 Ratio analysis, which means no more than acquiring the skill to be able to look at a mass of figures and make some sense of them.
2 Investment appraisal, which means being able judge the long term value of what we are proposing to do with our business.

3 Budgeting, which means organizing a company-wide planning process that will actually assist in the attainment of our
export targets.

Ratio Analysis – What's it All About?

The first thing to be clear about is what so-called 'ratio analysis'
is **not** about. It is not a sophisticated mathematical science which
will reveal to the manager mysteries the existence of which
he never even guessed at. To put the matter at its simplest, ratio
analysis will only tell you or anyone else, something that you
should have known already, something that was already there in
the figures to be analysed in front of you. So why bother?

There are in this world those natural entrepreneurs who have
that magical ability to see at a glance what is just the right decision
needed to make a profitable move. Such people do not need
ratio analysis. The other 99.9 per cent of the population (which
means us) will find it very useful to make the numbers say out
loud what would otherwise be an inaudible whisper.

The process of applying ratio analysis to a set of figures, and
they are not necessarily all financial figures, has these advantages:

1 It provides a simple and routine approach to 'reading' a sheet
of figures that might, at first glance, be no more comprehensible than a sheet of wall paper. We can settle down to the
task of analysis with the confidence of knowing that it only
requires patience and common sense to extract what we need
from them.

2 Because it is a routine process, it has the particular virtues of
any checklist (which ratio analysis really is). It enables us to be
reasonably sure that when we have finished the analysis we
have not missed anything that we should have noticed.

3 It enables us to look at individual bits of a set of reported
figures in a systematic way. That in turn enables us to make
comparisons between one aspect of a business and another,
because we can compare the results of different calculations.

4 Provided we do not forget the common-sense principles
used in devising the calculation of any ratio, we can at once

interpret the results of the arithmetic in terms of the overall business and commercial realities which are the proper concern of management.

Nevertheless, the application of the technique to any set of figures does demand something from the analyst. It requires that:

1 The analyst knows why the ratio is calculated in the particular way that convention has decreed. The underlying business principles must not be forgotten in doing the arithmetic.
2 The analyst must have a reasonable expectation of what a significant or non-significant result should be **in the context of the given figures**. For different companies or markets such significant figures might be quite different from the 'textbook' one.
3 The analyst must be prepared for the great majority of the calculated answers to be 'non-significant' but, at the same time, be vigilant for the few that suggest something of interest. Ratio analysis is akin to detective work; the skill is in noticing both the unusual event and the unusual non-event, just as Holmes did when the dog did not bark.
4 The analyst accepts that the results of the calculations are just sign posts, directing his attention back to the original data. Having got an interesting and unexpected result the analyst is then alerted to the possibility of something about the business which he or she might otherwise have missed. Having been alerted he or she can then investigate to see what lies behind that anomalous figure or group of figures.

Making Use of Some Standard Ratios

To use ratio analysis the manager must know what is being looked for, how a calculated ratio will help in the search and why the particular method of calculation is appropriate.

As illustrations we will use the performance of Matrix Materials Ltd over the years 1988 to 1994, which are shown in table 14.1.

This company commenced trading at the start of 1988. The table shows the turnover and net profit figures for each of the seven years, and the balance sheet figures for the **close** of each of those years.

Table 14.1: Performance of Matrix Materials Ltd (1988-1994)

£000s

Year	1988	1989	1990	1991	1992	1993	1994
Sales turnover	78	117	140	167	143	216	270
Operating profit	1	13	13	39	-35	33	9
Interest	0	0	0	3	4	4	4
Net profit	1	13	13	36	-39	29	5
Buildings	45	45	45	90	90	90	100
Plant at cost	32	32	32	50	50	50	70
less depreciation	3	6	9	14	20	25	31
Other fixed	12	12	12	20	20	20	26
less depreciation	1	3	5	8	9	10	13
Total fixed	85	80	75	138	131	125	152
Stocks	12	18	23	29	33	40	49
Debtors	13	20	23	28	23	36	46
Bank cash	-5	5	17	16	-7	18	33
less							
Trade creditors	14	19	21	23	21	31	47
Net current assets	6	24	42	50	28	63	81
Total assets	91	104	117	188	159	188	233
Financed by:							
Share capital	90	90	90	90	90	90	110
Share premium	0	0	0	0	0	0	20
Reserves	1	14	27	63	24	53	58
Total equity	91	104	117	153	114	143	188
L/T loans	0	0	0	35	45	45	45
Capital employed	91	104	117	188	159	188	233
RATIOS							
1 Sales/CE	0.86	1.13	1.20	0.89	0.90	1.15	1.16
2 Sales/FAs	0.92	1.46	1.87	1.21	1.09	1.73	1.78
3 R on CE	1.1%	12.5%	11.1%	20.7%	-22.0%	17.6%	3.9%
4 R on equity	1.1%	12.5%	11.1%	23.5%	-34.2%	20.3%	2.7%
5 Current R	1.4	2.3	3.0	3.2	2.3	3.0	2.7
6 Quick R	0.6	1.3	1.9	1.9	0.8	1.7	1.7
7 Net Cash F	5	18	18	44	-32	35	14
8 Payments days		51	56	56	65	50	55

Measures of performance

As was explained at the beginning of this book, exploiting an opportunity implies investing money in a business to obtain a return. That return is only obtained when those running the business turn the 'opportunity' into actual sales. So we will be interested in the ratio of sales turnover to capital employed, and also sales turnover to total fixed assets, so we get the ratios in lines 1 and 2 in table 14.1. We can see that the sales achieved as compared with the total investment in the company rose at first, as the company established itself, then fell off in 1991 and 1992, and then climbed back up again but only to £1,159 of sales for each £1,000 invested. There was a similar story when sales turnover is compared with the investment in fixed assets. However the significance of this second ratio will often depend on the nature of the business. For capital intensive businesses it clearly is important. Service companies may have very little invested in fixed assets – their 'investment' will be in people, in knowledge and in reputation, none of which appear on a balance sheet.

Measures of profitability

We are interested in what percentage return the management of Matrix Materials achieved with the moneys entrusted to their care. That can be looked at strictly from the point of view of the operating management, like this:

Operating profit before interest/total capital invested.

This is usually referred to as the return on capital employed or 'RoCE' though it is necessary to be sure as to which 'return' and which 'Capital Employed' is implied.

Alternatively, the return can be looked at from the point of view of the shareholders, the return on their equity investment. That is:

Net profit after interest/equity investment.

These give the ratios in lines 3 and 4 in table 14.1. From both ratios it can be seen that as might be expected the return in 1988 (the first year of trading) was low on either measure. From then on the returns improved, and it is very noticeable that the gearing from 1991 onwards benefited the shareholders' return as compared with the 'RoCE'. It is also noticeable that when the company made only a small profit or an actual loss the situation was reversed as theory suggests.

Measures of liquidity

One very popular measure of liquidity is the so-called 'current ratio', but the related measure of instant liquidity is the 'quick ratio'. It is also interesting to look at net cash flow to see the rate at which cash is or is not being generated. This last item is not, strictly speaking, a ratio at all. However that is true of several of the figures which can be routinely culled from a set of financial reports. In this case we get:

Current ratio: Current assets/current liabilities.

Quick ratio: Current assets less stocks/ current liabilities.

Net cash flow: profit after interest and tax, plus depreciation.

These are shown in lines 5 to 7 in table 14.1.

Interpreting these ratios for any individual company requires care. Major retailers with sophisticated stock ordering systems will sell their goods over the 'counter', before they pay their suppliers. That means that they can effectively run their business on their suppliers' working capital and will therefore show very low current and quick ratios. Exporters are in an opposite situation where the liabilities incurred with short-term export finance, or a large 'debtors' figure arising from open account exporting will distort the ratios.

The crucial consideration in all cases is the implication of any of these three measures on the company's **future** ability to pay its bills. In the case of Matrix Materials the current and quick ratios were quite acceptable except for 1988 (to be expected as it was the start-up year) and for 1992 as a consequence of the trading loss in that year. More interesting was the fact that except in the loss making year there was **not** a net cash **outflow**. For a company having trading difficulties that is important.

Measures of efficiency

Efficient management will keep the investment in both stocks and debtors as low as possible. That means in effect monitoring how often stocks are turned over, and how quickly customers pay. To establish the first we would need to have a breakdown of the stocks figure into finished goods stock (which can be compared with the cost of sales figures). That normally would give:

Cost of sales/average finished goods stock in the year

to show the number of times that stock was 'turned over' during the year.

We can estimate the average time spent waiting for customers to pay more easily from these available figures. We use:

(Average debtors/sales revenue) times 365

to give an answer in days. The 'average' will be the last plus the current debtors figures divided by two. This is shown in line 8 in the table, and of course there is no figure for the first year, 1993. You can see that it was fairly consistently about 55 days but this went up to 65 days in 1992. That was not sufficient to cause the net cash outflow but it certainly did not help.

Some General Considerations About Ratios

1 There is a very large number of ratios and similar measures that can be calculated. The books mentioned in Appendix C

will present many more, and other books on business finance will extend the list.

2 All ratios are the fruits of a common sense attempt to show something about a business. If there is an aspect of a business that is of particular interest then it should be obvious what calculation is required to show it.

3 The interested export manager will invent suitable ratios to assist in the analysis of the data available. That data can be drawn from the company's own internal records or from external market research.

4 However all analysis must be based on what data is available. In the case of the summary figures for Matrix Materials Ltd, it was not possible to calculate turnover of stocks because we did not have the cost of sales figures.

5 There are two types of mistakes that can be made in the use of ratios. The first is an unthinking reliance on 'normal figures'. We have already mentioned that non-exporting retailers will show unusually low quick ratios. Any assessment must take into consideration the company as a whole and the market in which it operates.

The second error is the elementary one of calculating the reciprocal of the intended ratio. This only happens if the analyst is not clear about why the ratio is calculated in a particular way in the first place.

6 And lastly, a reminder to keep things in perspective. In many books on management techniques a wealth of ratios are offered to the aspiring analyst, but you will notice that a large proportion of these are designed to help the 'outsider'. That is, the suggested ratios are a help to someone who has only **limited** access to published data about a company which might well be a remote competitor.

For the export manager concerned about the efficient operation of his or her own company, much of the information that would otherwise have to gleaned by indirect analysis should be 'on tap', from a well designed MIS, a Management Information System. Obvious examples are 'debtor days' or 'stock turn round' times but each Export Manager should be aware of the data regularly needed for the control of an effective export operation.

The Longer Term Assessment Task

What we have discussed so far are the ways in which existing data about **past** operations may be made more comprehensible. But if we refer back to the situation depicted in chapter 10 we can see that the forward planning problem facing Pretty Polly Plantations was assessing and evaluating events seven or ten years ahead.

The cash flow forecasts prepared then did demonstrate that the loans would be repaid and cash ultimately fed back to the UK parent company. But we did wonder then if it was altogether a good use of the money, when viewed in the longer term. The standard technique for assessing such longer term projects is known as 'discounted cash flow'. We briefly introduced the underlying principle at the beginning of chapter 10 when we talked about 'the time value of money'.

We will illustrate the technique using the example of the planned processing mill. But first we must go right back to the beginning, before the stage where the means of financing would be first considered. We start with the basic investment proposition:

1 The mill will require an input of cash at the beginning of its working life.
2 It will be some time before it starts to generate more cash than it absorbs.
3 It will be even longer before the mill reaches 'pay-back' when total cumulative cash out at last equals total cumulative cash put in.
4 Only then will the company see a net benefit, but that will only be for the period of life of the processing plant. After that the mill must be either closed or re-equipped.
5 So the parent company will have to wait for a return on the investment. Would it not be better off putting that money or those borrowings in some alternative investment, perhaps even Government bonds?

We will make the assessment by using two simple tools:

1 A planned schedule of cash flows for the mill. This schedule

will be strictly for the mill and will not cover the getting or repaying of any loans nor the paying of interest on any such possible loans. That financing has not yet been fixed.

2 The time value of money. As we explained in chapter 10, £1 of cash received or paid out is less significant the further into the future is the date of receipt or payment. The reason is that interest could be earned on that £1 in the intervening period.

So we will **discount** future flows, using standard discount tables, to find the 'present value' of those future receipts and payments. The 'discount rate' will be, at least initially, the marginal cost of capital which in the case of PPP Plc was the 18 per cent they would have to pay on any overdraft.

Doing the DCF Calculations

Step 1

We must draw up a list of the cash flows, those cash flows relating to the mill itself, forgetting for the time being where any outside cash might come from.

If you refer back to the cash flow forecast in table 10.1 you will see that cash receipts from sales did not start until Year Two (at $525,000) but then rose steadily before levelling off in Year Six at $2,700,000 each year.

The cash outflows started in Year One ($666,000 for the land, buildings and management) and then rose to a steady $1,650,000 from Year Six onwards. We are not concerned with the possible repayment of loans at this stage.

It is also necessary to take the whole future life of the mill into our calculations. PPP Plc are planning a ten year life for the plant which will then be worth only scrap but in Year Eleven they expect to sell the land and buildings for what they will have had to pay for them.

These prospective cash flows are shown in table 14.2. There will be a net outflow for the first three years but over the total eleven years there will be a net inflow of $5,304,000. Is eleven years too long to wait?

Table 14.2: Pretty Polly Plantations' prospective cash flows

Investment by PPP Plc ($000s)

Cost of capital @ (%) 18.00

Year	Cash outflow	Cash inflow	Net flow	Discount factor	Present value
One	660	0	(660)	0.847	(559.3)
Two	1,298	525	(773)	0.718	(555.2)
Three	1,564	1,305	(259)	0.609	(157.6)
Four	2,017	2,265	248	0.516	127.9
Five	1,657	2,655	998	0.437	436.2
Six	1,650	2,700	1,050	0.370	389.0
Seven	1,650	2,700	1,050	0.314	329.6
Eight	1,650	2,700	1,050	0.266	279.3
Nine	1,650	2,700	1,050	0.225	236.7
Ten	1,650	2,700	1,050	0.191	200.6
Eleven	0	500	500	0.162	81.0
Totals	15,446	20,750	5,304		808.3
					(=NPV)

Step 2

We now apply the discount factors to each net flow figure to allow for the time factor. The discount factors can be drawn from readily available tables or by means of a pocket calculator. The factors are based on a discount rate (that is, prospective interest rates) of 18 per cent per annum.

Multiplying the net flows by the discount factors we get the **present value** of each net flow. Some are negative and some are positive, so we call the total the **Net Present Value of the project**. You will notice that this net value is less than the earlier figure of $5,304,000 because PPP Plc will have to wait for those inflows.

Step 3

Assess the situation. The positive NPV of $808,300 is the value of the project to PPP Plc if they had to finance the project by borrowing at 18 per cent per annum.

It would be perfectly possible for the project planners to forget discounting. Instead they could calculate for each year how much needed to be borrowed, how much interest would be paid, how much cash came in and how much debt could be paid off. If they did that they would arrive at a cash surplus at the end of Year 11 equal to the un-discounted total. But PPP Plc would have to wait for that surplus and that means the 'Present Value' of that surplus is only the $808,300 of the NPV.

So PPP Plc could indeed borrow at 18 per cent and make a profit. This DCF calculation method makes it easy to compare the value of several projects with differing time scales and differing cash flow patterns.

Table 14.3: Net Present Value of the project

Investment by PPP Plc ($000s)
Cost of capital @ (%) 29.74 (29.74% = IRR)

Year	Cash outflow	Cash inflow	Net flow	Discount factor	Present value
One	660	0	(660)	0.771	(508.7)
Two	1,298	525	(773)	0.594	(459.2)
Three	1,564	1,305	(259)	0.458	(118.6)
Four	2,017	2,265	248	0.353	87.5
Five	1,657	2,655	998	0.272	271.5
Six	1,650	2,700	1,050	0.210	220.2
Seven	1,650	2,700	1,050	0.162	169.7
Eight	1,650	2,700	1,050	0.125	130.8
Nine	1,650	2,700	1,050	0.096	100.8
Ten	1,650	2,700	1,050	0,074	77.7
Eleven	0	500	500	0.057	28.5
Totals	15,446	20,750	5,304		0.2 (=NPV)

What would happen if the cost of borrowing went up? If we were to apply discount rate higher than 18 per cent, say 20 or 25 per cent, the NPV value of the project would be that much less. There will come a point where the NPV will be zero. That situation is shown in table 14.3

You can see from the table that an interest rate of 29.74 per cent, if used to discount the values of the net flows, gives an NPV of $200 which is as near to zero as makes no difference. What does that tell the project planners? It tells them two things:

1 That if PPP Plc financed the project by borrowing at exactly 29.74 per cent per annum they would break even on the project as a whole. Hence this discount rate is known as the 'Break-even Discount Rate' or more technically as the Internal Rate of Return, or IRR.
2 If PPP Plc were confident that they could always borrow, over the next eleven years, at less than the IRR rate of interest they would be confident of making at least some profit on the operation as a whole.

Now for a few final comments on this DCF technique.

DCF calculations are often presented as a bit of mysterious high finance. There is no mystery as the figure can always be checked by the more laborious method of forecasting all those annual borrowings and repayments. With a computer that is no problem although the presentation will not be so easy to follow.

The time value of money has nothing to do with inflation, being based purely on the interest that may be earned. If the project planners do wish to take inflation into account they can tackle it one of two ways:

1 They can base their cash flow forecasts on the current (non-inflated) expected figures and use a discount rate adjusted for inflation so as to show the 'true' interest rate.
2 They can base their cash flow forecasts on the actual prospective cash amounts (that is, showing the effect of inflation) and use the unadjusted interest rate (which does reflect inflation). That rate would be the so-called 'money rate' of interest.

The alternatives to the DCF technique for project planning all have some limitation. Conventional accounting budgeting methods ignore the time aspect unless the borrowings over time are also worked out in the way we have described.

The so-called 'pay-back method' only takes into consideration the payments and receipts up to the moment when the two cumulative totals are equal. What happens after that is ignored.

Bringing All the Figures Together

A business plan is a budget and vice versa. However it is more conventional to think of the two as different types of planning on the grounds that:

1 a business plan contains a strong marketing element and, partly for that reason, will be viewed as being of a speculative nature; and
2 a budget tends to be a financial statement, and in many fields of management activity is treated as a controlling device, not amenable to adjustment.

But any budget must be based on some plan if it is to be credible, which means that the speculative element is unavoidable. Any business is a dynamic operation which is continually adjusting what it is doing in order to adapt itself to a continuously changing economic, political and social environment.

Therefore the plan or the budget (whichever you prefer) must be simultaneously feasible and flexible.

Obtaining a Feasible Budget

This can only be achieved by an effective budget preparation process that will produce a business plan that:

1 Is targeted on agreed corporate aims that are unambiguous and genuinely desirable – so no megalomania and no ego-trips.

2   Is based on explicit and agreed assumptions about the economic, market and technological environment, so forming a coherent, basic marketing strategy.

3   Is complete in the sense that it involves all aspects of the business, brought together in a logical and coherent manner.

4   Is founded on a believable and feasible sales plan involving prices, volumes and also the possible variations around the central target figures.

5   Incorporates all the linked departmental budgets such as purchasing, production, stocks and transport.

6   Incorporates the personnel plan for recruitment, training and progression.

7   Leads to a working capital budget.

8   Leads to a capital expenditure budget derived from the basic, longer term marketing strategy.

9   Incorporates a cash budget, following the two elements above, incorporating cash flow forecasts consistent with all that has gone before.

10 Incorporates a master budget, founded on all the individual budgets, incorporating monthly budgeted profit and asset forecasts.

11 Has the commitment of all those affected by each individual part of the overall budget, that commitment being a necessary guarantee of feasibility.

12 Contains a mechanism for continual monitoring, comparisons of 'actuals' with 'budget figures' and a feed back mechanism that works quickly.

13 Incorporates a mechanism for testing and re-appraising the basic assumptions on which the budget as a whole and the marketing strategy in particular was based.

Underlying these principles that would normally guide the budget preparation process, there should be a pragmatic attitude, not to the preparation process itself, but to its implementation.

1   The budget or business plan is **a plan of action**. It is not the figures in the budget that are important, it is the implied actions and activities that will turn those figures into reality.

2   Budgets and business plans must be based on sales forecasts,

but sales forecasts are always wrong. The monitoring process has the task of revealing continuously that divergence.

3 A business is a dynamic process so it is to be expected that there will always be a discrepancy between actuals and budgets except in the case of pure spending departments like advanced research. If 'actuals' always match 'budgets' then someone is cooking the books!

4 With the exception of pure spending departments, a budget is **not a licence to spend**. That pernicious attitude towards budgets may be a feature of public sector bodies which are so often spending bodies only.

Whatever else the plan or budget is meant to achieve it must work, in the sense of enabling the company to achieve those business targets which were discussed in Part 1 of this book. That means ensuring that it all fits together in the end. One type of 'glue' that can enable the component parts of a business to hang together and pull together is what is imprecisely known as 'information technology'. We shall look at some of the implications of that in the next chapter.

Questions for Discussion

1 Using the figures for Matrix Materials in this chapter, and assuming that, (a) the cost of sales averaged 35 per cent of sales, and (b) that 80 per cent of 'stocks' were finished goods ready for sale, calculate the number of times stock was turned over each year.

2 Using the figures for Matrix again, note that the ratios for the return on capital employed and the return on the equity were the same up to 1990 but then diverged. Look up the definition of 'gearing' in Colin Barrow's or in any similar book – can you see how gearing explains this divergence?

3 A company has the possibility of purchasing one of its distributors, an acquisition that will generate a cash profit of £20,000 per year. However, these earnings are based on a licence agreement that will expire after five years, leaving only the disposal value of the distributor's remaining assets,

worth £5,000. To make the purchase the company will have to use invested funds currently earning 14 per cent per annum. There is no problem about remitting earnings to the UK.

Basing your answer on these figures, what is the absolute maximum that the UK company should pay for the distributor?

15

Information Technology and Exporting

Introduction

Is it just an expensive toy or can it be made to be something more?

The theme of this chapter is that 'Information Technology' in the context of exporting is not so much a matter of technology even though it is indeed about business information. The theme is that IT (as we shall call it from now on) is about: the exporting task; the people performing that task; and the organization of these two.

So where does the technology come in? The technology does three things:

1 It enables those people responsible for the running of an export operation to do what they have always done, but now more quickly, more reliably and at less expense – less **operating** expense it is important to emphasize. The capital expense is quite another matter.
2 It also enables them to do things that simply were not possible to do before or things which they always wanted to do but were just too expensive. Such things include keeping track of multiple, continent-wide deliveries by RoRo road transport to distributors 'Just-in-Time', or getting letters of credit right first time, every time.

3 But against those advantages, the technology imposes well defined constraints on the management (or more usually on the mis-management) of an export business and on the ways in which the technology may be beneficially implemented.

The Place of Technology in a Business

So why don't we just call in the experts? It is a sad but almost universal fact of business life that any project for an IT application:

1 will be delivered late;
2 will be significantly over budget; and
3 will not work as well as originally planned and may not work at all.

The reason for those three sad facts is not in the technology which is usually capable of delivering more than asked of it; nor is it the fault of the experts who will always be enthusiastic about providing ever more sophisticated system facilities, but it comes from the sheer management difficulty of organizing a business to be more profitable in a new way. One classic case of these difficulties was the London Stock Exchange's Taurus project in the early 1990s. This mammoth IT project was intended to replace the Exchange's victorian settlement system with an electronic, paperless one. In 1993, after millions of pounds had been spent, the planned Taurus system was abandoned as impractical.

So before we call in the experts we, as export managers, need to quite clear about what is required from any new development. That means being clear both about how it will increase the profitability of the business and how that increased profitability will be achieved in detail. That task is called 'system design' or sometimes 'systems analysis' and is the first step in the production of what is hoped to be a working system.

Implementing such a system will include the purchase of much hardware and software so it is necessary for those responsible for the project team to be able:

1 to analyse the needs and the potential of the business;
2 to give correct specifications to potential suppliers;
3 to be able to relate the technology to the non-technological business task; and
4 to organize the change over from one system to another with all the human, organizational and commercial complexities involved.

To sum up, getting IT to work in a business is about getting people and management systems to work in a business in a new way.

The role of management here is to be aware of the potential but also to be aware of the seductive attractions of 'state of the art' technology proffered by the technologists. For instance the EDI Association have recommended that when implementing an EDI application, the project team should not be headed by a technologist but instead by a senior manager with commercial responsibilities.

Therefore in this chapter we will list a number of aspects of the implementation of IT to provide a short checklist of possible technological constraints and of the business opportunities affected by them.

System Design: The Very First Step

The first step is to consider the system as a whole. Right at the outset it is essential for the planners to know in detail how the existing system works in practice, and what operating changes are proposed in order to enhance that system. This initial step of 'system analysis' is not so dissimilar from the budgeting process we looked at in the last chapter. It is the task of deciding what the company should be doing in the medium term and of demonstrating that what is proposed will be profitable. Because organizations operate both with formal, 'official' methods and informal, pragmatic adjustments to them, investigating the way a company actually works requires tact and patience from the analyst.

What is required is a clear picture for any part of the organization showing:

1 Who are the people involved?

2 What tasks do they carry out?

3 What are the inputs? – customer enquiries perhaps.

4 What are the outputs? – perhaps an order placed on a production department or detailed instructions to a freight forwarder or shipper.

5 What is the information base? Will the consignment details have been finalized when the order was accepted or will the production staff have to provide the information for completion of shipping documentation?

6 What other parts of the business are involved? Is there a Sales Order processing system (SOP) already in place and if so, is it the responsibility of the export department, the marketing department or the accounts department?

7 What is the permanent information base of the export department covering customer information, shipping tariffs and local market information, and how is it up-dated?

8 Who has responsibility for monitoring payments, currency purchasing and other 'Treasury' matters?

The final fruits of the investigation should be flow diagrams or 'procedures flowcharts'. Where decisions have to be made the methods or criteria by which those decisions are made should also be established.

The System Architecture

The second aspect to be decided is what sort of system? One major aspect that needs to be established is the degree of integration of the system and the extent to which outsiders are involved. Does the 'export department' limit its activities to preparing documents and instructing freight forwarders, or is it a total marketing operation covering everything from market research to operating foreign currency accounts? What are the links with shippers, banks, the Customs, and with overseas distributors?

These considerations will determine whether or not performance in that department requires only a modest investment in one or two 'stand-alone' PCs equipped with word processing and Spex 4. Alternatively, implementing EDI on an international scale will require detailed negotiations with suppliers and distributors and detailed considerations of communications software and hardware.

Central to these considerations will be the design and location of the data base. A very small exporter may require a 'data base' consisting of little more than Croner's guides, leaving practically everything else to the freight forwarder and the bank with whom he deals by correspondence. A fully integrated operation may allow distributors' own computer systems to interrogate the company's manufacturing system for information on stock availability and then follow this with an order sent directly to the company's SOP which can then generate the paper work.

Then follow questions as to whether any such integrated system should be mainframe or network based. What are the needs, the resources required and the system management implications? Associated with these questions will be others about system **structure** and in particular about the design of the data base – centralized or distributed, relational or hierarchical?

The Operational Requirements

How will the system be used in practice? The basic systems analysis must show how it will be operated. It may be largely a question of the degree of integration. Alternatively it may be more important to get the 'user interface' right, perhaps by using 'prototyping' at the design stage.

Highly integrated systems give scope to management both at the operating and strategic levels. For an export manager to be able to follow through an order from initial enquiry to confirmation of payment received, from his desk terminal, has obvious attractions.

At the strategic level a comprehensively integrated system should be able to support a Management Information System (MIS), which given well designed query facilities will enable the company strategists to access all aspects of the business.

Against these attractions is the fact that designing such a system is difficult and expensive, managing it requires the appropriate skills, and changing it may be very expensive. These considerations will be very much affected by the variety of activities carried out by the company. In 1993, Sainsbury's were spending £20 million a year on hardware and £50 million on running costs for software and staff even though it might have been claimed that it is only a 'shopkeeper'. It was for a retailing operation in one country, the UK, only, but it was a highly integrated operation, electronically linking 800 suppliers to 350 stores.

A non-integrated system has the opposing advantages of cheapness, flexibility and ease of management. It is relatively easy to provide a number of desktop PCs equipped with standard, off the shelf software; a spreadsheet, word processing, a data base, Spex 4, a laser printer and perhaps a CD-ROM disk drive for bought-in data. If the PCs are linked as a departmental network, or provided with modems to access subscription data services then the task of managing it is not too onerous. But even small networks do require some technical expertise to keep them trouble free.

With such a non-integrated system changes in methods, staff, and changes in the other departments of the company can be handled with little more difficulty than with a paper-driven system. Communications with other departments or outside bodies can be handled by the physical transfer of disks or tapes.

What Do Users Need to Know of the Technology?

The decline in the importance of the central computing department of larger organizations has come about with the development of networked, particularly linked networked systems, but also with the enormous increase in the availability of well written software for almost any function one can think of. One result of these developments has been that the less technical user has been increasingly insulated from the underlying technology that drives the system. The disadvantage of that change seems to be a lack of confidence amongst the non-technical about moving into new areas of IT applications such as Wide Area Networking possibilities or intelligent systems. Another disadvantage is being surprised by the way that more sophisticated software puts heavy demands on the hardware.

The Hardware and Software Base

Business users should be confident about the significance of processor developments – 'Pentium' for instance. Similarly the significance of clock speeds – a '486 running at 50MHz' for example, and why 'cache' memory might be useful. The basics of data transfer also need to be appreciated – the need for printer driver software or why, when mixing systems we need on occasions to make use of ASCII file transfers.

Knowing what is involved in the writing of software no longer requires an appreciation of the differences between assembler or 4GLs, unless an exporter decides to abandon his trade and go in for software writing instead. But knowing the difficulties and the process of designing software will lessen the frustrations of coping with what appear to be the idiosyncratic, not to say perverse, methods demanded of the user.

Nevertheless, even the least technically minded user, particularly if he or she wants to get more out of the software they have purchased, will sooner or later get involved in the operating system, such as the ubiquitous MS DOS. So what is an operating system? What does it do? What is the difference between MS DOS, Macintosh and Unix and when does it matter? And how does the operating system, the SOP package you have just bought, and Windows all work together?

For 95 per cent of the time these are strictly academic matters to the person in the export office. For the other five per cent, it is comforting to be able to understand the telephoned advice from the help line of your software supplier.

When communications over public telephone lines come into the picture, an outline knowledge of that technology is also helpful if only to understand articles in The Electronic Trader or the leaflets from software or service providers.

This book is about the principles of exporting not about the basics of electronic data processing (as it used to be known a long time ago). Fortunately, there is a wealth of literature available covering this subject, not to mention articles in periodicals at all levels of expertise. The trap to avoid is to purchase a book which presumes a higher level of knowledge than the reader possesses; such a volume will only produce a sense of intense frustration. So take some friendly advice before you buy.

Software Specifically for the Export Office

This is available to run on all levels of hardware from the stand-alone PC to what used to be called mainframes such as IBM's AS/400. Such export software is just one type of 'application software' and the 'application' as distinct from the 'system' is something that is of particular significance for EDI operations.

All types of application software have in common:

1 A facility to draw information off some file system. This may be nothing more than the disk files of documents stored on a word processor. Alternatively it may be a facility to tap a company data base or even automatically tap a remote source of information over public access telephone lines.

2 A user interface, for which the primary requirement is what is normally referred to loosely as 'user friendly'. The measure of that is: how long does it take the inexpert user to feel confident, and how infrequent and how unimportant are user's mistakes. This is the most difficult thing to evaluate when buying a new type of software as what is important and what is convenient will depend on the experience of the user and the type of work to be done. That will only emerge with use.

3 A processing capability. When a buyer is first presented with literature, with the manual or a demonstration of an unfamiliar piece of software, the capabilities of the package always

look impressive. It is only later that one discovers that certain, usually less common, operations can only be done in a round about way or with great difficulty. Discussions with existing users doing similar work to yours is always worthwhile.

4 An output capability which may be to disk, to a printer, to a modem and to another computer. This aspect should give the fewest problems, particularly with the almost universal availability of graphics printers such as laser or ink-jet machines.

Typical data base files an export support package will access would be:

Details of customers, agents and consignees.
Payments and sales terms or commission rates.
Other addresses; of forwarders, shippers, banks and so on.
Sales enquiry procedures.
Shipping and documentary procedures.
Product information, costs, prices, weights and cubes.
Packing and containerization data.
Product classifications, (CAP, Dangerous Goods?).
Declarations and signatories (names and titles).
Standard instructions for shipping and forwarding.
Freight rates, by carrier, mode, ports.
Insurance rates and tariff data.
Details of sales territories.
Banking instructions for collection.
Currencies.

Having drawn off the relevant data the software package should then be able to handle for any enquiry or order:

Product details and product pricing.
Quotations and pro-formas.
Enquiry processing and progress.
Order processing.

For handling an order the package should help with:

Monitoring progress.
Reporting on deadlines.
Consignment profitability.
Part shipment handling or consolidations.

Documentation that may be produced would include:

Order acknowledgements, invoices, packing lists.
Shipping documentation and instructions.
Dangerous goods notes.
Dispatch advice and delivery notes and labels.
Bill of lading or Airway Bill.
Company documentation as required.
Statistical declarations for VAT and Intrastats.

An important facility of such export software packages is the possibility of linking with the other company software and to generate general management reports.
   The links that would be beneficial could include ones with:

General sales order processing.
Stock control.
Warehousing.
Purchase ledger.
Sales ledger.

The management reporting possibilities should include:

Enquiry and current order analysis.
Sales management reports.
Production of price lists.
Control of commissions paid.
ECGD control.

Such reporting possibilities are only those specific to the export consignment. If the export software is linked with the general company software then all the facilities offered there will encompass the export activity as well as others. The obvious ones are budgeting and forecasting, and the automatic incorporation of all relevant accounting data.

What is implied by this list of all the good things that suitable software can provide is that the company, its organization, its management and its IT equipment of whatever type, is sufficiently well organized to do all these things.

That in turn implies that the management of the business is working to an agreed system of operations. By that is meant that individual members of staff know what their job is in detail, that the information and resources required are available, that these individuals know what is required from them and when and why, and that senior management is able to monitor the activities that will produce that budgeted profit.

In other words, what is required to make a computer system work is not technology but management.

Communications and Wide Area Networks

We have made frequent reference to the possibility of linking one company's computer with a distant one. The task is mainly a technical one and one that has been performed on a regular, but simple basis, since before 1970. Technical developments, the deregulation of national communications providers, the development of enabling standards and the simple worldwide proliferation of business computer systems have all made it much easier during the 1980s and 1990s. What was once a tricky technical task carried out by a limited number of experienced users is now there for any exporter to use.

Since it is largely a technical task a brief resumé of what is involved may help.

The carriers providing Wide Area Networks (WANs)

Longer distance communications, whether voice or data, must involve public access carriers. Outside North America these are usually the national telecommunications monopolies in each country. At the time of writing, in the UK we have the oligopoly of British Telecom and Mercury. Using these communications services one can send data over the same circuit-switched lines as are used for voice communication, to anywhere in the world.

However, digital transmission (as opposed to analogue) gives a more reliable signal and is usually offered with additional customer benefits as well. This is available on telephone lines featuring ISDN, the Integrated Services Digital Network.

Digital transmission of data will usually involve packet switching. The stream of data is automatically split into packets of uniform length which are then routed through the international network by the fastest route available, with the packets being re-assembled at the other end. The system is appropriate for computer-to-computer transmission. If the computers at either end are equipped with a PAD (packet assembler disassembler) the whole transmission routing is enhanced.

The lines used by subscribers may be public access or leased. The leased line, in theory, is for the exclusive use of the subscriber but some telecommunications authorities have been known to make use of 'leased lines' for their own regular, general user traffic.

The volume of traffic that may be carried by any line is measured by its 'bandwidth' and some telecommunications monopolies have in the past restricted bandwidths to prevent users of leased lines using them for voice traffic and thus infringing their monopoly in that field.

The service providers: the VANS

The communications possibilities outlined above are, in that basic form, only suitable for direct communication between two computer systems that 'understand' each other, as with voice communication. That does not serve the needs of a 'community' of computer users, all of whom wish to be able to communicate randomly with all the others. Such systems would be bank clearing systems, airline reservation systems, and the Customs Direct Entry system.

Since any digital communication system only transmits a succession of pulses, translatable into numbers, any receiving computer must be able to interpret the incoming signal. Such a signal might be an order acknowledgement, a fax transmission, or a stream of encrypted data only comprehensible to a particular computer program.

This problem is overcome by 'Value Added Network Services' or VANS. They operate (using public access digital lines) as a central clearing house for the messages of a group of trading companies, typically a group of purchasers and suppliers. Essentially they provide a 'store and retrieve' service for the messages going through the network. The messages are formatted to a particular standard so that a company transmitting a purchase order may be confident that the receiver will not only recognize it as a purchase order but all the details, names, quantities, part numbers and so on will all appear in the correct places, on paper, at the other end.

Telecommunications, WANs, VANS and EDI

The full exploitation of the communication possibilities using computers and digital transmission is achieved by the use of EDI or Electronic Data Interchange.

The essential features of EDI are:

1 It involves a group of trading partners who are exchanging a sufficient volume of data on a regular basis to make the investment, largely of management time, worthwhile.
2 Such a group has been typically a major purchaser, such as a retail chain, and a large number of suppliers. Examples of these are Tesco and Sainsbury's in the UK where nearly all

the suppliers are linked electronically to the purchaser.

3 The 'glue' that holds the group together will be a VANS working to a well defined standard. In the UK, Tradanet was a leading service provider using the Tradacoms standard. At the time of writing this was being overtaken in popularity by the EDIFACT standard.

4 The communication process is essentially direct from one computer to another through the VANS network. To put it more exactly, the communication is **application to application**.

5 The ideal mode of operation of two firms with a commercial relationship would be:

(a) Firm A's stock control software establishes that a particular item needs re-ordering. It automatically send an order enquiry to Firm B.

(b) Firm B's order processing software responds automatically to say that the item is in stock.

(c) Firm A's purchase software transmits the order, and at the same time ensures that the stock control system is updated.

(d) Firm B's SOP acknowledges the order and puts it in hand, fixing a delivery date which is notified to Firm A.

(e) The goods are dispatched from Firm B whose SOP system notifies the purchase system at Firm A. The SOP also notifies its Sales Ledger system, which then transmits an electronic invoice to the Purchase Ledger system of Firm A.

(f) The Purchase Ledger at Firm A, on confirmation of delivery (generated by the use of bar-coded labels on the goods), transmits the funds using, this time, one of the clearing bank's VANS.

However, it should be obvious that this fully automatic system is only a practical proposition when:

1 Both the companies already have well integrated computer systems. Effectively it also requires that most of the members of the trading group have such integrated systems.

2 There is a sufficient volume of standard traffic that makes the investment in management time worthwhile.

3 All members of the group have the motivation to conduct

their business this way. Often this is brought about by the pressure exerted by a major purchaser.

The advantages of electronic trading, as compared with 'paper driven' systems, are easy to see:

1 It eliminates data re-entry from paper documents, which is the major source of errors.
2 Increased staff efficiency. The task of staff is no longer handling paper documents. Instead they can concentrate on the management of the company's systems.
3 By closely integrating the purchasing, production, delivery and use stages it makes 'Just-in-Time' working more feasible, so reducing working capital.
4 The overall process can give shorter lead times between realization of the need to purchase to accepting delivery of the goods. Sainsbury's purchasing system, which is linked to the retail sales tills, interrogates the stock control system 10 times a day, and acts accordingly.

What We Have Learned from this Chapter

The lessons to be learned from the experience of applying IT to any business are very simple:

1 Applying IT is a management task rather than a technical one.
2 That management task is the familiar one of organization to produce a result. Disorganized companies will waste their money buying hardware and software if they haven't got the organization right.
3 IT simply enables managers to run their businesses in ways that they always wanted to, were it not that such ways were either too expensive or impractical.
4 The role of the technical expert is to ensure that the system actually does what management wants it to do.

5 The role of the systems analyst or system designer is to make the connection between business needs and the technical possibilities.

Questions for Discussion

1 A UK manufacturer exports one third of its products, a proportion that has grown rapidly over the last two years. The original computer system is now overloaded whilst the Export Department never had any system as such, only three 'stand-alone' PCs doing miscellaneous tasks.
What would be the relative advantages and disadvantages of:
(a) The Export Department having its own quite separate system?
(b) Having two systems (for UK and for export business) linked by a local area network or LAN?
(c) A single, 'mainframe' system with all terminals plugged into the central computer?

2 The General Manager of a company, 90 per cent of whose business is export, rather fancies the idea of EDI but has no idea as to whether it would be of benefit to his company. Who should he talk to, both inside and outside the company?

3 A small exporter employs an export manager (= chief salesman), one secretarial assistant in the office and one other sales person. In what specific ways would the use of computer based export software show a genuine benefit to the export operation? What type of hardware is likely to be required?

16

A Reminder of How it is All to be Fitted Together

Similarities

Management is a practical trade, and the techniques of management must be able to produce an objective benefit.

In chapter 4 we used the analogy of a business as a machine. The characteristics of a machine are:

1 that it costs money to set up and to run;
2 that it has lots of inter-connected parts;
3 it needs management to keep it running; but
4 it produces an output sufficiently valuable to make it all worthwhile.

It was the aim of this book to put that view of an export business in perspective, so that when we thought about the management of an export business we never lost sight of what was the overall aim of our work as exporters. It is a normal hazard of involvement in any business operation that we become so immersed in the day to day operations that these operations become an end in themselves.

What can happen then is that tasks continue to be performed long after the point at which they ceased to be beneficial to the company. We continue to exhibit in a market that has changed totally, we continue to push our distributor to take a product that is at the end of its life cycle or, worse still, we see our export business as business dedicated to filling documents and keeping accounting records.

So let us remember what we have covered in the chapters of this book.

1 Why are we in business anyway? We are there to make profit because making losses spells poverty.

2 We do that by providing goods or services to markets that want them.

3 To do that we set up a company which is there to run the business of providing those goods and services.

4 If the aim is to make a profit we must be quite clear what we mean by that term.

5 Therefore we need a system of information flows that will both get those goods and services to the customer and, at the same time tell management that they are doing it right.

6 Doing it right is the fundamental message that a balance sheet gives us. We can see if we have succeeded.

7 The profit and loss account tells us how we succeeded. Briefly, sales revenue was greater than total expenses.

8 But calculating a profit is not a straightforward task because any business is complicated and is changing all the time. We use accounting conventions to ensure the logic of our profit calculations.

9 Costs reduce profit, but management must be able to make sense of calculated cost figures. Are we calculating them for routine control or for planning changes to the business?

10 It is also necessary to watch the cash; how it flows in and how it flows out.

11 Having noted that we can forecast the cash situation; how it will flow in and out in the future.

12 But cash does not change on its own. All the elements of working capital will have an impact on the company's liquidity.

13 When we make changes to prices and to volumes we make changes to our profits. We need to have a clear view of that process and the most illuminating measure to use is 'contribution'.

14 The other hazard of a business is uncertainty about the future. But we do not have to give up at that point; we can take a view of uncertainty that will allow us to make rational decisions nevertheless.

15 Having got the business moving in the right direction, we can use ratio analysis to confirm that we have done so, we can appraise the future profitability of our longer term projects, and we can then put it all together in a coherent but flexible budget.

16 Since management is as much about the management of information as about the individual business activities, we can, if we are careful about what we are doing, apply technology to that information handling task.

Good luck with the exporting! Luck should not be necessary but it does help!

Glossary

AB
Aktiebolag. Swedish company either public or private

ABC
Activity Based Costing, a method of cost apportionment that attempts to relate all indirect costs to an identifiable activity

ABCC
The Association of British Chambers of Commerce

absorption costing
The usual method of costing manufactures whereby all manufacturing overheads are attributed to (absorbed by) the cost of the individual units produced

accrued expenses
Expenses related to an accounting period which have not yet been recorded (because no invoice yet received?) but are relevant to the profit calculation for the period

AG
Aktiengesellschaft. German public company

ASB
Accounting Standards Board

ASCII

American Standard Code for Information Interchange, the standard numerical code for any keyboard character or other function

ASCII file

A computer file in which text and data are stored as simple keyboard characters, with no additional codes peculiar to word processing or similar software. The file may therefore be read by other software different from that which originally wrote the file

balance sheet

A list of the assets and liabilities of a company at a specified point in time. Technically it is a list of ledger balances carried forward after the revenue and expense balances have been transferred to the profit & loss account

break-even

When costs exactly equal revenues so that profit is zero

budget

A quantified plan, agreed and approved, for the operations of a business for a specific period

BV

Besloten Vennootschap met Beperkte Aansprakelijheid. Netherlands private company

called up share capital

The amount that the company has required shareholders to pay on issued shares, which may then be either partly or fully paid

cash flow

The cash received and paid out by a business during an accounting period (see also Source & Application of Funds Statement)

CHIEF

Cargo Handling for Import and Export Freight, the Customs entry processing system for direct trader input

circuit-switching
The conventional telephone connection where a two-way circuit is allocated exclusively for the duration of the call

COGS
Cost of Goods Sold, often referred to as 'Cost of Sales'

company
A legal entity, normally formed by incorporation under the UK Companies Acts. It may be a private company ('LTD') or a public company ('PLC')

contribution
Contribution to fixed costs, is either price less unit variable cost (= unit contribution), or sales revenue less variable costs (= total contribution). Contribution to overheads uses direct costs in place of variable costs

cost
An expense attributable to any specified thing or activity

cost centre
A location, operation, or machine for which costs can be recorded for use in cost control

depreciation
The reduction of the book value of a fixed asset which recognizes the loss value due to the passage of time or obsolescence

DCF
Discounted Cash Flow, the principal technique for investment or project appraisal

dial-up circuit
A public telephone line as opposed to a private, leased line

direct costs
Costs that can be directly attributed to a specific product or unit of service

down-side risk
A view of uncertainty that considers only the adverse possibilities

EDI
Electronic Data Interchange, or 'paperless trading' with direct and automatic computer-to-computer links

EFT
Electronic Funds Transfer. Automatic payments between trans-action parties' bank accounts

equity
The ordinary shareholders' investment in the company; issued share capital, share premium and attributable reserves

EMV
Expected Monetary Value, an intrinsic value arising from a future event multiplied by the probability of its occurring. Applicable also to non-monetary values

expenses
Any financially measurable reduction in the asset value of a company. See 'cost'

FIFO
First-in-first-out, where stock issues are valued at the oldest purchase cost first

fixed cost
Any cost that is not a variable cost (so 'fixed costs' may change)

FRS
Financial Reporting Standard, issued by the ASB

GAAP
Generally Accepted Accounting Principles, (USA)

gateway
An interface between two computer networks so that terminals

logged into one can access the other, the networks becoming 'transparent'

gearing
The ratio of shareholders' capital to loan capital of a company; may be calculated in several ways

GmbH
Gesellschaft mit beschränkter Haftung. German private company

gross margin
Gross profit expressed as a percentage of sales revenue (see 'mark-up')

historic cost
The value of an asset recorded as the actual amount paid for it, as opposed to 'current' cost or 'replacement cost'

intangible asset
An asset that is non-monetary in nature and has no physical substance, eg. brands, development expenditure, goodwill, trademarks

INTRASTATS
Intra-Community Traders' VAT and Statistical declaration to the Customs & Excise on exports to Community countries

ICC
International Chamber of Commerce

IRR
Internal Rate of Return, the break-even interest rate which gives a zero NPV

ISDN
Integrated Services Digital Network, integrating packet- and circuit-switched services, voice and data and so on, so that, for example, a PC can make EDI connections directly

JIT

Just-in-Time. Precise scheduling of deliveries so as to avoid holding buffer stocks

LIFO

Last-in-first-out, where stock issues are valued at the most recent purchase cost

mark-up

Gross profit expressed as a percentage of cost of goods sold

net margin

Net profit (howsoever defined) expressed as a percentage of sales revenue

NIFO

Next-in-first-out, where stock issues are valued at the cost of the next (future) purchase

NPV

Net Present Value, the discounted value of future cash flows. A DCF measure

NV

Naamloze Vennootschap. Netherlands public company

packet-switching

Digital data transmission whereby the message is broken up into addressed packets of fixed length, which may follow different routes through a (international) network

parameter

A quantified characteristic of a population as opposed to particular statistical values of individual units, events, or samples

partnership

The relationship between two or more persons carrying on a business with a view to profit but not incorporated as a company

payback
The period of time required for a project's cash inflows to equal the cash outflows

PLC
Public Limited Company, almost always a 'quoted' company

prepayments
or 'payments in advance'. Expenditures for a benefit in a future accounting period, to be charged against profit in that future period but recorded as a current asset until then

prime cost
The manufacturing cost that includes only materials, direct labour and direct expenses (that is, excluding manufacturing overheads and all non-manufacturing costs)

probability
A value between zero and plus one, expressing an expectation about the likelihood of an uncertain future event, usually based on the 'frequency concept' of probability

profit centre
A segment of a business for which a profit or a loss may be calculated

Pty
Australian private company

random event
One that cannot be forecast, although it may be possible to forecast limits to its range or to forecast its average value

random sample
A sample drawn from a population in such a way that each member of the population has an equal chance of being included in the sample

registered company
A company incorporated under the UK Companies Acts

reserves
Profits retained in the business; may be distinguished by origin (capital reserve, revaluation reserve and so on) or whether distributable as dividends or not

revenue
Net invoiced sales less returns

ROCE
Return on capital employed

SA
Société anonyme. French public company

SARL
Società a Responsabilità Limitata. Italian private company

SARL
Société à responsabilité limité. French private company

share premium
Arises when a company issues shares at price higher than the nominal share value. The difference is the 'premium' and must be shown separately on the published balance sheet

SITPRO
The Simpler Trade Procedures Board

sole trader
A person carrying on a business with sole legal responsibility for its affairs (see partnership)

SOP
Sales Order Processing system, normally a computerized system

Source & Application of Funds Statement
A management report which reconciles the cash flows for a period with the calculated profit

SPA
Società Per Azioni. Italian public company

SPEX 400
A version of SITPRO's SPEX export documentation software designed to run on IBM AS/400 systems

SSAP
Statement of Standard Accounting Practice, issued by the former Accounting Standards Committee

standard cost
A predetermined calculation of what a cost should be under normal conditions. The difference between the standard and the actual cost is the 'cost variance'

stock
Any current asset held for sale or for conversion into goods for sale in the normal course of trading (see also UK/US terminology, appendix A

THE
Technical Help for Exporters

trial balance
A list of the debit and credit balances in the ledger accounts, the first step in preparing the final accounts for a period

turnover
Total invoiced sales less discounts given and returns credited

VADS
Value Added Data Service, a commercial VAN service that enables users to implement EDI. VADS include AT&T EDI, BACS, Barclays TRADING MASTER, BT EDI NET, GEIS EDI Express, IBM

expEDIte, INS-Tradanet, Midland TRADEPAY. Nowadays normally referred to simply as a 'VAN' (see below)

VANS
Value Added Network Service, a commercial communications service, offering enhanced facilities to subscribers, and running on a public access communications service (such as BT or Mercury in the UK)

variable cost
A cost that varies in direct proportion to the volume produced. Hence unit variable cost is a constant

voucher
Any documentary evidence supporting an accounting entry

WDV
Written Down Value, the cost of a fixed asset less cumulative depreciation to date

working capital or 'net current assets'
Current assets less current liabilities

Appendix A

Different Usages of American and British Terms

American	British
American	**British**
Accounts payable	Creditors
Accounts receivable	Debtors
Additional paid-in capital	Share premium
Amortization	Depreciation
Capital surplus	Share premium
Common stock	Ordinary shares
Fiscal year	Financial year
Income	Profit
Income statement	Profit and Loss Account
Inventory	Stock
Leverage	Gearing
Property, Plant & Equipment	Fixed assets
Real Estate	Land
Stock	Shares
Stockholders' equity	Shareholders' funds

Appendix B

Some Useful Addresses

The Institute of Export
Export House
64 Clifton Street
London
EC2A 4HB
Tel: 071 247 9812, Fax: 071 377 5343

SITPRO (The Simpler Trade Procedures Board)
Venture House
29 Glasshouse Street
London
W1R 5RG
Tel: 071 287 3525, Fax: 071 287 5751
Help desk: Tel: O71 287 1814, Fax: 071 287 1914

British Exporters Association
16 Dartmouth Street
London
SW1H 9BL
Tel: 071 222 5419

DTI: Overseas Trade Services
Kingsgate House
66-74 Victoria Street

London
SW1E 6SW
Tel: 071 215 5000, Fax: 071 931 0397

DTI: Export Market Information Centre (EMIC)
Ashdown House
123 Victoria Street
London
SW1E 6RB
Tel: 071 215 5444/5, Fax: 071 215 4231

DTI Export Publications
PO Box 55
Stratford-upon-Avon
Warwickshire
CV37 9GE
Tel: 0789 296 212, Fax: 0789 299 096

DTI: Single Market Compliance Unit
Room 602, Ashdown House
123 Victoria Street
London
SW1E 6RB
Tel: 071 215 6730, Fax: 071 215 6140

DTI: Business in Europe Branch
9th Floor, Kingsgate House
66-74 Victoria Street
London
SW1E 6SW
Tel: 071 215 4782/4786

The British International Freight Association
Redfern House
Browells Lane
Feltham
Middlesex
TW13 7EP
Tel: 081 844 2266, Fax: 081 890 5546

The International Chambers of Commerce (ICC UK)
14-15 Belgrave Square
London
SW1X 8PS
Tel: 071 823 2811

Association of British Chambers of Commerce (ABCC)
9 Tufton Street
London
SW1P 3QB
Tel: 071 222 1555

Export Marketing Research Scheme
ABCC
4 Westwood House
Westwood Business Park
Coventry
CV4 8HS
Tel: 0203 694 484, Fax: 0203 694 690

The EDI Association
148 Buckingham Palace Road
London
SW1W 9TR
Tel: 071 824 8848, Fax: 071 824 8114

Technical Help to Exporters (THE)
Breckland, Linford Wood
Milton Keynes
MK14 6LE
Tel: 0908 220 022, Fax: 0908 320 856

Prelink Ltd
Export House
87a Wembley Hill Road
Wembley
Middlesex
HA9 8BU
Tel: 081 900 1313, Fax: 081 900 1268

Overseas Promotions Support
Dean Bradley House
52 Horseferry Road
London
SW1 2AG
Tel: 071 276 2622, Fax: 071 276 2338

Export Credits Guarantee Department (ECGD)
2 Exchange Tower
PO Box 2200
Harbour Exchange Square
London
E14 9GS
Tel: 071 512 7000, Fax: 071 512 7649

NCM UK Ltd
New Crown Buildings
Cathays Park
Cardiff
CF1 3PX
Tel: 0222 824 000, Fax: 0222 824 003

Croner Publications Ltd
Croner House, London Road
Kingston upon Thames
Surrey
KT2 6SR
Tel: 081 547 3333, Fax: 081 547 2637

Euromonitor Plc
87-88 Turnmill Street
London
EC1M 5QU
Tel: 071 251 8024, Fax: 071 608 3149

FT Profile
PO Box 12, Sunbury House
Sunbury-on-Thames
Middlesex
TW16 7UD
Tel: 0932 761 444, Fax: 0932 781 425

Financial Times 'International Trade Finance'
Financial Times Business Enterprises Ltd
126 Jermyn Street
London
SW1Y 4UJ
Tel: 071 411 4414, Fax: 071 411 4415

SGS United Kingdom Ltd
SGS House, 217-221 London Road
Camberley
Surrey
GU15 3EY
Tel: 0276 691 133, Fax: 0276 671 683

Royal Mail International
49 Featherstone Street
London
EC1Y 8SY
Tel: 071 320 4000, Fax: 071 320 4141

The Institute of Linguists
24a Highbury Grove
London
N5 2EA
Tel: 071 359 7445

Institute of Translation and Interpreting
377 City Road
London
EC1V 1NA
Tel: 071 713 7600, Fax: 071 713 7650

Chartered Institute of Patent Agents (CIPA)
Staple Inn Buildings
High Holborn
London
WC1V 7PZ
Tel: 071 405 9450

The Patent Office
Industrial Property and Copyright Department
Hazlitt House
45 Southampton Buildings
London
WC2A 1AR
Tel: 071 438 4766

Appendix C

Further Reading: Books and Other Sources

Reading around this subject is an activity that involves basic background reading, regular updating, and using specific sources of reference. The three lists below are only designed to give a taste of what is available. Further research will then enable you to find something more exactly suited to your own needs. In that connection, do not forget to use the list of useful addresses, appendix B.

Basic background reading

Your starting point should be the other books in this series. For more guidance on the financial management of any business three books are suggested but from then on there is a wealth of published books relevant to the work of an export manager. Leafing through publisher's catalogues is the way to do it, so why not start with Blackwell Publishers' business catalogue (tel: 0865 791 100).

The Principles of Export Guidebooks series from Blackwell Publishers:

Ken Wainwright, *Principles of Marketing*
Julia Spencer, *Principles of International Marketing*
Peter Briggs, *Principles of International Trade and Payments*
James Sherlock, *Principles of International Physical Distribution*
Nicholas Kouladis, *Principles of Law Relating to Overseas Trade*
Len Groves, *Principles of International Marketing Research*
James Conlan, *Principles of Management in Export*

Colin Barrow, *Financial Management for the Small Business*,
    2nd edition, Kogan Page, 1991
Hitching & Stone, *Understand Accounting!*, 1st edition,Pitman,
    1984
John S. Gordon, *Profitable Exporting*, 2nd edition, John Wiley &
    Sons Inc., 1993

Periodicals

The selection of periodicals to keep up to date will depend very much on the business sector you are working in, since most of such publications are best described as 'trade magazines'. Therefore, just as a start:

Export Today, the official journal of The Institute of Export.
    Published bi-monthly, tel: 071 247 9812
Management Today, Haymarket Publishing for the Institute of
    Management. Published monthly, tel: 071 413 4566
Electronic Trader, the European EDI magazine, Hastings Hilton
    Ltd. Published 11 times a year on subscription only,
    tel: 081 742 2828
Overseas Trade Magazine, published 10 times a year, free.
    Available from DTI Regional Offices

Some Reference Sources

DTI, Export publications catalogue
DTI, Guide to sources of advice
DTI, Guide to export services
    Overseas Promotion
    Specific Export Help
UK Export Information Services
All from DTI Export Publications, Stratford-upon-Avon,
Warwickshire, CV37 9GE, tel: 0789 296 212, fax: 0789 299 096.

The DTI Euro Manual, CCH Editions Ltd, Telford Road, Bicester,
    OX6 0XD
EDI 93 – An EDI Yearbook, published jointly by the NCC, Basil
    Blackwell, the Blenheim Group
Common Market Reporter, and *Doing Business in Europe*, CCH
    Editions Ltd, Telford Road, Bicester, OX6 0XD
Companies Act 1985, Companies Act 1989, Her Majesty's
    Stationery Office, Publications Centre, PO Box 276,
    London SW8 5DT and HMSO Bookshop, 49 High Holborn,
    London WC1V 6HB, Fax: 071 831 1326 (also Edinburgh,
    Belfast, Manchester, Birmingham and Bristol)
HM Customs & Excise Integrated Tariff of the UK, HMSO Books,
    Subscriptions, PO Box 276 London SW8 5DT
Croner's Reference Book for Exporters, Croner Publications Ltd,
    Kingston upon Thames

Index

PAGE